Joke Hermes takes us on a fascinating intellectual journey, both sweeping in scope and attuned to intricate detail, to show that in the age of social media and rising polarisation, it is ever more important to listen seriously to the raw outpouring of emotion – hatred, rage, fear, but also fandom and appreciation – in audience talk about media and popular culture to understand their significance as contestations of identity, belonging and representation, that is, as the performance of 'cultural citizenship'.

– **Ien Ang**

With one fell swoop, Joke Hermes has rocketed forward the state of discussion about cultural citizenship. Written with characteristic accessibility and depth, the superb book brims and sparkles with offerings about identity, power, audiences, affect, and the values of stories and of listening.

– **Jonathan Gray**, *University of Wisconsin-Madison*

When democracies are threatened by screaming polarization, when engagement is obfuscated by capitalistic longing, when dreams for better worlds are becoming wake-up calls, Hermes' book offers a request as modest as it is ambitious: we must listen. Listening to audiences' everyday discussions is Hermes' attempt to recognize our affective lives, to trace our connections with strangers, to steer away from moralizing, ultimately to update understandings of popular culture and cultural citizenship – an elegant, eloquent, and essential response to our times.

– **Yiu Fai Chow**, Professor, *Hong Kong Baptist University*

This book offers an insightful and in-depth account of the complicated relationship between the powers of popular culture, democracy, media, and constructions of citizenship.

– **Francesca Sobande**

Joke Hermes has something powerful to say about cultural citizenship as world building in action – lean forward and listen in to her outstanding book.

– **Annette Hill**

CULTURAL CITIZENSHIP AND POPULAR CULTURE

Written in an accessible and engaging style, this book uses a series of case studies to show how popular media are important to us, as a source of pleasure and entertainment, but also in communicating about the world with others.

Social media platforms have changed how we talk about what we like and dislike in our popular media use. 'Cultural citizenship' shows how these discussions speak to 'belonging' and what we feel our rights and responsibilities are in today's polarized world. *Cultural Citizenship and Popular Culture* is based on audience-led research and does not privilege textual analysis as a starting point for taking popular media use's measure. Instead, it offers research tools to listen to others.

This book offers scholars and students of media and creative industries a means to understand their professional position as one in which they engage with rather than assume to know what users of popular cultural texts and products think and feel.

Joke Hermes is a Dutch media and cultural studies researcher. She has published widely on popular culture, audience research and feminist analysis of gender and diversity. She is a professor of Media, Culture and Citizenship at Inholland University and teaches media studies at the University of Amsterdam.

CULTURAL CITIZENSHIP AND POPULAR CULTURE

The Art of Listening

Joke Hermes

LONDON AND NEW YORK

Designed cover image: Joke Hermes

First published 2024
by Routledge
4 Park Square, Milton Park, Abingdon, Oxon OX14 4RN

and by Routledge
605 Third Avenue, New York, NY 10158

Routledge is an imprint of the Taylor & Francis Group, an informa business

© 2024 Joke Hermes

The right of Joke Hermes to be identified as author of this work has been asserted in accordance with sections 77 and 78 of the Copyright, Designs and Patents Act 1988.

All rights reserved. No part of this book may be reprinted or reproduced or utilised in any form or by any electronic, mechanical, or other means, now known or hereafter invented, including photocopying and recording, or in any information storage or retrieval system, without permission in writing from the publishers.

Trademark notice: Product or corporate names may be trademarks or registered trademarks, and are used only for identification and explanation without intent to infringe.

British Library Cataloguing-in-Publication Data
A catalogue record for this book is available from the British Library

ISBN: 978-1-032-26563-6 (hbk)
ISBN: 978-1-032-26562-9 (pbk)
ISBN: 978-1-003-28885-5 (ebk)

DOI: 10.4324/9781003288855

Typeset in Times New Roman
by MPS Limited, Dehradun

Thank you: Sacha, for teaching me about feminism as practice and for suggesting I might be interested in the books that became this book's most important references

Thank you: Noah, for teaching me that patience has merit and that creating is worth all the time and care that it needs

Thank you: Pieter, for everything else

CONTENTS

Acknowledgements — xi

Introduction: Democracy I — 1

PART I
I hear you: Popular culture, audience research and appreciative inquiry. Key concepts — 11

1 Identity: What cultural citizenship is and why studying it matters — 13

2 Power: Popular culture as an object of study
   WITH JAN TEURLINGS — 27

3 Affect: Researching popular culture and cultural citizenship. Rewriting qualitative audience research — 43

PART II
Decoding gender confusion: The litmus test of gender definitions in fearing the effects of popular culture. Three case studies — 59

4 Culpability: Affective-discursive analysis. Understanding the hatred of television character Skyler White 61
   WITH LEONIE STOETE

5 Innocence: Raising children to be media literate and fear of popular culture 76
   WITH SARIEKE HOEKSMA

6 Confusion: When the future (briefly) became female. Viewers discussing a woman being cast as Doctor Who 95
   WITH SOPHIE EEKEN

PART III
Listening with generosity: Another three case studies that take a broader intersectional approach and a conclusion **111**

7 Patriarchy: Good guys (or not). Feminism, auto-ethnography and *the Mentalist* 113

8 Responsibility: Content analysis with the help of fan-viewers: Sorting through the appeal of a decade of *RuPaul's Drag Race* 129
   WITH MICHAEL KARDOLUS

9 Storytelling: Meanwhile in the real world: Popular culture and cultural citizenship politicize online on social media platforms 144

Conclusion: Democracy II: (Searching for) *cultural citizenship as* (attending to) *worldbuilding in action* *160*
References *167*
Index *185*

ACKNOWLEDGEMENTS

Thank you, Annette Hill, Ann Gray, Jan Teurlings, Linda Kopitz, Toby Miller, Karel Koch and Jaap Kooijman, for the incomparable friends and intellectuals that you are.

Many thanks too to my co-researchers, co-authors and former students: Leonie Stoete, Sarieke Hoeksma, Sophie Eeken, Michael Kardolus and Erinn Rövekamp.

To the EjCS crew of these past years: Helen Wood, Jo Littler, Yiu Fai Chow, Anamik Saha, Erin Bell, Jilly Boyce Kay, Jess Martin and Annelot Prins.

To my lovely colleagues at Inholland, the University of Amsterdam, the Universities of Lund and Ghent, in ECREA and in the CoECI network and beyond, inspiring discussion partners and at times co-researchers and teachers, with special thanks to Peggy van Schijndel, Wina Smeenk, Natalia Berger, Emma Stoop, Ouafila Bejja-Essayah, Mirthe van den Hee, Pieter Breek, Koos Zwaan, Roos Gerritsma, Maarten Reesink, Jeroen de Kloet, Tommy Tse, Misha Kavka, Mark Deuze, Carolyn Birdsall, Linda Duits, Joanna Doona, Sofie van Bauwel, Frederik Dhaenens, Sander de Ridder, Tonny Krijnen, Geert Lovink, Hester Dibbits and David Craig.

I am especially indebted to Sacha Hilhorst, Florian Vanlee and Tamara Witschge for offering reading suggestions that built the core argument.

Garjan Sterk and Marianne van den Boomen: I owe a special thanks to you two for being there during a difficult period and for urging me to start work on this book. We continue to miss you, Marianne, but I know you would be very pleased that cultural citizenship is now meeting the digital world.

Zoë Papaikonomou, Gijs van Beek, Mariette van Staveren, Willemien Werkman and Marianne Wagemaker: you belong in none of these categories, but thank you for your shared reflection on the world; it has fed the argument presented here.

Thank you, last but not least, to Natalie Foster and Kelly O'Brien at Routledge as well as to Tarana Parveen for helping make this book a material reality.

I am deeply grateful to all of you.

INTRODUCTION
Democracy I

Have you heard of *Bridgerton*? It is a television series on the Netflix platform produced by Shondaland. Based on a series of regency romance novels written by Julian Quinn, it is the topic of heated discussion on Twitter in 2021 for its colourblind casting, its lack of historical accuracy and for (spoiler alert) sex without consent when Daphne uses Simon (the Duke)'s state of drunkenness to try to get pregnant. If you haven't seen it and have not heard about it, let me briefly explain: Regency romance novels are set in early 19th-century London. Like their supermarket sisters, known as Harlequin or Mills & Boon novels, they are love stories with often pleasingly independent heroines. Shondaland is Shonda Rhimes' television production company. Rhimes produced *Grey's Anatomy*, *How to get away with Murder*, *Scandal* and other well-watched tv series. Her work showcases diversity, whether in terms of ethnicity, size or sexuality. Now, for Netflix, Rhimes has taken on the romance novel which, as a genre, surely is placed at the very bottom in hierarchies of taste. These are novels that are read for sheer pleasure and not for any kind of status.

I am a fan: of romance novels and of Rhimes' work but not entirely sure about *Bridgerton* on television. Not because of Rhimes' slightly satirical take, which makes early 19th-century London strangely reminiscent of the world of Teletubbies but because romance reading is such a private pleasure shared only with like-minded fans. To be outed as a romance fan is one thing; to then have to hear people say deeply offensive things about romance novels and the series is quite another. This book is about understanding how media and specific texts are important to us, for ourselves and in communicating about the world with others. This is what I will call cultural citizenship. Initially, I understood the term to be a way to highlight the value of popular culture. It helps make clear that popular culture offers ways to discuss the world and reflect on it that deserve to be called 'citizenship.' The Twitter attacks on *Bridgerton* show that discussion of popular culture is important in another way as well. Apparently, when talking about what you do not like, you do so in forceful terms. If we agree that citizenship is a layer in popular culture talk, the strong emotions of others cannot be ignored. My goal in this book is to show how attending to cultural citizenship will help build connections and reaffirm democratic sensibility when we learn to hear the questions and arguments across condescension, confusion, anger, aggression and devotion.

A formal definition of cultural citizenship could go something like this: 'cultural citizenship' as a concept helps us understand public (and semi-public) discussion, civic connection and media culture beyond citizenship's modernist legacy of having to be rational, productive and measured. '*Modernist* legacy' refers to the continuing deep sense that media are important for democracies in a specific way: they inform us and enable us to be good citizens through the news and critical analysis. They speak truth to power. 'Modernist *legacy*' says: get over despair. The steadily declining rate at which newspapers and news are consumed is not a disaster. (Today's short news update consumption should also count towards 'being a good citizen'.) Stop disavowing that news and entertainment are now intertwined entities. On my part, I will get over an equally outdated postmodern flirtation that good quality news does not matter. I will even concede that political analysis can be exciting. It would be downright wrong though to think that drama and entertainment programmes are less exciting or less a space to learn. If media provide us with food for thought and talk, that food is digested into citizenship, regardless of its fast or slow food qualities.

Citizenship, whether civic, political or social, is generally understood as a set of rights and responsibilities. The associative link is to voting, the right to social benefits and 'good behaviour' that is attuned to the needs and safety of communities and living environments. Boring and important at the same time. It is invested with emotion though when we cheer on the national team in the soccer world championship, for example. Or when we lament the shortsightedness of governments and politicians. Or are alarmed by ongoing polarization and conspiracy thinking. The first chapter will say more about how we are aware of the emotional investments we have in citizenship but do not give it the attention it needs. It is my mission to show researchers, critics and professionals two things. Firstly, to understand how citizenship is far from the rational arguments-based beast it is often made out to be. Secondly, talking about popular culture is an easily accessible means to gain access to the emotions that hinder and afford belonging, taking responsibility and feeling heard. I am convinced that public professionals and social and cultural critics become better and more effective at what they do when they use the broad concept of cultural citizenship to follow the many everyday life routes that people take to think about their rights and responsibilities and what is best for most of us.

This is important because public professionals see a crisis of citizen disengagement unfolding. Why people would disengage, stop wanting to be volunteers or overshoot their goals in exclusionary activism may well become clearer when professionals allow themselves to tune in to the widespread and ongoing discussion of how the world is meaningful that is afforded by popular culture but that remains 'under the radar.' Feeding citizenship is important. How to belong, with whom to connect and how communities, whether smaller or larger, material or virtual, provide a home: those are all citizenship questions that many worry about. People dream of better worlds. Media offer space to do so, whether as viewers, commenters, producers, listeners, posters, tweeters or readers. In media and cultural studies, there is a long tradition of listening carefully to audiences in order to understand everyday meaning making. Such 'listening in' can be taken a step further. We can hone our skills as researchers, cultural critics and public professionals by understanding how the media engagement of others can be understood as taking up a felt responsibility and acting upon perceived citizen rights, as Dahlgren and Hill (2023) have argued. No matter that crises of participation and democracy have haunted political thinkers throughout the 20th century up to today (cf. Verba 1967). We can start listening to the conversations others are having via popular culture at any moment, whether in real life or on social media. We are offered a gift when we listen attentively to others when they react and respond to media texts, whether on the former broadcast media or on social media. However tentative, unpolished and sometimes offensive, this is where offers of participation and co-ownership of the public sphere are made.

It may feel awkward to understand this as citizenship. The modernist legacy includes a sharply defined image of citizenship as self-assured knowledge, authority and clarity of vision and the competency to present arguments in debate well. Connected to classic notions of masculinity, rationality and meritocracy, it has made us look down on emotionality, affect, unfinished arguments and muddled thinking (cf. Huyssen 1986; Littler 2018; Segal 1990). As a result, it is difficult to hear what others, outsiders, have to say. To feel underqualified to speak publicly is common. Dominant notions of what voices are worth listening to sell democracy short. It betrays democracy's core promise when representation is reduced to voting and voice and agency are reserved for elites, whether they are politicians, professionals, self-appointed loudmouths or entitled men. Listening to less self-assured and well-trained voices is possible: popular culture provides an arena for informal, unforced reflection that is nonetheless citizenship because it is occupied with rights, responsibilities and the relation between societal groups, with what is wrong with the world and with how it could be a better place.

Listening well is not easy. What others have to say can be difficult to hear. Living in very different worlds makes picking up on references a challenge. Viewpoints may be very far removed from the researcher's own. The first part of the book is therefore called 'I hear you.' Recognizing cultural citizenship starts with the willingness to hear what others are saying. How to do this? And why is it so intimately connected to making good on the promise of citizenship as it came into being over the past century and a half? The second part of the book offers a first set of three case studies that underline how listening well depends on keeping yourself as a researcher from moralizing. Jonathan Haidt (2022) suggests in *the Atlantic* that the more we moralize, the less we reflect. Easy though it sounds, not getting on your high horse is a challenge. The case studies in part II show how much being able to *hear* others depends on being aware as a listener of who you are and where you stand. It illustrates the difference between identity, being-identified and identifying-as that is discussed in part I. At issue is becoming more open in our thinking about gender. Turns out that this involves a small step for (wo)mankind but a very large one for women and men.

The third part of the book turns to popular cultural examples that I myself appreciate and have appreciated. Even there, it will turn out, there are no guarantees for finding like-minded and reassuring companionship. I have learned that I have to do more than listen carefully; I have to listen with generosity. This is also the theme of the conclusion to the book, based on the letters David Scott wrote to his dead friend Stuart Hall (Scott 2017). It is to listen while knowing you are given something. To receive is to become beholden, to start a relationship and to be in other people's debt. That makes it much more difficult than giving. Listening is not 'bestowing' attention or shining a light on grateful others; it is to realize your dependency on strangers. In the same article in *the Atlantic* quoted above, Haidt warns us that social media communication over the past decade has been weaponized. Painfully, the issues at stake can be entirely frivolous. As social media have become providers of information about people and issues and that information is assessed by likes and dislikes and vicious attacks that spread like wildfire when they 'go viral,' we have become fearful of stepping out of line. To be tone-policed into silence and to be threatened with rape are horrendous experiences. The lack of curation and fact-checking on social media moreover have made large groups susceptible to misinformation and disinformation. Hearing 'the silent majority' directly on issues that matter has therefore become all the more difficult. Shortcuts and back streets are necessary. If I do my job well, it will become clear how recognizing everyday discussion as cultural citizenship is a worthwhile project. But also that it needs to be grateful and humble in the face of rising distrust and anger. Like Haidt, I am motivated by the triple wish to find ways to rebuild trust, strengthen the reputation of academic knowledge and help unearth the shared stories we seem to be losing. They are an integral part of the different types of social capital that democracy needs.

Citizenship, popular culture and deep affective bonds to the world

Democracies exist as interlinked sets of material practices in specific places. Citizenship is simply the name for the contract that individuals have with the location-based governments that are called nation-states (Gunsteren 1998; Stevenson 2000, 2003). To have 'papers,' a legitimate ID and a working bank card gives you access to work, to housing and to living your life. Beyond that formal relation, citizenship hints at an implied contract that we have with one another as human beings to build and maintain societies (and ultimately a planet). As in a weave, there are warp and weft threads: the ones going lengthwise are crossed with the ones going from side to side. I find it useful to understand society as woven together and therefore in need of top-down and bottom-up connections but also of connections going across. Such horizontal connections can be formal (as in an owners' association of a housing complex) or informal (friends and family). And they can extend to unknown others. What do we expect of them? What implicit expectations and judgements do we have about how others (should) behave or think? Calling this cultural citizenship is to ask: what rights and responsibilities do people feel they have to others? What are they willing to give up and what do they feel they are owed? Answers help understand how safe or unsafe people feel. Where they feel 'at home' and where they are scared. What ambitions they have and what they hope for.

We tend not to talk much about these feelings and assessments. We live them on a daily basis though. In a representative democracy, we are far removed from the political realm and the discussions and considerations that precede decision making. Many in the Global North feel that their concerns are ignored. Small groups fight for their rights. Inquiring into cultural citizenship is to look beyond the political sphere for 'across connections.' They are less visible but important in how they feed a sense of well-being (or lack of it), in the life decisions people make and in the causes they support. All of these micro-movements and feelings 'trickle up' to political decision making (where ways forward are opened or shut down). They are connected to law enforcement, the regulating of care, schooling, work and support for the arts. Societies maintain their strength and resilience by allowing for lived realities to connect sideways, upwards and downwards. Media facilitate these processes. Research into placemaking provides great examples. Think, e.g., of neighbourhoods using social media to connect, work through (painful) change and influence local authorities (Breek et al. 2021).

However important and useful it is to inquire into how professionals and civilians broker relationships, there is also the need to delve one layer deeper and find informal means to make contact with those who do not automatically appear in the purview of professionals, or indeed with the views, thoughts and feeling that do not come in the correct packaging to be heard by those with social, cultural or bureaucratic power. While doing audience research, as I have throughout my work life from the mid-1980s onwards, I have witnessed how others, like me *and* unlike me, use media culture (and especially popular entertainment from sports to tv drama, to games, to social media) to relate to what is going on in the world. Popular and social media fare feed that deeper layer of ongoing reflection and assessments that is constitutive of worldbuilding. How to make contact with the deep feelings, ruminations and affective bonds that are part and parcel of worldbuilding through using popular media? Participative forms of media audience research suggest themselves as appropriate to gain access to tentative, raw and unformed feelings and intuitions through popular culture given how easy its lack of status makes talking about it.

In this book then, the 'cultural' in cultural citizenship refers to *popular* culture rather than culture in general or to Culture with a capital C. Popular culture is a highly suggestive term but not so easy to define well. Here it refers to the amalgam of cultural forms that are used less out of a sense of obligation but rather for pleasure and entertainment, a positive wish to be informed, to be virtually taken to other places and to be made to think or dream. It consists of a plethora of media genres, both fiction and non-fiction. It is not 'texts' in and of themselves that qualify as popular culture; it is practices of use that predominantly link media texts to pleasure and meaning making rather than to professional or other formal obligations. Popular culture spills over into all sorts of popular pastimes, be they shopping, sports or going to amusement parks. They are all practices, whether texts or not, that their participants can be asked about.

Popular culture tends to be discussed lightly or with trustworthy others. Popular culture's reputation may have changed from trash to perfectly ordinary forms of culture – whether we are talking about reality tv, sports, romance novels or, indeed, their television adaptations – but why discuss it with people who don't like what you like? Popular culture offers its users spaces to find one another at different levels of intensity, to commiserate, swoon or complain together, whether simultaneously or distanced in time and place. Different kinds of participant research give access to the stories that unfold there. They can be interviews, observation or participant design, or audience ethnography, as it is practiced here. Audience ethnography inventories, charts and tries to understand rather than offer cultural critique. It allows taking a stance against the still widespread and deeply held conviction that the media influence us. Despite over four decades of qualitative audience research in service of understanding the audience as 'active' rather than 'passive,' the dominant paradigm is still that the media are immensely powerful. Disturbingly, that particular mantra, the 'modernist' paradigm referenced above, has also taken over discussion of the use of social media. Haidt, whose work I find interesting and well-argued, warns convincingly against their fragmentary power. Indeed, the technology and manipulative powers of social media platforms are scarily impressive. Demonizing social media though is also a bad idea. There is an enormous variety of content produced by users of all ilks on social media platforms. Media, whether broadcast or social media, need not be reduced to Janus-faced monsters that are either good or bad for us (Jensen 1990). We are not merely the media's victims or slaves, even if we need new kinds of media literacy that teach appreciation and not just distrust, an argument that will return in chapter 3.

All popular genres and cultural forms allow for researching cultural citizenship: news, satire, YouTube and city building (Burgess & Green 2009; Doona 2021; Hartley 1999; Miller 1996; Yudice 2004). In this book, viewers, readers and users discuss entertainment. The more interesting discussions, not surprisingly, have clashing feelings on casting, characterization, storylines or other aspects of the storytelling that is at the heart of entertainment. Those clashes ultimately refer to issues of representation and identity. As such they are entangled with deep feelings of co-ownership. In this day and age of 'spreadable' media, pride, as much as disappointment and hate, are fuelled easily when they infuse a sense of belonging (or of being excluded). Studying cultural citizenship therefore benefits from using multiple starting points. Not so much in order to compare cases but to learn iteratively from case to case (or site to site) how we might better grasp what is going on in interactions with popular texts and practices.

It also pays to extend one's focus as a researcher from looking at specific text-related examples to a broader understanding that 'semi-public' conversations have changed because of the affordances of social media. Obvious though this sounds, it is important to understand how forms of discussion practiced on social media extend to the discussion of identity and representation in other domains. Two social media practices will illustrate this in chapter 9. They deal with online storytelling on a self-identified migrant community (Marokko.nl) and with racist folkloric practice in the Netherlands. In a similar vein, in chapter 5, parents talk about their (young) children's media use. It shows how, in the discussion of popular entertainment, deep convictions are present about our vulnerability to the images and ethics the media offer, implicitly and explicitly. This tells me that studying cultural citizenship benefits from double contextualization. The first is to understand that patterns and mechanisms found while studying popular entertainment infuse more 'serious' conversations. The second is that media texts and practices do not become meaningful as unrelated single entities. They work in unpredictable tandems and need to be understood cross-medially, as landscapes.

The structure of the book

The book consists of three parts. The first part is concerned with the basics of understanding and charting cultural citizenship in relation to popular culture.

Its keywords are identity, power and affect. As will become clear, 'identity' is a bit of a burden. Audience researchers always run the risk of 'identifying' (as in labelling) others and thereby closing themselves off from what matters to those they label. It precludes listening well. Power and affect have been assigned to different chapters to talk about the perceived power of popular culture (in chapter 2) and the difficulty of researching affect and emotion well (in chapter 3). In fact, all three terms could have been assigned to all three chapters. Understanding cultural citizenship and theorizing it as a form of listening for and charting everyday meaning making requires using them together. Without paying attention to identity investments and their affective load, the power of particular texts and practices is hard to grasp. What Arlie Russell Hochschild (2016) has called 'deep stories' will not be heard.

The keywords for the chapters in the second part of the book allude to deep questions of how to relate to others: culpability, innocence and confusion. The case studies all start from strong negative feelings: about the media in general and television in particular. Sometimes it is individual characters in a television series that become a magnet to voice outrage, even if that character and actor are also defended (Skyler White in *Breaking Bad*). Sometimes the media in general are seen as a minefield of dangers: across three small case studies, parents felt very uncomfortable when it came to their children's gender identities and media literacy. The casting of a woman as the thirteenth Doctor Who in the legendary British television series bespeaks confusion below its veneer of misogyny, transphobia and conspiracy thinking about authoritative media institutions.

The third part of the book counters the hatred and unease of part II. It employs forms of appreciative inquiry to give the paradoxical nature of our interaction with media and popular cultural texts and practices its due. How can I as a feminist be a fan of *The Mentalist*? How, as a loyal fan community, can we feel so critical of exclusion, e.g., in transgender representation, in over a decade of *RuPaul's Drag Race* seasons? And ultimately, how to understand the changes wrought by social media platforms in public discussion as changing cultural citizenship in new exclusionary ways? While there is 'aca' fandom in this part of the book in that some of the case studies are about media texts and forms that are close to my heart, fandom is not a big topic. There are many fans among the viewers, readers, media users and makers that are quoted in the chapters to follow, but it is their far more fleeting everyday media use and incidental conversations that I am interested in.

Three recurring labels need a short introduction. They are governmentality, neoliberalism and affect. Governmentality is the governing of citizens by themselves, literally, through mentality. More than self-discipline, it is also the ideals they aspire to. Under neoliberalism, it is the freedom and agency of individuals and collectives that are the targets of such governing (Dean 1999: 149). Neoliberalism, according to Dean, has a complex relation with neo-conservatism and populist, anti-governmental reactions, as well as with debates on morality and community. Where women are concerned, notions of individual valorization and self-actualization are easily linked to a deeply conservative gender agenda; not so with men. Affect provides the other side to key neoliberal terms that all suggest the possibility of mastery and control over the self and the body. Affect has to do with energy and how we become emotionally engaged through our bodies and how we are moved (Wetherell 2015). 'To be affected' refers to how feelings can communicate themselves as much as words. Reflecting on the use of 'affect' in cultural studies, Grossberg speaks of intensities, texture and timbre and how the discursive and the extra-discursive melt into 'the lived' (Grossberg & Behrenshausen 2016: 1002/3). However poetical, it makes clear how important it is to read as much for the extra-discursive and for discursive structure in how others reflect on their hopes, dreams and frustrations in talking about popular culture. As Ahmed puts it: '[E]motions do things, and they align individuals with communities – or bodily space with social space – through the very intensity of their attachments.' Rather than seeing emotions as psychological dispositions, we need to consider how they work, in concrete and particular ways, to mediate the relationship between the psychic and the social and between the individual and the collective (Ahmed 2004: 119).

In light of the enormous challenges our societies are faced with, cultural citizenship might seem of little consequence. Discrimination, exclusion and unequal chances, the destruction of the planet and the intransigence of our political and economic order seem far removed from popular entertainment. I would argue they are not. Understanding everyday connections and disconnections matters, as do the ways in which we use the media to bolster views and positions rather than to find information or to challenge what we think. Even single Facebook 'likes' can matter when the page is Pietietie, an online petition in favour of the racist tradition of Sinterklaas and Black Pete in the Netherlands. Those mostly carelessly given likes, the page itself made on a whim, mark a turn to deeply troubling populist conservatism that is paving the way for exclusionary rather than inclusive politics in parliament and in everyday life. They redefined who could belong and who could not. Reconstructing the affect and emotion in such discussions or in the hatred of a television character, the deep distrust of popular entertainment helps us understand how so many, in so many ways, feel they are 'strangers in their own land,' to reference Hochschild (2016) once more. It is not that there is a collective lack of civic imagination but there is a lack of recognizing where civic discussion is ongoing. We need to listen for and attend to cultural citizenship as it unfolds all around us. Perhaps then we can discuss how such listening can become part of, say, the media literacy curriculum in schools – but that is a topic for another book.

PART I

I hear you

Popular culture, audience research and appreciative inquiry. Key concepts

This part of the book offers a discussion of the key concepts with which it works.

Chapter 1 Identity: What cultural citizenship is and why studying it matters
Chapter 2 Power: Popular culture as an object of study
          With Jan Teurlings
Chapter 3 Affect: Researching popular culture and cultural citizenship. Rewriting qualitative audience research

1
IDENTITY

What cultural citizenship is and why studying it matters

This is the first of the three chapters that provide the basis for the analysis presented in the later chapters. Well, basis: these first three chapters provide a spiderweb rather than a scaffold. They are intended to provide a sense of context and intellectual history for the rest of the book. How to define cultural citizenship from a feminist perspective is this chapter's central question. By a feminist approach, I mean one that is sensitive to power and structural inequality and that is invested in dignity and respect for all. It nuances what citizenship can do (and tends to do). It puts into focus what a hit citizenship has taken in our current inhospitable world. I am thinking here of the deep fear of strangers that fuels conservative populist politics, as well as the fear of change which, among other forms, appears to be expressed in online hate speech, a sizable part of which is connected to popular cultural texts (Hochschild 2016; Keats Citron & Norton 2011).

Media and citizenship have been discussed at great length. That discussion will almost entirely be absent here. As a hint to how it is an important part of the background against which to read this book, think of the belief in strong public (news) media for democracies, however naïve and archaic such a belief may seem today. Equally, the discussion associated with early cultural studies about the power of audiences versus the power of media and its uneasy division of a popular culture project and a public knowledge project is relevant but not discussed here (Corner 1991). We now know that the two are deeply intertwined and also that it has not especially worked to turn an older notion of powerful media on its head and exchange it with powerful audiences or the importance of everyday conversations.

The idea that it matters what audiences *do* with media, remains a key insight. I at least continue to feel inspired by John Fiske's suggestion to think of popular television in terms of semiotic democracy, John Hartley's DIY citizenship and television as a transcultural teacher, Toby Miller's warning to see how cultural citizenship is resistance and discipline in equal measure, Néstor Garcia Canclini or Anne Cronin's linking of the consumer and the citizen (Fiske 1986, 1989; Hartley 1999; Miller 1996, 2001; Canclini 2001; Cronin 2005). In roughly the same period, Mica Nava, Nick Stevenson, Bryan Turner and Herman van Gunsteren among others pointed out that we needed to rethink citizenship in a more global and cosmopolitan frame (Nava 2002; Stevenson 2000, 2003; Turner 1993; Gunsteren 1998). Their work too was important and deserves more than the brief shout-out it is given here.

Briefly, and in order to provide a road map for the rest of the chapter, cultural citizenship can be found when reconstructing what fuels ongoing conversation and discussion, and how, in and through those exchanges, we connect with others, with places and spaces, with stories and ideas. Cultural citizenship is fed by an ongoing everyday politics of learning and listening connected to testing and rewriting normativity, truth finding, generosity and honesty in our relationships with others. Rereading texts for this chapter, I came across an essay by Nick Stevenson in which he writes that: '(q)uestions of citizenship for Hermes move beyond liberal distinctions between the individual and the state to explore the construction of the ways in which personal identities emerge through the interface of popular culture and politics' (2003: 341). Indeed, here again, I will argue that identity, identification and self-identification need to be studied carefully to understand that citizenships concerns us as persons rather than in a functional capacity.

I define 'identity' as how a person sees themselves and is seen by others. This comes from Woodward's useful discussion in her *Questions of Identity* (2004: 13). Rather than personality, which some would define as a person's core self, identity is the interface between a social role, the way a person performs that role, the emotions and feelings they have and how others perceive them being that particular person. Identity always depends on difference (what I am not), and on community (being the same as some and different from others). Woodward points to Erving Goffman's perspective on the self as dramaturgical: identity is a performance (Goffman 1959). Woodward further suggests we understand identity as 'interface between the personal (-,) the social (-) and the social, cultural and economic factors which shape experience and make it possible for people to take up some identities and render others inaccessible or impossible' (Woodward 2004: 18). The extent to which we have agency or are at the mercy of others, is dramatically different. Identity, therefore, always needs the lenses of power, ideology and the myths we choose to believe in to become understandable. Often without us being aware of this, social expectations and conventions structure our options, whether we comply with them or resist them.

Identity seen thus is an integral part of (everyday) meaning making, which is what audience researchers like myself are interested in for how it allows us to understand how societies function. Hall summarized that, 'in fact, meanings are produced at several different sites and circulated through several different processes or practices (the cultural circuit). Meaning is what gives us a sense of our own identity, of who we are and with whom we 'belong'- so it is tied up with questions of how culture is used to mark out and maintain identity within and difference between groups (-)' (Hall 1997: 3). Circular logics as implied here are frowned upon in scientific circles. In cultural research and in the humanities, it is more or less a fact of life that this is how we come closest to understanding (and critiquing) social reality. Meaning making and identity formation imply each other. Culture is specifically the space where they meet. Cultural citizenship is therefore also where we need to shift from identifying others to the right to self-identification.

About identity

Although they write about slightly different subjects (social and cultural capital, 21st century feminism and media, diversity and inclusion), a number of feminist scholars and activists have shown me how cultural citizenship can best be studied and practiced and how that entails an open and non-agonistic understanding of identity. In practice, identities are contested the moment they become socially visible. They are a burden or a responsibility, a banner or a shield. In *Thick* (2020) Tressie McMillan Cottom rewrites Bourdieuian sociology. One of the book's chapters ('Dying to be competent'), shows how ideology, ideas and images others have of you, can be a matter of life and death.

McMillan Cottom shares her experience as a pregnant black woman. The chapter starts out in a lightly ironic tone as a discussion of competence, and often finding oneself to be incompetent in the most mundane of ways. Don't we all? The argument shifts to how 'competence' is neoliberalism's pipedream which for some reason we like to be sold back to ourselves. ',,, for some of us being competent has always been an illusion. (-) For black women, racism, sexism and classism, have always made us structurally incompetent (MacMillan Cottom 2019: 81). There is a complication four months into the pregnancy and she starts bleeding. 'Bleeding is against company policy almost everywhere. When you are a black woman, having a body is already complicated for workplace politics. Having a bleeding, distended body is especially egregious' (2019: 82). At the obstetrics clinic, there is, unusually, a very long wait. When the doctor finally arrives, he looks at her, says she is probably too fat and spotting is normal. Go home. She starts hurting. Calls the clinic. Does her back hurt? No. It is my ass that hurts. Ah, probably constipation. She does not sleep, keeps bleeding and is finally admitted for an ultrasound in a hospital. Another doctor again dismisses her and a night nurse, almost as an aside, mentions she has been in labour for three days. 'You should have said something,' she scolds. Well, she did but institutions cannot see black women as competent, as having a relevant diagnosis about anything, including their own bodies, as persons. No one paid attention.

There is no happy end to this story, and instead of support, care or sympathy, more scolding: 'Just so you know, there was nothing we could have done, because you did not tell us you were in labour.' Everything about the structure of medical care had filtered her through assumptions of incompetence (idem: 85). The assumption of black women's incompetence includes all who are identified as such, whether a superstar or a researcher.

This is why talking about identity matters. This is why we need to understand exactly how identity is different from *being identified* or *identifying* (as a woman, as a feminist, as a full-bodied person). Talking about identity matters because the differences made by us and to us are instructive. I have had babies in hospital, and as a white woman was treated respectfully until I tried to poke out the eyes of a gynaecology intern who wanted to flatten a rim in what up till then had been my vagina. I have never felt so divested of any say over myself or my body. Likewise, I have experience being overweight in health care where it is a sure sign of lack of competence and control over your body. I have had doctors look at me and say that I am fat, no wonder you have these complaints. Only, in my case, the doctor talked of BMI and genetics, there was a conversation of sorts. Tressie McMillan Cottom and I were never identified in the same way, our positioning as a woman of colour in the United States and a white woman in the Netherlands precluded that from happening. While I identify with her as a woman and as a feminist, I also understand that my experience is one of partial, intersectional privilege and therefore profoundly different.

Having your sense of self ignored, your dignity stepped on and denied, is something most of us will recognize. Multiply by ten if you are also a woman of colour or divide by ten if you are slim and able bodied, or present as male, and there you are. Then start thinking about how limited we are in how we address the pressures we endure from different groups and communities. How rights to dignity and equality are often trampled. The feelings this produces need to be talked about to address the neoliberal lie of 'liberating individuality' that denies discrimination and systemic exclusion. Communities guarantee identities for good and for bad, including 'liberating' individual ones. Citizenship is the interface of that belonging, a way to address what we owe a community and what it owes us. It is the space of the politics of inclusion and its dual requirement that we feel we belong and that we are allowed our uniqueness (Shore 2018). Neither of these is likely to occur if we are not seen.

Identity and popular culture

The rest of this book turns to talk rather than experience. Much of that talk is about identity. It starts from inhabited bodies that 'become' through feelings, emotions, thoughts and affect. Bodies that try to manage how they are seen.

They have to understand who they feel they are so that they know how they want to be seen. They often feel hindered, challenged and threatened by others and occasionally loved and cherished. Regulating these clashes (and sometimes savouring the pleasure of connection), especially when it comes to identity, identifying and identification, is another way of defining cultural citizenship: the –often unaware – reflection on the world, on your rights, privileges, responsibilities and dues that unfolds in using and talking about popular cultural texts.

Like Tressie McMillan Cottom, Amia Srinivasan (2021) manages to shift lenses from debate to theory, to living conditions and back again, going from the particular and the material to logics that can be found worldwide. She argues that feminism must be a political practice that recognizes that a hard distinction between the genders is useful some of the time without needing to subscribe to an essentialist definition all of the time. Positions and identities can overlap as much as they can clash (Yuval-Davis 2006: 202). Srinivasan disentangles the balancing act between self-identifying and being identified and how reflecting on power is to engage with how hatred and disgust are fed. Her book title may sound like a ridiculous question: do we have the right to sex? My first thought was: yes! We all deserve to be loved in deeply intimate ways. The correct answer of course is *no*: we have no *right* to sex; it is not part of any citizenship.

Or is it? Srinivasan's question pertains to incels (involuntarily celibate men), who form a (prominent, online) community primarily in the United States and who think they are entitled to the bodies of others and to their willingness to engage with them. Their caricatures of 'Stacys,' 'Chads' ('attractive' people who can 'get' anybody and 'Beckys' (unattractive needy feminist types) are a violent and misogynist rewriting of the sanitized world of popular culture characters. Reading Srinivasan makes clear exactly why how we use popular culture to talk about who we are and who we want to be, is not innocent.[1] I am not suggesting that popular culture has a more or less direct effect on us as media audiences. Such a denigratory shortcut hardly serves the goal of understanding complicated, ongoing processes of meaning making and identity formation. These processes hardly ever depend on single texts. Nor are single texts so straightforward that they cannot contain both promise and disappointment. Or that they can withstand 'mainstreaming' when they become successful and their radicality is contained. Take super woman Sooraya Qadir, better known as Dust, who saves lives while wearing her niqab. Only in Sarah Alfageeh's original comic version can she take care of herself. In the tv-series *X-men* she has to be saved by her male colleagues, as a disappointed Kauthar Bouchallikht points out (Bouchallikht 2018).

Popular culture matters when it comes to the mundane practices of reproduction of standardized identities. There is no denying that media representation is often a conservative force. As a consequence, the codes in popular culture that feed the ongoing conversation among many of us are weirdly twisted. That makes wanting to use popular culture for a project on cultural citizenship a risk. It limits exploring how we might talk better with one another, and adds to the challenge of being a good ally. The work of McMillan Cottom and Srinivasan, of activist experts such as Zoe Papaikonomou and now parliamentarians such as Kauthar Bouchallikht inspires and helps (Papaikonomou & Dijkman 2018; Bouchallikht & Papaikonomou 2021). Their work makes clear that identifying and theorizing cultural citizenship through discussion of popular culture is both important and limited. However large the collectives that we belong to, they have to make do with what is available. It will take another project to explore how we can have more examples of interesting strong women of all colours, of non-binary representation and of the complexity of identities and allegiances. It is on my list.

Citizenship, feminism and affect

Cultural citizenship as a concept came to matter to me because I identify as a feminist who happens to love popular culture. Clearly, this is a paradox. It is possible to defend popular culture for its occasional inclusion of emancipatory examples and embracing of marginal gendered and sexed identities. In general, though, it is a domain that appears to always tend to reinforce an exclusive normal that is blind to inequality, discrimination, misogyny and violence against all who are not straight, white, young, limber and what is considered to be good-looking. This is not what I wish to defend. On the contrary, I want to defend that whatever is presented textually, audiences will use on their own terms and in ways that they see fit, for good and for bad. It seems to me that they do not believe much of what they see and hear either. Nor is popular culture a guaranteed gateway to a happier view of the world. On the contrary and as the chapters later in the book bear witness to, fear, hatred and frustration are what is voiced via the shared worlds of popular texts, celebrity gossip and sports. Beyond the venting there is also meaningful discussion. While hardly in equal measure, a range of arguments can be found in real-life and in online discussions of popular media texts, characters and practices. Despite its many faults, popular media culture functions as a domain in which we can attain forms of exchange that are hard to achieve elsewhere. Popular culture feeds and tests our collective imagination, the bedrock of citizenship and community-building.

Like popular culture, citizenship is a loaded term. It has been built for men more than for women and is invested in 'hard identities' rather than soft ones. Possibly because they are built on sameness and equality rather than difference. You have the right to vote, or you don't. Soft identities allow for openness, inclusion and change. They are not bound up with exclusive (national) domains or (racial) groups. The marketing-speak of 'target groups' makes clear how hard identities are categorical. It destroys the potential of large collectives whom they lock into definitions of who they are in essence. To attain (or at least imagine) a different kind of citizenship and a broad-minded sense of identities, the lens of social roles (of which all of us can have many) is promising. It is a central part of Habermas' theory of the transformation of the public sphere and his subsequent work on communicative action (1985a, b).

Relying on Habermas' work is not without its problems. I prefer his feminist critics and interpreters, notably Nancy Fraser (1985, 2013). If cultural citizenship is to be a useful tool for understanding hopes, dreams and critique people share, can it be taken further to address prerequisites and obstacles to social change? If yes, for me it would need theorization from a progressive feminist perspective. Ten years ago, I would not have added 'progressive' to 'feminist'. It would have felt like an unnecessary precursor and almost a pleonasm. Not so today. Although feminism has never been entirely a left-wing politics, today, in the wake of the current wave of 'identity politics,' there is strong investment in essentialized identities and differences, the like of which I have not seen for over thirty years. In as far as cultural citizenship is about listening and understanding, it can hardly be about taking a position or about identifying (as in 'labelling') others. It is, of necessity, a call to respect self-identification. To insist on such a right is to challenge the deep meaning of citizenship as a contract between a community and individual actors. Identity in the context of citizenship is embedded, after all, in the rights and responsibilities that the group (or collective, community, nation or state) bestows on individuals and guarantees.

This link between communities, individuals and accorded rights is a complex one. Think only of Covid-deniers in recent years who spread their fears and alarm widely through misinformation (Drazkiewicz & Harambam 2021). They identified as critics of government policy. Respecting this identification only on rational grounds would have immediately denied a significant part of it. Instead of limiting discussion of citizenship, identity and community (via Habermas' notion of communicative action) I propose to include feelings, emotions, affect, ideology, power and their interconnections up front. They converge, in a way, in the right to self-identification. Granting individuals such a right becomes meaningful when we understand society as allowing many communities to exist and flourish alongside and overlapping one another. No matter that they can also be at cross purposes. The bottom line is that if there are no groups or communities to identify with, identities have no meaning.

Useful suggestions to build discussion about the right to self-identification, have been provided over the years. Negt and Kluge (1990), for instance, wrote about counterpublics in the 1970s that evolved around what now would be called self-identification. Warner (2002) more recently understands counterpublics as discursive communities that come into being around public issues. This entails that identity has less to do with origins and far more with beliefs and convictions. These may well change over time, much as Grossberg (1992) suggested how we think of what it means to be a fan. He likened being a fan to managing an investment portfolio. A form of property that changes through investing and losing interest, and that fluctuates in value. Coming from a different direction, Jonathan Gray underlines how dislike, fandom's opposite, is likewise 'political' in nature and therefore related to questions of citizenship. He considers Habermassian 'romaticization of rationality and suspicion of emotions' perfectly useless, whether in relation to politics itself or to popular culture (2021: 216).

Whether they are called counterpublics or discursive communities, whether we speak of fans, anti-fans, dislike-mindedness or citizen roles, popular culture links to politics, however unparliamentary, and can be oriented as much towards social critique or lifestyle choices. Communities offer a sense of belonging by supporting the identities that fit us but cannot be assumed as given or as an always positive presence. While, as individuals, we need the protection of communities, we also need respite from their – sometimes invasive – forms of social control. Indeed, when we are outsiders, we may need protection from exclusionary forms of politics that deny us the right to self-identify, e.g., when we are attacked for our views on Twitter or other platforms.

This is why this project needs to be a *progressive* feminist project. There cannot be first and second-class persons. We cannot go back to colonial times when we have not even managed to fully decolonize. We cannot disavow what we have learned about class and race (Skeggs 1997; Vergès 2021). It cannot be that some of us qualify and others do not. This means that I agree with Thomsen and Essig (2022) that even though I am deeply troubled by the views of 'trans-exclusionary radical feminist,' I cannot start using the acronym TERF as an insult. Such actions will be used against all feminists in irreparably divisive ways. Transness, moreover, incites a true panic that reverberates widely outside (as well as inside) feminist circles. It is one of the (unexpected) finds of chapter 6 in which the choice for a cis-straight woman as an actor to play Doctor Who is traced in online reactions to the BBC Reveal video. Meanwhile, however difficult, it is clear that in this book I will need to depend on the self-identification of others wherever I can.

Two guiding principles for understanding how 'cultural citizenship' can be used well, unfold here. Both address how self-identification is a zone of trouble, intertwined as it is with identitarian politics. The first principle is that the only way to deal with identity politics, inclusion and exclusion, is to remain in dialogue and exchange. Chantal Mouffe's agonistic politics, to fight without becoming antagonists or foes, serves as a model here (Mouffe 2018). The second principle is to be aware that mechanisms of racism, classism and sexism are structural and systemic. Intersectionality too easily focuses on individuals and on feelings and affect without seeing the larger picture. Different forms of discrimination and inequity attach to one another and produce divisions, rifts and inequality across identity categories (Thomsen & Finley 2019). Therefore, while learning how to listen for cultural citizenship, the feminist researcher will always have to go back to structural analysis.

Self-identification has great advantages for cultural analysis but there are also major pitfalls. I am not talking here of methodology but of politics. However counterintuitive and painful this sounds, when citizenship is defined as the right to belong on one's own terms, it can serve exclusion rather than inclusion. For the past two decades, there has been a widespread belief that we should pursue inclusion. An entire diversity and inclusion industry has sprung up, that is well able to make money, even if it rarely delivers what it promises (Chen 2020). Inclusion is imagined as an easy, happy state of being. Amia Srinivasan disagrees and writes that, on the contrary, 'a truly inclusionary politics is an uncomfortable, unsafe, politics' (2021: XV). When we dream of inclusion and belonging, we insist on a guarantee of safety and commonality 'before the fact'. That stops us from dealing with diversity and accepting differences. Insisting on commonality, whether as women, as intellectuals or as people of colour is to push aside 'all those who would trouble (our) domestic idyll' (idem). The challenge for citizenship, for feminism and for change is to deal with the fact that overall agreement and goodwill are the stuff of naive dreams. We are not, deep down, all cut from the same cloth. We will always have to work at accepting difference, at not being understood immediately, at knowing that all relationships are coloured by inequalities and power imbalances. So, while self-identification is a crucial right, to be accepted on your own terms is not. It is always also up to others to recognize and respect that self-identification.

In self-identification, the personal becomes political. In listening to others, including the outrageous things that people will say, we can learn how that is the case. Their intentions might be questionable. As citizens, it behoves us to pay attention, to try to understand and sometimes respond or engage. As researchers, we are offered a chance to learn about the social scripts that have moulded emotions and desires as much as rational behaviours. It offers access to cultural citizenship.

Uses and drawbacks of citizenship as a concept

Renato Rosaldo considered cultural citizenship an oxymoron: 'a pair of words that do not go together comfortably. Cultural citizenship refers to the right to be different and to belong in a participatory democratic sense' (1994: 402). Developed much later than the other 'citizenships' and founded in anthropology, cultural citizenship depends on its earlier brethren and sisters.

Discussion of citizenship will usually reference Habermas' work on the structural transformation of the public sphere, his later work on communicative action and Marshall's 1950 distinction between political, civic and social citizenship. All three citizenships relate to equal rights and duties as defined by a nation-state (rather than a right to difference). Habermas' basic premise is that to be a citizen is to be part of the 'lifeworld' where ongoing conversation can be taken to separate realms that allow for discussing truth, morality and sincerity. The citizen also participates in the 'system' (the state and the economy). Citizenship thus principally allows for translating lifeworld creativity and dialogue into system solutions and procedures. If the lifeworld and its connected discursive spaces work well, the work of governments is fed and criticized and when necessary, innovated.

In his earlier work, Habermas pointed to the historically important role of media, public discussion and literature in co-building early capitalism (with its need of shipping news) and the modern state. He does not mention their dependence on the colonies and slavery, what it was the ships transported to make money for the West. Race like gender is effaced from his account. While early entrepreneurs and industrialists are key players in this transformation, it is the first journalists and literary critics who teach the new middle class to talk and discuss, and reflect on themselves. Famously, Habermas described the Vienna coffee houses of the 17th and 18th centuries as a space of free speech in which the liberal Enlightenment could unfold. 'They were essential social institutions of political modernity—caffeinated pathways out of clan society and into a cosmopolitan world,' says Gopnik (2018). Imagine first being introduced to coffee and then drinking a lot of it. The coffee houses must have been rowdy spaces, full of loud and over-excited males. For the non-white, non-cis-male with no means, as for women, this was, of course, a space of exclusion. A cynical observer would add that it celebrated colonialism and slavery (the coffee bean), patriarchy (no women) and money (no jobs requiring a presence elsewhere apparently). How the coffee house was ever elevated to a pure space of discussion and arguments (rather than excitement), begs the imagination. The reference to heated discussion though suggests a bridge to today's online world, where discussion will get out of hand, is often toxic but also a space of exchange. Jumping ahead, cultural citizenship as I see it, in that light links easily and comfortably to Habermas' historical reconstruction.

A new group of men moving into politics during the French Revolution (1789): this is the best-known association with citizenship coming into being. Women in this period are pictured as knitting while cheering on beheadings (or being beheaded under the guillotine). Some of them organized the Parisian 'salons' that were as much a place of exchange of ideas and debate as the coffeehouses. Habermas did not include these salons in his earlier work (Kale 2002). Neither does Marshall in his reconstruction (discussed next). To write (upper-class) women out of this history (Landes 1988; Maza 1992) is to suggest that the start of several centuries of emancipation was a male affair, an injustice to be sure.

Marshall also took a sexist view of citizenship. He defined it as 'full membership of a community' (1950: 8). He understood it to consist of three parts: civil citizenship (consisting of the rights necessary for personal freedom, such as freedom of speech), political citizenship (the right to participate in the exercise of political power) and social citizenship (the right to a modicum of economic welfare and to share to the full in social heritage and to live the life of a civilized being to the standards of society) (1950: 11). Initially, in the Middle Ages, he argued, these rights were all wound together as the state itself combined political and social functions as well as juridical ones. Over time civic, political and social rights differentiate to form into shapes that are recognizable today.

Once established, citizen rights are not very stable. Early poverty laws, for instance, provide a link forward to what will become social rights but they were also divorced again from a right to a decent income as a result of encroaching capitalist market logic (Marshall 1950: 23). Indeed, those who had no work and thus no income, lost citizen rights and were interned in workhouses (in Britain, Germany, Norway) or what were called colonies for re-education (in the Netherlands) throughout the 18th and 19th century Likewise, the right to education is slow to become attached to citizenship. Note that this is not a right of children. It is, in Marshall's view the right of adult citizens to have been educated, so that they can take up their duties as citizens.

All of this recurs in work on media and citizenship. Developing an argument about television and citizenship Murdock (1990: 13) refers to how the exercise of full citizenship needs resources of information, experience, interpretation and explanation. Television viewers will need to be at least minimally educated to do so. This is exactly Marshall's reconstruction: farmers and artisans become gentlemen, the poor are disciplined, and poverty, the root of much evil, is contained in a bid for civilization. Marshall pays little attention to how civilization is intertwined with disciplining and normalization (Donzelot 1979; Foucault 1975). He thus neatly avoids the family, which, as Foucault and Donzelot have shown, became a relay of government rather than its model (Donzelot 2008: 119). The family, in turn, takes us to how incredibly blind Habermas' work is to gender, gender roles and gendered forms of oppression and abuse.

Reading Habermas' theory of communicative action against the canvas of Marshall's reconstruction makes clear why Habermas needs such an intricate constellation in which the citizen is only one of four roles each of us has access to. In distinguishing between the different spheres of the public, the private, the political and the economical and their signature roles (the worker, consumer, citizen and client), Habermas attends to the complexity of contemporary society. Crucially, he argues that when we communicate in a lifeworld situation, we live, however counterfactually, in the expectation that we can challenge each other on the validity, normativity and integrity (or authenticity) of what we say. In system contexts, on the other hand, we know that other 'media' as he calls them, money and power, operate.

It is Nancy Fraser who opened the feminist discussion of Habermas' theory of communicative action in the 1980s. Tracing discussion of citizenship for my project of 'tooling' cultural citizenship to understand how social change is hindered and might be helped, her work offers crucial insight. Feminism, for Fraser as for me, entails wedding the ways in which ideological and symbolical structures are reconstituted and anchored in material reality and understanding. Habermas seeks to circumvent ambivalence when he distinguishes material and symbolic reproduction but it stops him from seeing how much (re)production is both - whether in families or in work contexts (Fraser 1985: 101). He does not see that the nuclear family is a key site for the reproduction of social relations that directly serves economic goals or that power builds the nuclear family. 'It seems to me a grave mistake,' Fraser writes 'to restrict the use of the term "power"' to bureaucratic contexts' (Fraser 1985: 109). An understatement, it seems to me.

Crucially, in Habermas' account, the citizen only surfaces in the interaction between the state, (the system), and the public sphere. In Fraser's summary: for Habermas, exchange between the public and the private can occur because of the institutionalization of roles: the worker and consumer link the (official) private economy and the private sphere while the roles of citizen and client link the public state and the public opinion institutions (Fraser 1985: 111–112). While it is questionable whether this sophisticated account holds true for today's neoliberal state and financialised capitalism, it does show how the citizen's is a role of reflectivity. The citizen is not a worker, a client or a consumer but a *role* that takes up critique and debate regarding welfare, care, labour, consumption and production. With wilful disregard for the integrity of Habermas' theory, I abstract only this one piece. *Cultural* citizenship is a *role* that allows for diffuse forms of exchange between public and private, system and lifeworld issues. Women's experiences of Habermas' roles, needless to say, have been very different from those of men (Fraser 1985; Hochschild 1989; Pateman 1992). Habermas' citizen is a debater who can hold their own in dialogue with others, a participant in public debate and political culture (Fraser 1985: 115). Child rearing, any of the responsibilities really women take overwhelming responsibility for, is not his thing (Fraser 1985: 117).

(Cultural) citizenship as performance

Judith Kulynich suggests how to build a new vector of feminist use of Habermas' insight by adding performativity to deliberation. Her definitions of citizenship, politics and identity are broad and include how power runs the gamut from interpersonal violence to state bureaucracy. She uses Foucault's theorization of power as productive and insidious, normative and disciplining, to bring out implicit gender and racial norms in bureaucratic societies. Oppression, she argues, is reproduced by people 'simply doing their jobs or living their lives (who would) not understand themselves as agents of oppression' (Kulynych 1997: 319).

Contrary to Habermas' denial of gender's importance, Kulynych suggests we try to realize the extent to which power shapes gender and therefore identity. That it does so, moreover, in such complex ways that understanding and undoing power relations defies straightforward political deliberation. It makes it impossible to define social or administrative change as simply entirely good or bad. Therefore, participation needs to involve more than procedure (as Habermas sees it), it needs to include performance and rules of conduct. Democracy requires more than problem-solving or decision-making. Therefore, it needs forms of deliberation that are open-ended enough to allow for imagination, creativity, critique and change.

Habermas is interested in open deliberation's 'signal function' as a means for 'effective problematization' that enables agenda setting for formal political fora (Habermas 1996: 359). Kulynych points out how this requires 'suitable dramatization'. It has been difficult for outsiders to address the 'cultural common-sensical' that governs these processes (Kulynych 1997: 327) especially when they are seen as overly emotional. Kulynych writes that:

> (s)peech evocative of identity, culture, or emotion has no necessary place in (Habermas') ideal speech situation, and hence persons whose speech is richly colored with rhetoric, gesture, humor, spirit, or affectation could be defined as deviant or immature communicators. Therefore, a definition of citizenship based on participation in an ideal form of interaction can easily become a tool for the exclusion of deviant communicators from the category of citizens (1997: 327).

That means that cultural citizenship is a useful concept separate from and in addition to other citizenships. It can track (heated) feelings about change whether positive or negative. Both are important. Cultural citizenship is not upfront connected with specific genres, texts or practices. Even though humour has become a strength of the populist right, this is not true of all comedy, satire or humour (Nieuwenhuis & Zijp 2022). Think about *the Daily Show*, *Key and Peele* reruns or *Fleabag*. The signature of shows, texts, says little about how they will be talked about and on what mill they will be fodder. The key insight here is that cultural citizenship comes into being when popular cultural practices, texts or forms are used for reflection, whether critically or affirmatively. Such reflection is always also performative and connected with identity construction. Hallsworth sums up well. 'Cultural citizenship: a mode of citizenship that (can be) define(d) as the capacity to speak and be heard, and which cultivates a sense of belonging. (It) transcends the political and legal entitlements and responsibilities that define the state-citizen relationship' (Hallsworth 2022:2).

If popular culture is the exercise ground for cultural citizenship, it needs to be understood for what it is and how we have studied it. The next chapter, therefore, tackles popular culture and how it allows for the analysis of social power relations. Reconstructing the history of popular culture research will touch on how affect (rather than effect) came to be a key term. Belonging and the populist divide over claiming particular forms of belonging (or the loss of a sense of home) will return throughout the chapters and in the conclusion. The popular, after all, offers a sense of place in the world. The challenge is how to reconstruct what goes on in those virtual processes of placemaking.

Note

1 For the incel online community see: https://www.vox.com/2018/4/28/17290256/incel-chad-stacy-becky.

2
POWER
Popular culture as an object of study

With Jan Teurlings

> People griping about nonwhite actors in Bridgerton but not fussing about the Duke wearing riding boots to a ball?! Riding boots!
> (Fredericks 2020 on Twitter)

Popular culture offers unique access to understanding cultural citizenship, simply because it offers simple access to the views of others. Whether in fiction or non-fiction popular culture represents the worlds we live in (or fear to live in, or dream of living in) and we love it for that reason. We know who we are, as our identities are reflected back to us in countless scenarios and from a myriad of viewpoints. As popular culture is either produced for consumption or via platforms that earn their money by having us use them, its producers are always invested in seeking bigger numbers of users. It is easy therefore to feel connected when using popular culture. We know that others will be watching, reading, playing and doing what we are doing.

Beyond the fact that popular culture is easy and fits the purpose of tracking cultural citizenship, it is also a field that has enormous significance in audience research. Either as an object of concern (media effects research by social psychologists and communication scholars) or as a terrain on which hegemony is achieved in a balancing act (cultural studies). This chapter charts how popular culture has been studied in media and cultural studies and how studying popular culture has changed over the past 40 years, the decades that span Joke's academic life.

As a political science student, she was intrigued by the idea that engaging with romance novels could be a form of academic activism (and indignant about the prejudice against women, women's fantasies and this particular genre). That moment is long gone, popular culture research has become a mainstream activity. While this could suggest that popular culture itself has become accepted and is no longer a field of distinction is not the case. Jonathan Gray's (2021) *Dislike-minded* book proves this by analyzing conversations with many who have well-founded objections against popular texts. In an IAMCR roundtable discussion on the power of the popular, the authors of this chapter, Jan Teurlings and I, agreed that the study of popular cultural texts and phenomena does seem to have become entangled with other discussions. Among them discussion of governmentality (the way we rule ourselves and our ruled through mentality) and affect (the interpersonal energy of emotions).

While earlier discussions of popular culture focused on pleasure and meaning making, and the emancipatory potential of popular culture's practices of use, today's discussion feels more fragmented. Much of what used to be subsumed under the label of popular culture (games, social media platforms, tv series) is now studied in its own right and to diverse ends. Popular culture as a whole is hardly ever addressed. Such studies might well point to the literacy of critical audiences (Teurlings 2017) or to how taste is constructed via discussion of popular culture as in *Dislike-minded* (Gray 2021). There is also an interest in affect, in the sensory and emotional appeal of (popular) texts, but that needs research tools beyond the merely textual. I am not focusing on popular culture itself either. It is important though to show why popular culture is such an exceptionally useful field to track cultural citizenship in more detail.

This chapter will provide context to how popular culture has been studied as an arena of hegemonic rule, normalization and resistance. The ultra-brief reference to the work of Fiske, Hartley and Miller in the first chapter suggested as much. Cultural citizenship largely exists in and as that meeting of forces that shape identity and forge submission as well as fantasy selves. To understand power as productive and insinuated in the very fiber of everyday life is to add to feminist insight and to the understanding of a range of forms of identity activism. There is never mere oppression, there is always a little or a lot of something more. Hence the need for cultural citizenship: as a tool to understand contemporary society and especially as a tool that helps make clear why societies globally seem routed towards polarization and public displays of anger rather than to conversation and agreement. Not only is that an effect of social platform algorithms (Haidt 2022), it has to do with a lack of being able to hear the stories of others. To get there though, the history of popular culture research will provide insight into the richness of this field of study. Largely, this chapter will follow Jan Teurlings' and my own argument on how the study of popular culture has changed (Hermes & Teurlings 2021). The *Bridgerton* tweet above was the opening call of the article we wrote after the conference roundtable, it will return towards the end of the chapter.

Losing sight of popular culture

Although popular culture has been studied for almost 50 years, it seems the terms in which it is, have changed almost beyond recognition. On the surface, it would seem that we never really left the terrain of the popular. When analyzing the way Twitter controversies shape public discourse, it is clear a 1980s scholar, magically transported to 2021, would have no trouble approaching Twitter as a cultural forum (Newcomb & Hirsch 1983) where different views and parts of society meet and interact. That same 1980s scholar would also approach Twitter as neither entirely top-down nor entirely bottom-up, operating instead somewhere in between the abstract forces of the cultural industries while generating and requiring activity and enthusiasm 'from below.' Twitter comments are neither high culture nor the kind of authentic folk culture associated with premodernity. All of this to say that yes, Twitter can be considered – *is*, actually – popular culture.

However, Twitter is not studied *as popular culture*. Instead, we look at it and other social media platforms as a place where the free labor of users is exploited (Terranova 2000; Fuchs 2010); as a powerful advertisement platform that manipulates voting behavior through targeted advertising (Tufekci 2014). We look at it as a network that can manipulate public opinion through the creation of botnets (Bastos & Mercea 2019); a place where filter bubbles reinforce existing opinions (Pariser 2011), or as a platform that allows populist leaders to bypass the traditional media of old (Enli 2017). All these forms, notably, hinder open conversation. Popular culture serves the study of 'more important' phenomena that threaten democracy and society.

An interesting example is the recent *Popular culture and the civic imagination. Case studies of creative social change* (2020), edited by Henry Jenkins, Gabriel Peters-Lazaro and Sangita Shresthova. Its intentions come close to this book. Notably and commendably, Jenkins also spends his time on The Civic Imagination Project, 'to explore ways to inspire creative collaborations within communities as they work together to identify shared values and visions for the future,' taking a step away from being a popular culture scholar to being a community worker and activist (http://henryjenkins.org/aboutmehtml). What we see in recent work like this is that, even though the words 'popular culture' figure prominently, the entire conceptual framework that came with the initial discussion of 'popular culture' and 'the popular' has been relegated to the background: the topological distinctions between elite, mass, folk and popular culture; the culturalist insight that popular culture is actively produced; the Gramscian idea that popular culture is the place where common sense is produced and formed. Notwithstanding exceptions, what remains is a 'fun' object ('popular culture') without the conceptual framework that tied everyday practices of meaning making to engaged research of power structures. Or a zone of exploitation, subjection or exclusion, of course.

How did that change occur? And what does it mean if popular culture is to be used for developing understanding of cultural citizenship? In answering these questions, the focus will be on how the cultural studies project transformed, arguably the interdisciplinary domain that introduced and disseminated the term. The point of reference here is what came to be known as cultural studies in the 1980s and 1990s and originated in Britain (focused on class and ideology), Australia (work on policy, governmentality and the creative industries) and the USA (fans, genres and affect). While less easily identified, it originated elsewhere too, for instance as studies of youth culture and music in Scandinavia or multiculturalism in South America. Work that approaches popular culture as folk culture (as in ethnologist approaches, e.g., at German universities) or uses literary methods has been left out of this overview. The cultural studies of the 1980s and 1990s, published in *Cultural Studies* and, by the end of the decade, in the *International Journal of Cultural Studies* and the *European Journal of Cultural Studies*, understood popular culture as a linking pin. It connected what Williams called a structure of feeling with concrete and identifiable cultural texts. Popular culture was understood as giving access to the hearts and minds of 'ordinary people,' to what connected those who did not have automatic access to the public space of politics and information. In entertainment, politics and the popular were understood to merge.

Cultural studies' modes of political engagement changed, as did the popular culture objects that were (and are) studied: from soap opera to reality TV, to games and social media today. A genealogy of the *debate* on popular culture, in the precise Foucauldian sense of the word, is 'a history of the present,' one that explains how the present moment came into being (Foucault 1977: 31). From a vibrant, engaged form of scholarship emerged something completely different, in which recognition of the merits of popular culture – understood as texts-in-action, the text/style/object-related practices that are energized by the shared use of music, TV series, clothes – have been drastically altered and perhaps even been lost. Even though the focus here is how popular culture objects have been approached, it is worth pointing out that as a field of objects that energize and connect, popular culture itself has also changed, for various technological, economic and political reasons.

The merging of popular texts and politics that is characteristic of cultural studies work, is prefigured in Hall and Whannell's collection *The popular arts* (1964) and Fiske and Hartley's *Reading Television* (1978). Both books depend significantly on semiotics, where later work merged semiotics and Marxism with an ethnographic approach. They need to be credited with making well-read 'low cultural' texts worthy of serious academic attention. Popular television as in police series, westerns, Ian Fleming's James Bond novels, jazz and advertising, are all discussed. 'Popular culture' itself, as a label, is put to new use to undo the ideological force of the high-low culture distinction and expands the much more restrictive use of the term by historians such as Burke (1978). The key element that changed is that the commercial nature of these widely used and appreciated texts no longer counted against taking them seriously.

Early work on popular culture in cultural studies, in its enthusiasm to defend the relevance and importance of this new domain of critical work, developed a penchant to cast different kinds of everyday, often media-related practices as transgressive and resisting dominant culture. These claims may not always have been entirely convincing. A certain level of 'optimism of the will' was required by researchers and readers, but it was not an impossible task. There were enough links to progressive ideas in the popular culture of the 1970s–1990s to at least warrant the option of reading popular cultural practices as progressive (via oppositional or aberrant decoding). In today's context that feels more problematic. Gamers out to bully women journalists (Seymour 2016); conspiracy theories; the deep commercialization of making your own online influencer video: all of these examples either do not read as a political agenda, or when they do, do so as a deeply exclusionary and right-wing one. The occasional hopeful reading of e.g., *RuPaul's Drag Race*, as an emancipatory moment that queers gender conventions and offers a highly diverse range of ethnicities in competitors on this television show, also points to host RuPaul's deeply neoliberal convictions. Fans and viewers combine their love of the show with the criticism that it discriminates against darker-skinned queens and trans women as contenders (see Chapter 8). All of these changes within popular culture and in its users as well, go a long way in explaining how we lost sight of the popular as a domain of energy and possibility. At least as important are a series of paradigm shifts that gradually shifted the object of cultural studies.

Before proceeding to an overview of these paradigm shifts, a word of clarification. This reconstruction might be interpreted as a story of betrayal – a once vibrant approach was betrayed by subsequent scholarship – and a call to return to the origins. This is not what this chapter wants to do Each of the changes identified below responded to earlier problems and offered valuable ways forward. It was, in other words, not a question of betrayal but of scholarly work responding to paradigmatic deficiencies and societal changes (and in some instances, changing political priorities). The net effect of this work of advancement has been a gradual redefinition and reorientation of the field, which in turn necessitates a defense of sorts for returning to it.

Uncritical celebration rather than critical reflection

The first movement *away* from studying popular culture through the lens of the popular did not take place as a result of a paradigm shift, but rather as the result of unease with the direction the study of popular culture had taken. It is easy to forget how soon this sense of unease emerged. Already in 1988 – a year after John Fiske published *Television Culture* – Meaghan Morris published her *Banality in Cultural Studies* essay, which became the programmatic text in the anti-celebratory approach to popular culture. 'I get the feeling that somewhere in some English publisher's vault there is a master-disk from which thousands of versions of the same article about pleasure, resistance and the politics of consumption are being run off under different names with minor variations' (Morris 1988: 15). Morris' critique entailed more than the complaint that the celebratory takes on popular culture were repetitive and decontextualized. She also argued that the use of interview material amounted to little more than a 'vox pop' technique, in which the interviewer becomes the spokesperson (and thus privileged interpreter) for what the interviewee 'actually' means: 'The people is a voice, or a *figure of* a voice, cited in a discourse of exegesis' (1988: 16, *emphasis in the original*). Or, in one of the harsher judgements in the essay, 'the people are [... ...] the textually delegated, allegorical emblem of the critics' own activity' (ibid.: 17). Thus, instead of giving a voice to 'the people,' the scholars of popular culture were depicted as having become narcissistic ventriloquists, who make ordinary people utter the words they want them to speak. The result was a left populism that was mechanically transposed on any given situation and lost its critical bite.

The loss of critical purchase was also at the center of Jim McGuigan's book-length critique *Cultural Populism* (1992). In a recent interview, he recounts the context in which he intervened:

> In the 1980s, interpretation of the culture of 'ordinary people' in cultural and media studies had become peculiarly reverential and even celebratory [... ...]. I had myself gone along with the rather more positive estimation of contemporary popular culture until the point – probably when reading John Fiske – when I thought, come on, this has gone too far! Critical judgement had been abandoned too easily
> (Moran & McGuigan 2020: 1005–1006).

McGuigan did not challenge the importance of studying popular culture: he remained attached to the idea that 'the cultures of ordinary people are of paramount importance' (ibid.: 1007). (One might wonder who is and is not included under 'ordinary people.' Are we, as intellectuals? Should we not speak of ordinary or everyday culture?) Regardless of having second thoughts about McGuigan's choice of words, it is useful to underline how he was not alone in considering the knee-jerk celebration of popular culture an undesirable evolution of an otherwise correct idea that popular culture was a terrain not to be neglected by politically engaged intellectuals. These early criticisms of the cultural studies project on popular culture represent a corrective moment, more interested in a return to the source than in abandoning it: not a loss of the popular but a reappraisal of it. As a corrective moment, it also came with its own set of limitations. The work of John Fiske conveniently served as a shorthand for all of cultural studies, which does not do justice to the wide variety of nuanced empirical work that was dismissed as celebratory and populist. Neither did his critics give John Fiske any credit for the wave of scholarly enthusiasm and inspiration that his work undeniably generated, or the complexity of his reasoning.

Institutionalization: from popular culture to audience research

Looking back, the earliest engagement with popular culture from a cultural studies perspective to gain widespread renown was at the Centre for Contemporary Cultural Studies (the CCCS) in Birmingham. There is the famous *Resistance through Rituals* (Hall & Jefferson 1975) collection on youth culture and how its rebellion against established class culture is afforded by making wayward use of consumer culture. The attraction of the CCCS books and earlier stenciled papers lies at least in part in the surprising tolerance for consumption and what could easily be demeaned as trivial pastimes and interests, given the keen interest in Marxist philosophy at the Centre.

At the CCCS, the importance of everyday meaning making and of popular culture was never a given, nor was their significance ever underestimated. Rather, both were felt to be in need of theoretical understanding. With regard to conceptualizing popular culture, Gramsci's writing (1971) on civil society, common sense and organic intellectuals was important, as was Althusser's work (1971). Althusser offered ideology and recognition as concepts, while Gramsci solved Althusser's problematic distinction between science and ideology, as well as the associated notion of false consciousness. He also insisted on common sense as fragmented, disjointed and contradictory (and thus open to change). In an essay originally written in 1977, Hall, Lumney and McLennan explicitly bring both arguments together: 'Because Gramsci does not work with a true/false consciousness or science/ideology model his thinking is directed towards the contradictory possibilities within spontaneous, non-systematized forms of thinking and action' (2007: 284). Allowing for contradiction might well be the single most important contribution to critical thinking that made studying popular culture at all possible. It will return as a key element in the next chapter on methodology. It is in and through contradictions and paradoxes that the daily work of understanding the world and making it one's own, finds its shape.

'Contradictory possibilities' also allow understanding how exceptional a collection *Resistance through Rituals* is in combining a Marxist perspective, extensive ethnographic description and a somewhat romantic rendering of the spirit of independence amongst young people. Together with Dick Hebdige's slightly later *Subculture. The meaning of style* (1979), *Resistance* established the political significance of youth culture. *Subculture. The Meaning of style* in turn established the 'reading' of culture as a valid method of cultural research that Meaghan Morris would be so very critical of ten years later. Its implied method is ethnographic, even if Hebdige does not offer a methodological account. Like Marxism, feminism is an important source of inspiration for CCCS researchers. It allows for a different type of argumentation, as becomes clear from the work of the CCCS women's group in *Women take issue* (1978). It is far less celebratory though of popular culture and resistance against dominant culture than the work of the men is.

The famous example of Angela McRobbie's chapter in *Women take issue*, in which she wrote about talking with girls about their bedrooms, provides a link to popular music but also to acquiescence with patriarchal rules. Both returned, popular music and women's popular culture, in work undertaken in the United States. American media and cultural studies scholar Larry Grossberg wrote about popular music and resistance. He would also introduce the notion of 'affect,' which was to provide a new direction for cultural analysis (defined broadly) by the end of the 1990s. Unaware of the work in Birmingham, UK, Janice Radway studied romance reading in the United States, following a remarkably similar logic to the CCCS Women's group (Radway 1984). She, too, understood women's reading of romances as only a temporary bid for freedom that at the same time rewrites dominant ideology. Romance reading rebuilds masculinity as both caring and spectacular, as part of a fantasy shared by novels and readers.

In the early 1980s, studying popular culture was a political act in itself. Authors engaged with social power relations and subordinate groups by doing research among different groups of popular culture users. Taking the perspective of its users (rather than that of popular culture's critics) was commonly referred to as 'ethnographically inspired.' Whether it was Ien Ang's work on *Dallas* (Ang 1985), the prime-time soap series, Radway's work on romances (Radway 1984) or Morley's on television viewing (Morley 1980, 1986). Their seminal texts all start from the experiences of actual viewers and readers, who talk about cultural texts that are not deemed very worthy. Their work countered established notions about the utter lack of quality in popular entertainment that John Hartley dates back to the 19th-century tenets of class culture. It also countered how these tenets were upheld by what he calls the knowledge class: schoolmasters in the 19th century, intellectuals of the 'fear' school in the late 20th century (Hartley 1999: 124, 133, 134). While Morley, Ang and Radway offered a combination of ethnographic method and engagement with texts, the method part of their work was not what attracted others to this new field of study. They were read as alternatives to the dismissive and pessimist 'mass culture' paradigm (Jensen 1990) and fed a gleeful sense that consumer culture might not be all bad.

Notably, the double political agenda their work served was a feminist one rather than the Marxist one in the earlier work at the Centre. Ang suggested that melodrama's tragic structure of feeling allows for emotional realism, a new term with which to approach how media texts become meaningful. Rather than reduce reactions to the soap series as sentimental drivel, and a typical example of women's culture, Ang offered an account of the kinds of imaginary identification involved in engaging with media texts. Morley focused on both class and gender in his work, carefully noting how masculinity in the home is a mode of power. While attacked for interpreting romance reading as a form of proto-feminism, Radway showed popular culture to be a space of negotiation that temporarily rewrote patriarchal rule and ideology, in that romances challenge that it is always women's task to care for others emotionally, and not men's.

While Ang, Morley and Radway are seen as media and cultural studies scholars, it is earlier work at the CCCS that established academics studying popular culture as 'organic intellectuals' (Fernandez Castro 2017). 'The popular' and 'common sense' had come to be considered valuable categories. Morris correctly identified the sleight of hand taking place, from the voice of the people to the academic as a mouthpiece. She was too irritated, however, to see how ethnographic insight had simultaneously come to be valued in cultural studies, stemming from academics' personal engagement with specific popular cultural texts as well as with a strong wish for non-patronizing forms of research. As Richard Hoggart said when talking about literacy in 1998: 'You see you're always torn if you come from my kind of background. (... ...) Perhaps excessively, you don't want to appear to patronize. You want to understand better. So I wanted to avoid two things in *The Uses of Literacy*. One was the dismissal of working-class culture as though it was nothing, was worthless or crude. And the other was sentimental acceptance, which is just as bad' (Gibson & Hartley 1998: 14).

The early 'organic intellectuals' cared about specific texts and their users. As the focus on media use grew stronger, there was a move away from 'the popular' as such while criticism of the new popular culture research intensified. Curran criticized what he called 'the new revisionism' in mass communication research for its lack of historical awareness of earlier pluralist communication research that held similar tenets regarding audiences' appreciation of media texts (1990: 158). When Simon Winslow and Stephen Hall reviewed the second edition of *Resistance through rituals* a decade and a half later, they reiterated a sense of disappointment that has come to haunt cultural studies: 'We did expect Hall and Jefferson to deal directly with the main flaw of the BCCCS's work, which for many of its critics is the assumption that youth subcultures have the irrepressible ability to avoid the compulsions and seductions of the consumer culture they inhabit, always nimbly moving beyond its chain of signification and processes of identification to fashion their own meanings and identities as methods of resisting the dominant order' (2007: 395).

While early popular culture research presented a happy and irreverent mix of disciplinary backgrounds, ranging from the literary to criminology, sociology, political economy and psychoanalysis, the 1990s proved a period of attrition and disciplining of an unruly field. For Curran, the fact that researchers did not understand their compliance with consumer culture, pointed to how the new cultural studies work was really just a new chapter in the tradition of mass communication research. Winslow and Hall spoke of post-war sociology and a similar failure not to take mass cultural and consumerist manipulation into account. Others felt that the link made to ethnography is erroneous. Although the new audience researchers might well have been inspired by how critical anthropologists took Geertz's 'thick description' further to question the power relation between researcher and researched (Clifford & Marcus 1986; Geertz 1973), they were not actually doing fieldwork. Often, the power of popular culture was such that researchers felt deeply familiar with what they studied and used personal experience rather than long interviews or participant observation in a more formal sense. This is not incommensurable with ethnography (Hammersley & Atkinson 1989). It did differ greatly from the lengthy fieldwork that, exceptionally, Marie Gillespie (1995) conducted in East London about television among the families she had come to know as a school teacher or that Sarah Thornton (1995) conducted in clubs studying club culture.

Over two decades, work that started from engagement with forms of culture that were presumed to be worthless brought about the revaluation of 'the popular' and popular culture, and then again lost the claim of transcendent value in popular culture as a phenomenon in and of itself. Neither Ang nor Radway understood romances or melodrama as in themselves empowering, but they did appreciate how these particular texts allowed audiences to use their agency and imagination to make them empowering. Ten years later, neither Gray (1992) or Gillespie (1995), nor Hermes (1995) understood the video recorder, television or women's magazines as 'prime movers.' In the first instance, their interest was in the audiences they studied. How specific (sub)cultural forms inspire audience members was to be culled from how informants talk about their lives and media preferences rather than from the media texts or practices themselves. Media texts and technologies were credited with providing instances of resistance. Gray, for instance, noted how her informants explained their complicated cookers to her when talking about household technologies, but claimed they could not program the family VCR. A case of calculated ignorance, she argued: not knowing how to do this meant one chore less on their plates. However telling, this was a minor countermove compared to the much grander claim made by Fiske for popular cultural texts. The shift away from the 'power of the popular' was mirrored in a much stronger emphasis on method: cultural studies was no longer a free space in academia that attracted radical thought. While all of these newer authors related their work to everyday practices of meaning making and the power relations that shape these practices, they were more accurately labelled as politically engaged than as radicals or organic intellectuals.

In another decade, 'aca(demic)-fans' will reclaim free space and, much to the amazement of outsiders, such subjects as 'Buffy studies' become part of the academic curriculum (Hills 2002). Here a different logic returns us to popular culture as text where unexpected discoveries can be made. Here, too, the operative suggestion is that the gap between literature and pulp is not as wide as is believed. In this case, it leads to the emancipation of exceptional texts and not their users, and while it broadens what may count as 'high culture,' it leaves the distinction between high and low culture intact. Otherwise, popular culture studies will mostly turn into audience studies.

Governmentality. Foucault, again

The influence of governmentality studies presents a second decisive shift away from popular culture (even though, as we will see, it did not abandon the notion entirely, but instead reinterprets it by linking it to its strategic use in the wider field of culture). The influence of governmentality studies came rather late, considering the long-standing influence of Foucault on cultural studies. The focus initially was very much on Foucault's earlier work on discourse (Foucault 1970, 1972). When his later work on power/knowledge, governmentality and practices of the self was used, it was interpreted in such a way that it always led back to discourse. (Hall's chapter in the Open University textbook *Representation: Cultural representations and signifying practices* (1997) is a good example of this tendency to 'discursify' Foucault). This changed around the 2000s, when the exhaustion of the Gramscian influence on cultural studies opened up a space for reinterpreting Foucault's work. The concept that generated the most scholarly enthusiasm was governmentality. This brought a radically different approach to culture, a paradigm shift that was less interested in conceiving culture as the site of the creation of common sense, than as a field crisscrossed by strategic power relations.

A cursory glance through the table of contents of the 2003 collection *Foucault, Cultural Studies, and Governmentality,* a fairly typical selection of the work being conducted under the rubric of governmentality at the time, illustrates this new orientation of culture towards strategy. There is an article on how new communication technologies have been strategically deployed in order to reconfigure the home along neoliberal lines (Hay 2003). Mary Coffey (2003) offers an analysis of the role of museums in the reconfiguration of Mexican society towards neoliberalism. Samantha J. King (2003) analyzes the rhetoric of cancer survivorship as embodied in initiatives like 'Race for the

Cure' and examines how such consciousness *cum* fundraising events redefine citizenship away from the State and towards individual ethical notions. As diverse as these analyses might be, they all approach cultural phenomena as strategically deployed in pursuit of some higher good, usually involving some large-scale but low-intensity transformation of society. In this sense, the governmentality approach to culture represented a return to earlier strands of sociological analysis that stressed the instrumentalist character of cultural goods (e.g., Vance Packard's *Hidden Persuaders* (1957), but also to some of the work of Bourdieu that stresses the role of symbolic goods in establishing and maintaining different social positions (e.g., Bourdieu 1980).

Two observations are worth making here. First, almost unnoticed, the governmentality approach to culture eliminated the adjective 'popular' from its conceptual apparatus. (It is worth noting, in this context, that Tony Bennett's contribution to the above collection is simply called 'Culture and Governmentality'). Read positively, this meant that cultural studies widened its scope to also include phenomena that were previously considered to be 'high culture.' Yet, more often than not, this also had the consequence that the entire notion of the popular was evacuated from the discipline. To be sure, governmentality scholars still scrutinized popular culture objects, ranging from computer games like *Civilization* (Miklaucic 2003) to reality TV shows like *Judge Judy* (Ouellette 2004), but they did so without invoking the popular as a recognizable entity, phenomenon or field.

The evolution of Tony Bennett's work is a good example of this switch away from the popular towards the wider field of culture. His earlier work was heavily invested in the notion of the popular, e.g., in his writing about James Bond as a popular hero (Bennett 1982, 1986). But by the early 1990s, he had made the switch away from the popular to study one of those classic loci of high culture: the museum, which he analyzed from a governmental point-of-view (1995). The series of essays gathered in *Culture: A Reformer's Science* (1998) is the culmination and further theorization of how the governmental turn impacted cultural studies' understanding of culture.

This does not mean that the notion of popular culture was abandoned in its entirety within governmentality studies, even though it was given a much diminished and certainly much less prominent place. True to form, governmentality studies at times invoked the opposition between high and low culture, but only to the extent that the difference was strategically deployed by those wanting to intervene in a social field. In Bennett's words: 'Rather [..] than speaking of a contest of high culture versus low culture, the logic of culture, viewed governmentally, organizes a means for high culture to reach into low culture in order to provide a route from one set of norms for conduct to another' (1998: 79). Consequently, if – and this is a big if because occasions were scarce – governmentality scholars used the term popular culture, it was always from the viewpoint of how the notion was strategically deployed.

Whereas in earlier times, the popular had been connected with both power and resistance, it was now cast adrift, or back to being seen as what needed to be 'reformed.'

Affect

The move towards affect theory constitutes the final and definitive turn away from earlier efforts to understand popular culture for its own sake. While not named as such, affect was always part of studying popular culture as a political moment. Ang traced an intricate relationship between the melodramatic text (and its tragic structure of feeling that defines happiness as always transient and short-lived) and the emotional realism it affords. This ultimately revolved around the kind of energy soap opera offers its viewer: it seems to be a kind of warmth, a feeling of recognition and being recognized. That feeling, however, was couched not in terms of affect but in terms of ideology – an Althusserian rendering of the power of television as ideological state apparatus. Likewise, when Valerie Walkerdine (1986) wrote about watching *Rocky II* (the movie) with the Cole family, she pointed to how the film offers a fantasy of transformation, drawing together the text, psychoanalytical insight and theorization of identity and subjectivity. The actual popular text is crucial to the unfolding psychic processes. Psychoanalysis, however, is not an approach that is much favored in cultural studies. As a theoretical apparatus, it goes against the radical contextualization and Foucauldian understanding of subjectivity that is enthusiastically taken up by the field. Psychoanalysis' association with textualist approaches in film studies has not helped. Nevertheless, in analyses like Ang's and Walkerdine's, there is a notion of affect at work.

Discussion of affect as such emerged in cultural studies in the mid-1990s to fill a void. When Larry Grossberg spoke of affective sensibility in relation to music fandom (Grossberg 1992), he used it to critically intervene in a discussion of identity and representation that felt too mechanical to him. According to Grossberg, affect is a subjective feeling, which 'gives 'color,' 'tone' or 'texture' to our experiences' (1992: 57). He used the concept of affective sensibility to think of identity outside of modernist and essentialist parameters, as historically and culturally constructed, as fluid and fed by (popular) culture. As a term, affect locates the 'doing of popular culture' (rather than popular culture as text) between subjects by following in Spinoza's footsteps; it aims to recognize energy and change in 'being affected.' While 'emotion' is used to refer to the social performance of feelings and sensations, affect refers to the power of moments of connection, whether positively or negatively (Wetherell 2012). While arguably this could tie in with engaging with the popular to understand its power, this is not what happened.

A 1999 article by Sara Ahmed illustrates this perfectly. Just before Ahmed's work turned to affect, she wrote about 'becoming' by focusing on how texts interpellate readers and construct them in doing so – which as a reader we may also resist. Her mode of analysis was to read popular texts against philosophical 'master texts.'

> It is my position that a close and critical reading of master-texts such as *A Thousand Plateaus* is of fundamental importance to Cultural Studies. This is not because I think we should keep a canonical narrative in place of the production of (high) theory. Rather, we need to attend closely to texts which have been read as originary and as charting a field. In the case of *A Thousand Plateaus*, the critical appropriation of models of becoming, bodies without organs, bodies as machines and desire as positivity, all mark its powerful dissemination in cultural theory.
>
> (Ahmed 1999: 49)

The crucial text here is the philosophical one in which Deleuze offers a complicated and little accessible account of capitalism and/as schizophrenia. Ahmed's retelling of the narrative of *Dances with wolves*, the 1990s movie, was used as ammunition against it. Ahmed was not interested in the film's appeal as popular culture, she was interested in the homology between the two (very different) texts that allowed her to develop what reading 'skeptically, critically and closely' as a feminist (idem 49) might mean in relation to engagement and the power of phantasy, and against essentialized notions of identity. Much can be recognized here, but not in any known configuration of what was previously known as 'doing cultural studies.' Partly it is Ahmed's unique approach. Equally, it was a sign of the times that we had moved far away from the exhilaration and pleasure that early cultural studies found in subcultures and youth culture and in popular entertainment.

From pleasure to power to affect and identity

While cultural studies stopped studying popular culture in order to understand 'the popular' as a field that allowed for the study of power relations and meaning making, and started using it, among other things, as a means to confront high theory, neoliberal politics was consolidating. Initiated in the Western world by politicians such as Thatcher, Reagan and Kohl, in the 1990s, neoliberalism became part of British Labour's creative industries policy (Hewison 2014). Culture, regardless of its provenance, was felt to be an 'expedient' for all sorts of policy initiatives and governmentality in general (Yudice 2004). The broad field of media and cultural studies keenly felt that it needed to turn away from what was now deemed to be too naive an approach to mediated culture. It did not help that the new reality genres that offered a public presence to non-professionals, or 'ordinary people,' and then the new digital platforms that allowed for amateur production, after a brief moment of anarchist hope in the late 1990s, could be seen to close down rather than open multiple identity formation (Ytreberg 2004; Lovink 2002, 2011). To understand the politics of the new media culture as allowing for broad fantasies of new selves and different worlds, felt like a small part of a troubling and much larger whole. There were exceptions, of course, that recognized the political power in media as information and in the pleasure of cosplay (Andeweg 2017; Fox & Ralston 2016; Gn 2011) but the moment of 'the popular' was past.

Today, when popular culture is referenced in the hybrid field that includes cultural studies but also sociology, popular culture and the popular have become part of a research tradition, as in John Storey's work, or props for quite different arguments. When Wood and Skeggs write about reality TV, they discuss class and gender (Storey 2018; Skeggs, Thumin & Wood 2008; Wood 2017). When Jo Littler makes her case against meritocracy and unveils it as neoliberalism at work, she references the ultra-rich as they populate TV programs and popular figures such as the 'mumpreneur' (Littler 2018). When Gloria Wekker deconstructs the politics of race in the Netherlands, the yearly Sinterklaas festivities and its caricatural Petes in blackface serve as an example of popular culture as a deeply conservative and exclusionary force (Wekker 2016).

It is well possible that had Stallybrass and White (1986) come across Sinterklaas when writing their *Politics and Poetics of Transgression*, they would have interpreted the Petes in Blackface in terms of carnival and exhilaration. Referencing medieval examples, they would have cautioned that these were raucous and uncouth times that did not particularly score well on inclusion or emancipation. In as far as the popular has carnivalesque traits, Stallybrass and White might have argued that these have to do with temporarily stepping out of line, suspending the normal order and turning power relations upside down. That contemporary scholars approach such popular energies with distrust has very sound political reasons in times when QAnon believers storm the US Capitol. In the current conjuncture, it seems that the Right is simply better at reading and using Gramsci. Cultural studies, on the contrary, seems to have lost its sense of how texts might energize and produce collectivity and utopian connections. Of course, cultural studies also gained critical awareness through its understanding of governmentality, and through its theorization of affect and how the senses are involved in processes of meaning making.

The 'moment of popular culture' was relatively short-lived but highly influential. It is a foundational moment in the history of cultural studies and it allows the use of popular culture as a field, defined decades past, as still an arena or a space for discussion of crucial importance to cultural citizenship and identity formation. This old discussion also offers a clear route towards understanding the discursive and the affective as involved in one another. The next chapter will tackle how to respect each of these perspectives in relation to one another methodologically, a challenge in and of itself. Interlocking changes in the mediatic and political environments, changing political engagements and changing scholarly views, changed how media and cultural studies approached popular cultural texts and practices. Methodologically, these changes consolidated into a move to audience studies. This was as much a response to changing media technologies as it was an attempt to attenuate and empirically ground some of the more grandiose claims made in the 1980s.

Popular culture is a key site for the production and reproduction of hegemony (Storey 2018: 3). It provides us with easy means to reflect on what binds and what divides us, whether such forms of cultural citizenship take progressive or conservative forms (see chapters 4 and 5). It affords wholehearted immersion and excitement over issues that are deeply political, but quite possibly more properly belong in other realms. The opening quote of this article, one of the many tweets about the Shondaland series *Bridgerton* for Netflix (Chris Van Dusen 2020) proves this point: *Bridgerton* is based on a series of romance novels, one of the ultimate 'pulp' genres. As a Netflix offering, it has become 'drama.' In the hands of producer Shonda Rhimes, it also became a political vehicle to suggest that racial diversity requires only the smallest leap of the imagination. On Twitter, however, the series becomes a *cause célèbre* to vent outrage over historical inaccuracy: not just about whether or not the English nobility might have been a more diverse group of people than is assumed, but about its costumes and musical scores as well. An astounding wish for authoritative, historically correct storytelling seems to motivate the twitterers. The point seems lost that *Bridgerton* might simply be an instance of 'the popular,' of that which gives us energy and hope and a sense that everything might be better (and to h*** with historical accuracy and other norms, codes and prescriptions). A pity really, that without the popular, we are all dancing in our riding boots (which, for the uninitiated, is truly extremely uncomfortable).

3
AFFECT

Researching popular culture and cultural citizenship. Rewriting qualitative audience research

Methodology often feels like a challenge. It is a moment of reckoning, of justifying how particular cases were chosen, questions asked, material collected and analyzed. It can be more than a moment of accountability; it can be a moment to consider storytelling and why we do research. In cultural studies, there is space for an author to be visible in her narrative. Thinking and writing about methodology can be turned into a moment of self-reflection and identification. This is helpful in producing better theory and stronger forms of cultural critique and making them as convincing as they can get.

My story as a researcher and a cultural critic hinges on doing giant jigsaw puzzles. When I theorize practices of everyday meaning making, I use the writing and research of others for inspiration and validation. The theoretical emphasis can shift. Sometimes practices of everyday meaning making are best seen as fueled by relations of power. At other times, imagined identities, affect and emotion help come to a critical understanding of how media are used in a particular way or, indeed, why work and life practices are organized the way they are. In this book, the case studies all turn to cultural citizenship, to how we inform ourselves and are informed by media texts and by others about what is right and wrong in society, and how we imagine better worlds or the collapse of the current one.

Whether I talk about empirical analysis, data collection, the reading of interview transcripts, notes or logs of online discussion, thinking about a good data set, how to assemble it and take it apart again in analysis, has its charm. Philosophical and theoretical points of departure provide a compass. This chapter addresses different forms of listening to others talk about media, whether 'live' in (long) interviews, or online or in participative research and design projects. It will point to how 'doing' data analysis is underdiscussed,

DOI: 10.4324/9781003288855-5

and, secondly how overly formalized methods leave (too) little room for contextualization and for the kind of storytelling that allows for theorization. After discussing how method is literally the backbone to doing research, how it steers what we do when and how an example is offered that leads into a summary of five methodological guiding principles.

Methodology as the gateway to better theory

Methodology links a particular philosophy or theory to an appropriate research method and bridges philosophical notions to practical and applicable research strategies (Byrne 2001: 830). This chapter connects this book's philosophy and theory to its methods and offers a justification for doing so. My philosophy is easy enough to label. It is feminist post-structuralism as discussed in chapter 1 where my points of departure for 'tooling' cultural citizenship for social critique and change are presented. To offer as succinct a description of this book's theory is more of a challenge. The method, it will turn out, is easier again. It is a form of discourse analysis that recognizes that understanding affect is as important as it is to understand arguments in the general patterns of social storytelling that feed identity formation and community building. Also straightforward is that the approach is inductive: rather than look for universal laws deductively, I look for local patterns in meaning making. Among the many forms of discourse analysis that exist, this one is a form of affective-discursive analysis.

Picking up from the first chapter and against the background of how the study of popular culture changed to converge and then diverge from engagement with audiences to include the role of understanding affect, I will first return to the basic theory underlying cultural citizenship (Figure 3.1).

We live in a world that is less focused on conversation and debate (and political citizenship) than on what Rosaldo (1996) would recognize as 'the right to difference' and therefore cultural citizenship. Current forms of polarization, often referred to as identitarian politics, the spread of conspiracy theories and hate-speech, the way in which humour is abused to shame and exclude others, all suggest that we cannot stay with Habermas' binary system-lifeworld theory. Neoliberal ideology has made us overrate our own achievements and well-being against our responsibility for the communities we belong to. It makes sense therefore to draw the system-lifeworld distinction in such a way as to show that personal life is weighted down (and perhaps also buoyed up, who knows) by both system and lifeworld logic (as shown in Figure 3.1). Doing so makes visible how e.g., gender and race matter to the social structure but are relegated to personal burdens or privileges. That is to say that Habermas' theorization of power situates it in the system part of society but that it makes itself known as an exclusion in the lifeworld and as feeling in the domain of personal life.

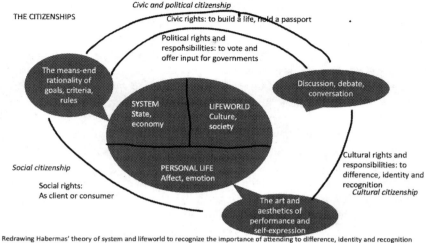

FIGURE 3.1 Redrawing Habermas' theory of system and lifeworld to recognize the importance of attending to difference, identity and recognition.

This points to how and why identity has become a crucial field for feminist social criticism. Identity is linked to material reality, social positions, belonging and having access to shared cultural knowledge to narrate who you are. It is connected to how we envision our life's trajectory and that of the communities we recognize in the world. Identity today funnels the full range covered by the four citizenships: from our civic and political aspirations (who can belong, how do we want to be governed), to social rights and cultural rights of self-expression and recognition. Popular culture is one of more fields that allows for the open and unforced exploration of identity and identity narratives connected to the citizen roles identified by Habermas and Fraser. This is what I have called cultural citizenship in that such exploration will touch on hopes, fears and critique. I have also called it cultural citizenship because partaking in popular culture, is to be part of its communities of use (Lindlof 1988). Even when we never discuss what we have seen directly, our use of popular media infuses not only our view of the world but our contact with others. Whether it concerns the use of terms, tropes or examples, or direct referencing of values, ambitions or politics.

For a Habermassian, this is far too messy a presentation. The terms that are used, however, are not that far removed from Habermas' second part of *The theory of communicative action* (1987) and his later *Between facts and norms* (1996). A Habermassian will recognize the use of identity against the background of cultural and social reproduction and socialization, important aspects to lifeworld interaction. As Kemmis argues we should understand system and lifeworld as interconnected. They create mutually constitutive conditions for one another, if rather one-sidedly (Kemmis 2006: 104). System imperatives put pressure on lifeworld reasoning and sentiments. Understanding system and lifeworld dialectically, benefits from paying close attention to how individuals experience themselves under conditions of late modernity, with its emphasis on such semi-rights as emancipation and a public voice, as well as neoliberal insistence on the accountable and enterprising self. Gender is important here. The pressure on women to perform well socially is very different from the pressure on men, as women have to do it all: be emancipated, caring, morally accountable, fit-bodied entrepreneurs who stand by their men (Gill & Scharff 2011; Littler 2018).

This multi-faceted investment we are under pressure to make in ourselves (to be slim, successful, a good mother) is usefully thought of as part of 'the personal' (and not just 'the individual'). For one, personal life links through to privacy, a typical concern of our times. Secondly and perhaps even more importantly, personal life opens up to the interest these past two decades in affect and emotion. It allows understanding of today's forms of informal conversation and interaction as based on the performance of the personal and the exchange value of the authentic. Neither is easily understood from the roles of the client, the consumer, the worker or the citizen. The Marxist discussion of the 'free labour' of media consumers has made clear that our social roles merge when value can be extracted (Terranova 2000). It seems more useful to try and understand platformized media society as historically connected with new roles. Two extra axes of exchange suggest themselves. One is afforded by talk of popular culture in which we all to some extent become social critics (Teurlings 2018). The professional connects the personal and the lifeworld. The other axis is the ongoing counterbid against how 'feeling,' 'real life' and 'authenticity' have come to be for sale, first on television and then on online media platforms. Intuition is pitted here against system rationality. System and the personal connect. Such experiential wisdom challenges a dangerously limited conception of value as basically economic, rather than an integrated whole that also comprises the social, the cultural and ecological. This role might be called the activist. In broadening conceptions of value, the activist role can serve many causes. Adding them to the citizen 'role repertoire' provides an open connection to how emotion and feeling are assimilated into citizenship understood broadly (as the conglomerate of roles of the voter/debater, consumer, client, worker, professional and activist). This is to say that citizenship can be understood as a project that unfolds in what Margaret Wetherell calls affective-discursive practice (Wetherell 2012, 2013, 2015).

If, in Habermassian terms, the lifeworld is to feed system politics and government, we need to understand how the personal cannot be equated with or subsumed under the lifeworld. We need to understand the personal and the lifeworld at their own merit. In order to be able to do so, we need to understand discourse as rational debate *and* as affect and emotion in all three domains. I do not know what the men in Habermas Vienna coffee houses talked about. I do know that much of today's urgent and excited uncoerced 'lay' exchange takes place online. Media and popular culture feed those discussions with examples, insights and (sometimes false) theories. The various case studies this book is based on, strongly suggest that in large part online discussion is not fundamentally different from in-person conversation although it escalates more easily. Methodologically the challenge is the same: to analyze those discussions well.

Reconstruct the affective and the discursive in everyday meaning making

Audience research has many forms. In cultural studies, it links through to political engagement. As such it is close to action research. With Kemmis (quoted above, 2006: 104) I understand theory to be a powerful resource for developing insight and understanding. My methods of choice, therefore, need to allow for participation that I can test against theory as an 'orientation towards inquiry.' Action research according to Bradbury and Reason 'is grounded in lived experience, developed in partnership, addresses significant problems, works with (rather than simply studies) people, develops new ways of seeing/interpreting the world (i.e., theory), and leaves infrastructure in its wake' (2003: 155). Opening up 'new communicative spaces' is important (Reason & Bradbury 2006: xxii).

Much of what I do does not fully qualify as action research but some of it does. Doing the kind of analysis presented here leaves infrastructure for those interviewed and for my students who in some cases have become teachers and extend respectful ways of working with others on their questions rather than the other way around. Some of this work also gets translated into direct practice-oriented research, for instance on media literacy or practical citizenship skills. Those projects hardly ever build enough material for academic publication but sometimes they do as in the telenovela project for a Moroccan-Dutch news website presented in chapter 9 or in an older project on digital storytelling for sex education (Borghuis et al. 2010). Generally, developing tools to study affect-in/and-discourse-as-cultural-citizenship accords well with the methodology, aims and values of other (feminist) action research family members. Potentially awareness of cultural citizenship as a tool can help publish more action research than is currently the case.

Unsurprisingly, as I want to attend to everyday meaning making, I will turn to ethnography for methodological insight and especially to how it has been used in cultural studies. To bring more definition to how we might study affect, phenomenology might be useful to increase sensitivity to the different ways in which affect, emotion and feeling make themselves known. I understand them to be different in the sense that affect exists between persons, and between persons and things. Feeling is set in motion by affect. It is becoming aware of the world through and in the body. Emotion is the social performance of feeling. The work of Sara Ahmed and Rita Felski is inspiring here, if focused on texts and social phenomena rather than on talk and discourse for which I would turn to Margaret Wetherell's work (Ahmed 2006, 2004; Felski 2015, 2020; Wetherell 2013).

Following Wetherell's argument, I would say that language and talk limits us in how we can share intensity and the presence of our bodies as defined and shaped in affective encounters but language and talk do not close us off entirely. We can talk about unease, anxiety or excitement. Cultural studies research, at its best, uses talk both literally and recognizes the echoes of excess and feeling, whether excitement or pain. Phenomenology with its close attention to orientations and the contemplation of objects as these become 'present' to us, can work well in media and cultural research but leans more heavily on a first-person perspective (introspection and experience) than on a second (discussion and debate) or third person (analysis and interpretation) one. All three perspectives are compatible with action research and serve the need to be reflective, query one's own position, invite the insight of others and decode conversations as they unfold in terms of arguments, the negotiation of meaning and the kind of shared feeling that suggests we are included (or its absence, and bodily knowledge of being excluded).

My version of affective-discursive analysis is built on two books that do not use that term. They have taught me method and methodology, and doing careful and caring research. One is Martyn Hammersley and Paul Atkinson's (1983) *Ethnography. Principles in practice*. There are three editions after this one. I have lost the 1983 book, a slim beige volume that starts, as I remember it, by discussing objectivity and subjectivity. As the earliest edition I have been able to find (a 1995 second one) opens with a discussion of positivism, naturalism and realism, I am probably wrong. Still, Hammersley and Atkinson helped me move out of the jaws of the useless argument familiar to all action researchers, that posits that science needs objective truth (which exists somewhere and is knowable) and an overly relativist argument, often a caricature of a post-structuralist approach, which understands science to be part of the mechanisms that link power to knowledge. Neither an absolute nor a relativist perspective appeal to Hammersley and Atkinson who opt for reflexivity and for understanding the researcher as active sense-maker. Along with those we study, we interpret the world. The difference is in being systematic, in zooming in and out and in being able to both accept and step away from our own presence in a research situation in order to assess what 'facts of life' we are coming across (Hammersley & Atkinson 1995: 19). That is neither objective nor subjective. Scrutinized for being too narrow-minded or short-sighted, checked against the recollections and interpretations of informants and knowledgeable others, reflexive knowledge adds to our understanding of the sentiments, stories and structures that govern the social world.

Ann Gray's (2003) *Research practice for cultural studies* is the other book. Even less a formal, 'recipe,' type book, it distinguishes between the use of methods and research as a process. The chapter titles summarize what is at stake: from the grasping of lived cultures, to articulating experience, we can gain a sense of how community is imagined. As discussed in chapter 1 of this book: community and identity buttress processes of meaning making and are fed by mundane, everyday, habitual practices. In the second part of *Research practice for cultural studies*, Gray turns to storytelling. Narrative, she writes, is the stuff of life (2003: 107). We live in stories that tell us who we are, that speak to who we want to be. In sharing images, ideas, hopes, ideals, we embed them in stories, no matter how disjointed we tell them. We continually build shared worlds. Making contact with others and studying these instances where world and identity building meet one another, need to be talked about frankly and openly. That way, according to Gray, cultural analysts are able to share insight, into 'facts of life,' methodology, and how our politics and agendas as academics and co-citizens are made stronger (2003: 188–190).

Initially, writing about popular culture for me was a way to defend it and show how it is used for empowerment. Over the years, as popular culture became more accepted and less looked down-upon, the wish to defend shifted to understanding it as a complex domain that we also need to be critical of. Somewhat uncomfortably, a more critical understanding included finding how the (post) feminism of television series such as *Ally McBeal* and *Sex and the City* had its uneasy corollary in viewer comments. Slighting actor Calista Flockhart for being underweight, or a male character for being a wet noodle and thus reasserting the measuring of men by their sexual prowess belie what a feminist perspective stands for (Hermes 2006). Can one be a feminist without practicing solidarity or challenging gender conservatism? Can one be a feminist audience researcher and maintain one's integrity when not respecting others for their gender views? It is a fine balance between critique for what people say, the codes, stories and discourses they refer to and condemning them for who and what they are. Understanding how popular cultural texts and practices are used to maintain and spread misogyny and racist exclusion (e.g., Hilhorst & Hermes 2016) is important. Using audience research to declare others racists or sexists, is not.

The key insight ultimately is that all forms of discussion that are inspired or energized by popular culture, benefit from being understood as cultural citizenship. No matter how far they are removed from my worldview and ideals, they are all part of an ongoing conversation that links the personal to the lifeworld, to everyday and to governmental political realities, turning the fears, hopes and dreams of speakers into spare change for the public political domain. They all need being understood for their affective as well as their discursive impact and power. To take a broad view of comments, rants, exchanges, painful to read as they sometimes are, is to create distance between what people say and who they are. Our preoccupation with the personal and with authentic selves appears to spiral us into much harsher assessments of others than a fierce debate would. The world over we see conversation and discussion stop while the violence and pain of exclusion take over as societies polarize. To offer tools to enable the countering of such processes is my goal. Empathic understanding of the feelings involved will surely, in the short or long run, allow for better counter-offensives.

Moving beyond business as usual

Attending to affect is a methodological challenge. Standards for reporting on methods and results, tend to keep their distance from all things felt. Add to that that media and cultural studies research has at times been attacked for lack of methodological rigour and it becomes clear that 'business as usual' is not an option. Here is what I know: empirical work on everyday media making that is sensitive to inequal power relations, requires a double, dialectical engagement. It starts as a combination of description and reflection. Its engine is the analytical move to bring these together and theorize processes and outcomes. While 'analysis' sounds reassuringly technical, it is also a complex intuitive process that relies on a researcher being able to imagine what kind of stories or narratives are suggested across interviews, comments and (online or offline) discussions. In systematically examining and testing the theoretical understanding that emerges, analysis gains rigour and value. It cannot be done without wide reading on the themes that come up across the material, however unexpected. It usually involves gradually focusing or even fully changing central research questions. Without wanting to canonize any one approach, Grounded Theory offers great examples. (It is explained briefly below.)

Empirical research is open-ended and therefore risky. You may not find anything exciting or not be able to move beyond the obvious. This needs to be accepted. There is no way to know at the outset where the research process may take you. This may sound disturbingly mystical and the opposite of transparent. In practice, qualitative empirical research mostly requires honesty and documenting thoughts, impressions and decisions on steps taken. This is made easier once you have acquired the habit of writing research memos (as advised by Hammersley and Atkinson and by almost all handbooks on qualitative research). Let me illustrate all of this by using part of a paragraph on the methods of data collection and data analysis for a project with Sarieke Hoeksma which is also the basis for chapter 6. Its subject is how parents talk about the power of the media over their children and their below-the-surface feelings of helplessness and fear. They are not sure they can counter images in media content or keep their children from following their innate sense of who they are and what they want. Beyond explaining well how affect is important to audience research, it will lead into a number of the methodological principles for analysis on which this book is built.

Sarieke Hoeksma interviewed six parents, two of them a couple, five of them white. All were cis-hetero presenting people with, according to themselves, liberal views on child-rearing and gender. Sarieke was interested in getting a sense of how more gender and sexual diversity (non-binary, gay and trans characters) could be introduced in children's television in the Netherlands. I am interested in diversity, inclusion and how they are talked about as an instance of cultural citizenship in action. While it was Sarieke's project, I participated in the analysis of the material. The writing up of the research (below) is mine. My heartfelt thanks go to Sarieke for allowing me to be her partner in the project and the use of her material here. She is credited as co-author of chapter 5. Here, I will use parts of the description of our research methodology for data analysis to serve as an example of what methodology accounts tend to present and what they leave out.

The interview material was transcribed in full and analyzed using Glaser and Strauss' Grounded Theory as developed in the 1960s of the last century and further streamlined as a method of analysis in the 1990s (Glaser & Strauss 1967; Strauss & Corbin 1990). *This approach consists of three rounds of coding the data (open coding, axial coding and selective coding). In open coding key words simply were* boys, girls *(often including* 'typically'), aggression, pink, tough *and descriptions of television and tv use:* good versus bad television; viewing habits; what children prefer; nostalgia; commercialization. *In axial coding, recurring themes were identified. They included* nature versus nurture; to be yourself; to be protected; risk zone; gender experiments are a phase. *In selective coding, these themes were clustered and needed to be regrouped when the nature-nurture distinction while present throughout most of the material did not bear much explanatory weight, which we had expected it to do. (The three selective codes* 'Be who you are,' 'Big, bad world' *and* 'Do not hold me accountable' *will return in chapter 5.)*

While organized procedurally as a form of grounded theory, the method of analysis closely resembles how Potter and Wetherell describe reconstructing 'interpretative repertoires' or the narratives that function as shared cultural resources. In their definition, interpretative repertoires consist of 'recurring .... collections of phrases and terms that people use to describe and evaluate a situation or action' (1987: 138).

Potter and Wetherell underline that language utterances are acts and that language is functional at all times (1988, 169). The fact that discourse is used to serve concrete ends, means that it will be variable (idem, 171). Such an approach to discourse, talk or texts of any kind, allows a researcher to move beyond the categorization of individuals (at the level of attitudes e.g.) and to attend to how variability points to cultural logics that informants and researchers reconnoitre in uncoerced talk. When done well (in lengthy interviews) *and with enough informants to test for chance connections as well as oversight, this is an approach that allows the reconstruction of shared social and cultural knowledge. Contradictions in viewpoints as expressed by informants become a research asset rather than a reason to distrust informants or dismiss part of what they say as insincere or untrue. Trying to do justice to the lived reality of gender politics is no mean feat after all and hard to do without landing oneself in logical and moral pitfalls.*

To validate our findings, we cross-referenced quotations belonging with the three repertoires with the original interviews to ascertain that the repertoires occurred throughout the majority (and preferably all) five interviews. After all, in long interviews such as these, we expect to be familiarized with the full scope of an informant's cultural knowledge. As we were interested in broadly shared beliefs and ideas that structure child-rearing practice and the governing of television viewing, we feel that Morley's observation applies. That is, in the absence of participant observation, we can make do with the stories that respondents choose to tell us as these stories are not only 'limited by,' but also 'indexical of the cultural and linguistic frames of reference which respondents have available to them, through which to articulate their responses' (Morley 1989: 24). In addition, Potter and Wetherell remark 'that variability need not be a consequence of deliberate or intentional processes. Much of the time people in their lay explanations will not be strategically planning, or self-consciously adjusting their discourse in a Machiavellian fashion, but just 'doing what comes naturally' or saying what 'seems right' for the situation' (Potter & Wetherell 1988: 171).

Our own position and contribution to the research encounter matter. Methodological discussion in discourse studies suggests we need to make clear how our own position and research agenda are not leading in the analysis of the material (Henwood 2007 271/272). Both of us are highly concerned about gender conservatism in children's television and the lack of 'alternative identities' that are offered either explicitly or implicitly. Our research agenda includes practical advice and suggestions to (future) children's television makers. We had assumed to find support for our own position and hoped to act as 'cultural intermediairies' between parents and professionals (Hesmondhalgh 2006; Maguire & Matthews 2012). This was not to be. The material and analysis do underwrite the need to better understand gender conservatism and that parents (and children) lack safe routes to change. They also tell us that we had wrongly assumed that our informants would be 'like-minded people.' In fact, a variety of competing views appear to exist of how gender identity is constructed and what child rearing in a mediated-saturated society should look like.

The example shows how we needed to rethink the agenda for our research and professional practice as we became aware of how much further we were removed from the preoccupations of the interviewed parents than we had expected. We abandoned the ship and did not write up the material as a journal article. The small number of interviews was always a risk. When you are overextending what your data can carry in terms of interpretations and conclusions, there is nothing for it but to let go. When Sarieke found a job in television production, it was the end of the project.

Looking back at this extract, it seems to me we never really acknowledged what our disconnect with the parents meant. Even a simple visual summary of the coding of the material shows that we did not follow the rules going from one phase of coding to another. We did not take the parents' fear of television influencing their children very seriously. While we did gain depth in our insight, we kept having to abandon our interpretation of what we thought the parents thought and felt (Figure 3.2).

Especially going from open coding to axial coding, we did not pay much attention to *how* television was meaningful and a source of anxiety. Had we done so in axial coding, we would have had the parents' fears return in axial codes far more meaningfully than as a typically modern, effects paradigm assessment of television that assumes that the medium influences viewers who may not be entirely passive but are, ultimately, at the mercy of powerful media. Looking at the codes, 'be who you are' follows from *to be yourself* and the ways in which nature versus nurture was resolved into 'nature over nurture.' 'Big bad world' is linked to protection and risks but hardly with the affective load carried by risk, protection and the dangers of television. The 'do not hold me accountable' repertoire' simply is not directly carried by the key terms we found. It follows from the inflection in what the parents said rather than from the actual words they used. Had we attended solely to discourse and not to affect and sentiment, we would have fully missed what the parents were trying to convey. It would have been impossible to contribute anything at all to the reinvention of gender representation in children's television. A sobering realization as it says nowhere in grounded theory or in qualitative methodology handbooks how we should attend to

Open coding	Axial coding	Selective coding
boys		
Typically boys	nature versus nurture	
Typically boys	to be yourself	'Be who you are'
girls	to be protected	
Typically girls	risk zone	'Big, bad world'
Typically girl	gender experiments	
Aggression	are a phase	'Do not hold me accountable'
Pink	Tv is dangerous	
tough		
what children prefer		
good television viewing habits		
bad television viewing habits		
Nostalgia		
Commercialisation.		

FIGURE 3.2 Coding scheme: parents talking about the power of the media over their children.

feeling and how we are oriented towards dominant interpretations and views of, in this case, television and parenting.

As one among a series of smaller case studies on parents, children and media, there is more material that allowed the inclusion of this small case study in this book. This offers me the opportunity to discuss using surprise, disappointment and outliers in data collection as a means to theorize and assure research quality (in terms of validity) (cf. Miles & Huberman 1984, ch. VII Drawing and verifying conclusions). In conventional terms, the very different outcome from what we had expected and the overall homogeneity and agreement across the group of parents (whose living conditions and type of employment varied), do prove the validity and independence of the analysis. By offering long quotations in chapter 5, it will be shown how the interviews attest to the fact that the researchers' agenda 'does not obscure other meaning frames and relevancies that are important to understanding people's orientations to, and ways of acting within, specific encounters and local situations.' They also show that we attended 'to the ways in which participants' themselves orient to, and invoke contextual frames, in social encounters.' (Henwood 2007 272). Small consolation but an important one.

In terms of the theory sketched earlier in this chapter: talk about children and television from the perspective of concerned parents connected the personal to lifeworld issues. The perceived danger of television's manipulation is also a system issue (it addresses the [ab]use of power). In addition, in moving from discourse analysis to affective-discursive analysis, the powerlessness the parents felt became become visible. We started recognizing that they found themselves in an impossible situation. Their feelings of helplessness can be traced in their not following up on their own experiences. Cultural citizenship (what would be the best possible world for most of us) could not be translated into political citizenship that relates to the system medium of power. Doing so would have added to a negative, conservative agenda they did not support. They did not want to stop change in the realm of identity construction but saw no way forward either.

This example is included for showing something else as well. Not only the parents' feelings but our own were more important than we gave credit for. We felt so betrayed by the material. Not by the parents who had generously given their time and had all been open and willing to query their experiences, feelings and ideas about gender, media and children. We felt betrayed by their shared common sense that it was dangerous to diversify gender representation. We were abhorred by their resolute disclaiming of responsibility for how their children embraced gendered identities and their lack of commitment to what we had assumed to be a shared progressive ideal. It makes clear how affect and emotion are not only to be found at the informants' end of empirical research. It shows what is entailed by the radical self-reflexivity that both action research and cultural studies research requires of researchers.

As I remember that first edition of Hammersley and Atkinson's *Ethnography*, it strongly suggests making preconceived notions explicit in order to enter the field as open-minded as possible. Slightly different from what phenomenology would call 'bracketing' (Ahmed 2006), it is an exercise in undoing expectations. It turns out that this is really difficult to do. Pre-conceived notions of 'progressive persons' and their views on gender wreaked havoc, as did pre-conceived notions of parenting. As a researcher, I often fail to contextualize to the extent that I should because it is so difficult to listen really generously. It may have made Sarieke and myself overly receptive to the possibility of gender conservatism. It also seems to be the case that the formalization of research procedures makes inclusion of the intuitions and feelings of researchers harder. Recognizing an unspoken wish for change that seems impossible can be important but is hard to include in a codebook. The more formal research approaches thus tend to play into the hands of dominant power structures that come with a vocabulary and established narratives. To illustrate: it was our intuition that when interviewed parents invoked the nature-nurture distinction, they were offering a rote observation. Had we not dug deeper, a different structure of meaning making would not have emerged. Looking back, I fear we skirted the very edges of the basic rule of respecting your informants and identified them in loaded terms.

I imagine that if we had used a more formal version of discourse analysis, the way for example that CDA (critical discourse analysis), is practiced these days, we would not have caught on to how parents were a bit sick of having to perform 'good parenthood.' They offered some of that by explaining about their 'rules' and when and how they allowed their children their freedom. Their frustrations would have come across as simply conservatism. Given that family and friends had introduced us, we could contextualize the material and shift and tilt frames. We could open up to how we were 'oriented' in phenomenological terms, to television, television viewing, parenting and gender representation. While our assumption that parents would feel that the media are dangerous was correct, they were ahead of us and had stepped out of the nature-nurture frame that has long been used in everyday conversation to suggest that as a parent you do have a measure of control. Neo-liberal accountability has taken over. While that is often used to suggest personal success, our parents used it to announce their imminent failure. Interestingly what they felt they were failing at was protecting their children by not having them embrace mainstream gender identities. They felt guilty in advance for setting them up for failing to fit in. The idea that they could also fight conservative moralism and gender policing was inconceivable.

Principles for practice

I have tried to illustrate how methodology bears thinking about beyond how data were collected (and why) and what method of analysis was used, necessary though it is that such things are reported on. Methodology, as the twin side to theorizing one's material well, is the locus of quality control, of taking a sufficiently broad outlook without losing focus, of allowing for the imagination without giving up on a chain of evidence. It is to think about what proof needs to be entered, when to clarify what patterns were discerned, what stories they led into and how those might be tried on for size. By that, I mean that emerging narratives, sensitizing concepts and the theorization of the material need to be validated by offering quotes or other instances from the data as well as references to the literature and earlier research that either challenge or confirm what was found.

Five connected methodological principles guide my own work. It starts with having an idea, the early collection of inspiring articles, or screenshots of images or quotes found on social media or newspaper clippings. Then there is the decision to set up a project, collect data and analyze and theorize them against the available literature. The most important principle is to assess your own pre-conceived notions as a way to practicing self-reflexivity throughout these steps by taking intuitions and frustrations seriously. This is linked to the second and third principles of listening generously and contextualizing well what others say. The fourth principle is to be aware that contradictions and paradoxes are one's friends in data analysis. They point to where informants (like researchers) are engaged in ongoing work to make sense of the world, to 'unfinished business' and to where change is wrought and can materialize. Audience 'work' after all is both performative and interactive practice (Hill 2007). Connected but slightly different is the fifth principle which is to cherish surprise by engaging in appreciative forms of inquiry.

Appreciative inquiry is how Rita Felski suggests we surpass 'the limits of critique' (Felski 2015). Focusing mostly on literary criticism, Felski argues that a 'hypercritical style' has 'crowded out other forms of intellectual life' (2015: 10). She feels we are faced with an epistemological dogma that requires ever digging deeper to uncover truths. As if we ourselves as critics and academics are victims of gaslighting by commercial capitalist culture and the political establishment. Her goal is to restore interpretation to 'the many possible ways of trying to figure out what something means and why it matters (-). We do not need to throw out interpretation but to revitalize and reimagine it' (Felski 2015: 10). Like Felski, I would like to take part in creating 'new imaginaries' (2015: 187), based on appreciative inquiry rather than suspicious reading. A project of creating new imaginaries through appreciative inquiry will serve the type of emancipatory agenda that cultural studies has helped build much better than suspicious reading which is more likely to harden than to soften social divides. It simply consists of '(e)mpirical investigation, a willingness to be surprised and attention to as many actors as is feasible' (Felski 2015: 189). If we are not shackled to 'protocols of professional pessimism' (2015: 128), such as the lingering suspicion that popular culture tends to be conservative, we may well discover a diverse and possibly emancipatory field, where 'inspiring alternatives and new vocabularies' (2015: 150) are to be found. I hope for differently critical shapes of thought that do justice to cultural forms without particular artistic merit beyond their power to please and entertain.

Appreciative inquiry need not be naïve or complacent. When Felski suggests we need 'sustained attention to the sheer range and complexity of aesthetic experiences, including moments of recognition, enchantment, shock and knowledge,' there is no reason not to extend that approach to popular culture (Felski 2015: 191). Surely, we can work with its emancipatory and conservative sides, without coming to an ultimate judgment. What Felski describes as 'aesthetic experiences' …

> "… speak to academic as well as lay practices of reading: they connect us to our lives as social beings, while also inviting us to reflect on the distinctive qualities of works of arts: what spurs us to pick up a book or to become utterly engrossed in a film. We cannot do justice to these qualities (-) as long as we remain in the thrall of a suspicious hermeneutics. Sometimes serious thinking calls for a judicious decrease rather than an increase of distance – a willingness to acknowledge and more fully engage our attachments."
>
> (Felski 2015: 191/192)

Recognizing how the everyday pleasures of popular television might be used to develop new frames of analysis is to respect popular culture for being a space where audiences feel an 'emergent sense of rights to roam across media storytelling' as Hill puts it (2021: 8). A space in which we rely as much on our feelings and emotions – on affect – to guide us, as on rational decisions. This in turn requires a concept like cultural citizenship, to understand the multi-layered and contradictory forms of engagement that Peter Dahlgren and Annette Hill have charted (Dahlgren & Hill 2020, 2023). In discussion of the other citizenships, after all, emotion runs against the grain. They are seen as involving the danger of not seeing facts or recognizing reasonable alternatives which lessens the probability of reaching consensus (or rational dissensus). Popular culture however does feed the imagination and offers us images that can be crucial to the legitimation of political acts, whether voting, either or not following the news, or undertaking political action inside or outside of representational and governing bodies.

How to ensure that researching popular culture can take up that responsibility? Beyond taking methodology utterly seriously, we need how to engage with the knowledge of others, invite them into dialogue and disseminate (new) knowledge. We are not the only ones to have elevated suspicion and distrust to an art. Media and data literacy training in American schools and elsewhere does the exact same thing. Addressing this issue, danah boyd is sceptical about whether 'we know how to educate people who do not share our epistemological frame' in order to undo what she calls 'gaslighting': the feeding of misinformation and untruths to distort a person's worldview, a common online practice (2017, n.p.). American teenagers are taught to question the information they receive and to find out the truth for themselves. Often this goes wrong. Assessing sources is not always easy and sensational stories that spread widely may appeal to fears and convictions, and become irresistible. Add to that the implication of self-reliance that experts should not be trusted. Boyd warns us that '(a)ddressing so-called fake news is (-) going to require a cultural change about how we make sense of information, whom we trust and how we understand our own role in grappling with information (idem).'

If we want to strengthen dialogue across divides, we need to work with what counts as common sense today. We need to replace 'but is it true' with 'why or how would this be true'? We need to come to terms with the fact that we are cared less about by others than we hope is the case. That includes our governments. Disinterest is a far bigger problem than outright maliciousness and bad intentions. Evil is sexier than lack of care and solidarity. Empowerment comes from listening, showing genuine interest and care and constructive forms of feminist criticism. It benefits enjoying who we are, including our gender and sexual identifications, to name but two. It is to overturn critique as a form of condemnation into a form of understanding.

This chapter concludes the first part of the book. It has offered a sense of how popular culture for the past half century has been a terrain for cultural studies' research of everyday meaning making. For me too it provides a service. Immense field that it is, it offers a wide choice of accessible topics. Better than the weather, it allows for the exchange of all kinds of sentiments and opinions or simply for the venting of frustration, hatred and anger. All these utterances give access to how others experience their rights and obligations as citizens, even if they would be amazed to hear me say this. In the coming chapters discussion of gender is the main topic. Turns out that women are the problem. No surprise there. Interesting though how much emotion permeates assessing and controlling the gender performance of others. It will make clear how seriously we take our cultural citizen rights and responsibilities, as viewers, parents and fans.

PART II
Decoding gender confusion
The litmus test of gender definitions in fearing the effects of popular culture. Three case studies

Chapter 4 Culpability: Affective-discursive analysis. Understanding the hatred of television character Skyler White
    With Leonie Stoete
Chapter 5 Innocence: Parents talking about what popular culture might do to their children
    With Sarieke Hoeksma
Chapter 6 Confusion: When the future (briefly) became female. Viewers discussing a woman being cast as Doctor Who
    With Sophie Eeken

4
CULPABILITY

Affective-discursive analysis. Understanding the hatred of television character Skyler White

With Leonie Stoete

For Netflix, the series *Breaking Bad* (AMC 2008–2013, dir. Vince Gilligan, available on Netflix) was important in establishing its platform in the Netherlands halfway through the 2010s. Even though the series had been on Dutch linear public television, the possibility to 'binge watch' it, made it reach a much wider and younger audience who had long been turning away from programmed tv. Via my students and my family, *Breaking Bad* became part of my television menu. It is beautifully made. The landscapes and *mise-en-scene* are extraordinary, and the characters – well the characters are pretty awful. I happened to like the vulgar and utterly sexist brother-in-law Hank (no one else did) but felt no bond with Walter White, the central character. Walt is a chemistry teacher who is diagnosed with cancer. To pay for treatment and leave his family (and unexpectedly pregnant wife) with some savings should he die, he starts cooking methamphetamine with a former, dropout student, Jessie. Those interested in the self-ruination of a man caught in his own deeply conservative notions of 'what a man's gotta do,' should see the series and read Jason Mittell's compassionate interpretation of Walter White in *Complex TV* (2015). This chapter will quote him extensively but is dedicated to Skyler, his wife.

While *Breaking Bad* became a talked-about series, Skyler White rapidly climbed online lists of most-hated female characters. She is not meant to be particularly likable as she struggles to come to terms with a partner who is sick and bent on taking on a life of crime. She also has a disabled teenage son to raise and a baby. In the narrative, she is one of the major obstacles in Walt's way. To me, that felt like a deeply dishonest and typically modernist way of portraying women as basically a hindrance to man's self-development. Discussion in class and in my living room was therefore the start of looking at

DOI: 10.4324/9781003288855-7

how others discussed Skyler White. Leonie Stoete collected material on Reddit and we co-authored the paper that is an earlier version of this chapter (Hermes & Stoete 2019).

Discussion of Skyler White on the online platform Reddit reads like an introduction to misogyny. It is deeply uncomfortable how not just the character but the actor playing her, are attacked. It is as if Skyler White, the character, is half of a celebrity figure, the other half of which is actor Anna Gunn. The Reddit discussion about her is analyzed as a test of cultural citizenship as a lens. That is to say that we were interested in how rights and responsibilities are addressed. It turns out that commenters do not address their own responsibilities. They clearly feel the right to pass judgement on Skyler/Gunn. In the chapters to come, this same skewed understanding of citizenship will return. Yes, the Reddit discussion can be read as reflection but only when the underlying stories (or speaking positions as they will be called in this chapter) are reconstructed.

Actors such as Gunn, meanwhile, are caught between a rock and a hard place. Her plight, more about which below, speaks to how a century-long process of emancipation afforded by popular media (from print, to radio, television and online platforms) enabled the introduction of a new range of feelings and emotions into public and semi-public debate. Analyzing discussion and attacks on 'composite celebrities' such as Gunn/White also show perfectly how discourse and emotion interweave. A bit unfairly cultural studies audience research has been accused of not attending to affect (Gregg & Seigworth 2010). But even when it is not theorized at length, affect is what colours the Reddit discussion and its interpretation. The chapter starts with a discussion of celebritiy as a phenomenon. It then turns to analysis of *Breaking Bad* Reddit posts, to conclude with a discussion of cultural citizenship as a form of gossip culture.

Celebrities: caught in the middle

In everyday media talk, celebrities figure as key characters (Hermes & Kooijman 2016: 483). Celebrities provide fixed points in shared narratives that serve social cohesion and identity formation (Driessens 2012: 642). Fictional characters, it seems, may do the same and become celebrities in their own right. Skyler White is a case in point. A Facebook page called 'Fuck Skyler White' has more than 31,000 fans, 'with posts and comments dripping with violent, misogynist hatred' (Mittell 2015: 347). Those discussing Skyler White do not always make a clear distinction between Gunn and the fictional character of Skyler. They become a single entity – a composite celebrity, to coin a new term, to whom viewers address their deep dislike and hatred.

Celebrities, says Marshall, are 'the production locale for an elaborate discourse on the individual and individuality that is organized around the will to uncover a hidden truth' (Marshall 1997: 4). We study celebrities to understand the value of individuals, to determine when and why they deserve social recognition. They feed reflection on norms and social rules. As such, celebrity is 'implicated in new categorizations of the public sphere [...] connected to the heightened significance of popular culture and democratic culture. The celebrity embodies the empowerment of the people to shape the public sphere symbolically' (ibid.: 7). Marshall's empowerment of the people is understood here as cultural citizenship 'in action' but also as literally a threat to actor Anna Gunn.

Celebrities are not used by audiences in gender or colour-neutral ways. Differences are stark, in academic research as much as in the media (Holmes & Negra 2008: 1). 'Boys will be boys. Girls will be hounded by the media,' Holmes and Negra quote *New York Times* journalist Alex Williams (2008) as saying. Others attest to considerable slut-shaming and 'star testing' in everyday discussions of celebrities. Femininity, we can conclude, is policed far more restrictively than masculinity (Allen & Mendick 2012; Jackson, Goddard & Cossens 2016; Wilson 2010). As a composite celebrity Skyler/Gunn provides a link between celebrity culture, everyday sexism, gender ideology and neoliberal governmentality.

Gunn is not a celebrity actor. She sees herself as a professional doing a job. In a reaction to the overwhelming volume of hate mail and threats uttered on social media forums, Gunn (2013) wrote an open letter to *The New York Times* (Aug 23):

> Playing Skyler White on the television show 'Breaking Bad' for the past five seasons has been one of the most rewarding creative journeys I've embarked on as an actor. But the role has also taken me on another kind of journey – one I never would have imagined. My character, to judge from the popularity of Web sites and Facebook pages devoted to hating her, has become a flash point for many people's feelings about strong, non-submissive, ill-treated women. As the hatred of Skyler blurred into loathing for me as a person, I saw glimpses of an anger that, at first, simply bewildered me.

She continues her open letter by analyzing the narrative logic of the series, which makes Skyler her husband Walter's antagonist. 'I was aware that she might not be the show's most popular character. But I was unprepared for the vitriolic response she inspired. Thousands of people have "liked" the Facebook page "I Hate Skyler White"' (ibid.)

Gunn pinpoints the confusion and mixed feelings inspired by female characters who do not adhere to the traditional code of 'standing by your man,' referring to 'other complex TV wives' such as Carmela Soprano (*The Sopranos*), and Betty Draper (*Mad Men*). 'Male characters don't seem to inspire this kind of public venting and vitriol' (Gunn 2013, n.p.). Key to the extraordinary situation Gunn finds herself in is that she, the actor, is seen as accountable for the actions of the character she plays, and thus the barrage of online hatred becomes personal. 'Could somebody tell me where I can find Anna Gunn so I can kill her?' reads a post she finds online. Skyler is an uncomfortable character, Gunn (2013) concludes, a 'measure of our attitudes toward gender'; and she is 'glad' that the public discussion 'has illuminated some of the dark and murky corners that we often ignore or pretend aren't still there in our everyday lives.'

Gunn's letter deserves following up to further air those 'dark and murky corners' of gender ideology. This chapter does so by turning to a discussion of Skyler on Reddit across a number of threads that are part of the subReddit thread 'Breaking Bad' (r/breakingbad). It will become clear how Skyler is both a fictional character and the composite entity Skyler/Gunn who links celebrity, gender ideology, and neoliberal accountability. When Leonie Stoete and I decided to turn to Skyler, it was an unusual thing to do. In the then academic literature, attention was mostly given to Walt's process of moral decline which will end in a life of crime that spins completely out of control (cf. Pierson 2014; Blevins & Wood 2015; McKeown et al. 2015). Later this was remedied, among others by Melissa Click (2019).

'/r/breakingbad'

The subReddit '/r/breakingbad' has over 200,000 subscribers. While discussions of Skyler as a character can also be found on dedicated Facebook pages such as 'I hate Skyler White,' Reddit makes it much easier for a researcher to find discussion on a topic. 115 Reddit threads discussed Skyler (rather than merely mentioning her name in plot recaps and so on). Posts had garnered 2–270 reactions per thread. Top scoring threads (in 2016) were: 'Anna Gunn has been amazing this season' (609 reactions) and, 'the moment every BB fan decided they hate Skyler' (900 reactions). Clearly on Reddit Skyler was a hotly debated character who is defended as well as hated, with many lauding Gunn's acting.

Following a grounded theory approach (Strauss & Corbin 1990), threads were integrally included in a long document to allow for open coding. This resulted in a coding scheme in which all content that is of interest is assembled. The open codes included the praise and swear words used for Skyler; technical terms used to describe decisions of the production team regarding Skyler's character and Gunn's acting; references to Skyler being a mother and being in a relationship with an impossible man; and so on. A second round of (axial) coding collected all the codes and sorted them into meaningful clusters. A last round of selective coding reconnected original quotations with an appropriate label and analysis of the logic of the clustered quotations. A grounded theory approach mixes well with discourse analysis, as it does not sort individuals into specific positions, or link quotes to the intentions or attitudes of individuals. Rather, it finds the best possible way to reconstruct the underlying shared cultural knowledge from which individuals draw. Margaret Wetherell and Jonathan Potter (1988) employ a similar approach and remark: 'there is no sense in which we could have divided our respondents into three classes (...). Each respondent selectively combined different repertoires' (Wetherell & Potter 1988: 178). Redditers likewise selectively use speaking positions that reflect different types of shared cultural knowledge. As will become clear, these speaking positions are infused with emotion.

In relation to Skyler, three speaking positions are important: 'savvy viewing'; 'moral realism'; and 'public shaming.' The 'savvy viewing' speaking position is characterized by talk of how to read the narrative of the series and its production. It makes full use of the complexity of the *Breaking Bad* characters and storylines. Here, Reddit posters speak from a position of inside, technical knowledge – as 'savvy viewers' (Andrejevic 2008; Teurlings 2010). These quotes bespeak the critical repertoire of television analysts. A second manner of speaking is far more personalized and reminiscent of how celebrities are talked about by gossip magazine readers (Hermes 1995; McDonnell 2014). This is 'moral realism' (see also Ang 1985). Ang uses the term 'emotional realism' to explain how melodrama is felt to be of practical use to viewers as characters remind them of people that actually exist, however, exaggerated the storylines might be. Celebrity gossip, likewise, 'makes morality meaningful' (McDonnell 2014: 89–109). In the 'moral realism' comments presented here, characters in television series are understood on two levels of abstraction: they refer to archetypes that embody moral codes (or their opposite), and they are seen as standing in for real persons who can be judged for their life choices and behaviour. This is the performance of cultural citizenship in discussion as an exercise in practical morality.

Of special interest here is a third category of talk that connects the commenter to the character and actor in which the character and actor are merged into a composite celebrity. These quotes show how codes of 20th-century professionalism are superseded by 21st-century celebrity culture. Before the advent of social media platforms, we also expressed ourselves forcefully about public figures we disliked. In this sense, celebrity hating is a common enough phenomenon (Johansson 2015). Today's wide dissemination of such feelings changes the impact of such discussion though. This third group of comments shows how the Redditers suggest it is their right to hold an actor or character to account. Skyler/Gunn is understood as a member of 'the elite' and therefore fair game. The underlying shared cultural repertoire thus combines the populist politics of social media culture with a neoliberal politics of accountability that is imported into personal life (cf. Bennett 2012).

Social media logic here dissolves what was left of the distinction between the private and the public. In addition, it dissolves the status of the professional, which up until a quarter century ago would have shielded the private individual behind the professional persona. It is as if to play a character in a television series is to urge others to look at and respond to you, to seek status and celebrity, which in turn gives others the right to judge and hold you to account. We have called this third speaking position 'public shaming,' yet another way of performing cultural citizenship.

Discussing the three speaking positions below verbatim quotes as used on Reddit are given as illustrations of the argument. Misspellings and factual errors have not been corrected. Where Redditers included comments in brackets, they have been left in. Nothing has been added to the quotes. We have anonymized the quotes. Although Reddit employs a fair use policy which means that material can be used for educational and academic purposes, stylistically congruent pseudonyms are used to protect the privacy of the Redditers while respecting the fun Redditers clearly have in devising screen names.

Savvy viewing

Savvy viewing is to discuss the series in terms of depth and complexity (or lack thereof). It distinguishes good script writing – which may result in liking or hating Skyler, but with the understanding that hatred appears as a consequence of how the character has been written and is necessary for plot and narrative development – and bad writing and/or acting which results in irritation, as the root cause for viewers' dislike of Skyler. Generally, the savvy viewing position is the one most commonly found on Reddit (and not just about *Breaking Bad*) (see also Teurlings 2018). It comes closest to a more formal citizen style where one uses rational arguments. The online forum context allows for showing appropriate enthusiasm. 'Skyler was one of the best-written female roles on television and I loved LOVED that she wasn't a saint' (dolfs_sisters_group). The hatred voiced against Skyler, according to Oldwhoresandweed, 'is a testament to how good the writers are and Anna Gunn's acting is.' Others feel she is a badly written character, which makes her come across as a 'bitch'. According to Redditer Oxthorpe, Skyler is 'underwritten and obnoxious [...]. Skyler's job in the story was "be pregnant" and "stand in the way". It's a thankless role.' When asked by another Redditer to elaborate why the series would be more enjoyable without Skyler, William Trollope says:

> Erm … …. how about another wife character that doesnt make you want to punch the screen every 2 seconds? I am not even speaking about her deeper plot, from the first second I saw her on screen with every move she makes, she is extremely annoying. It's just a badly made character.

Gunn's acting is discussed in similar terms. The hatred towards the character is her achievement, according to some. Oldwhoresandweed and Willldbeasthybriddd laud Gunn's work: 'I HATED Anna Gunn's character and as a result think that she's an absolutely amazing actress' (Willldbeasthybriddd). Vintage_Ant agrees: 'If one likes or dislikes a character to that extreme, that means the actor is doing a fantastic job.' Victoriangent loves both the character and the actor:

> I should say I actually have loved her as a character and actress since the beginning. I totally get her anger and can see the sadness in her eyes just grow and grow as the seasons roll by, and I don't feel that the show needed to change or spell out anything differently.

Others suggest simply that Gunn poorly portrayed an otherwise normal and neutral character, turning Skyler into a bitch she was never intended to be. ThePeskyHeckler:

> The reason most people think that Skylar is a bitch is because Anna Gunn is a bad actress. Vince Gilligan has said, multiple times, that they never intended for her character to be a bitch. They never wrote her that way. And yet she still comes off as a bitch. That problem, my friend, is a result of the actress failing to portray the character as she was intended.

Savvy viewing takes commenters further to suggest that Skyler needs to be hated in order for us to feel sorry for Walt. WasHere states: 'Initially the writing is designed to help the viewer sympathize with Walt's decision to turn to cooking meth.' Skyler is an obstacle 'that Walt had to act against, and we like Walt, so we hate those obstacles' (WasHere). In addition, zjparatsov says, we are invited to see things from Walt's perspective:

> We have been viewing this from Walt's side of the story. We have seen the events that transpired and have an understanding of why he went into the meth business. So when Skyler freaks out, she seems like a total bitch to us. If it was told from Skyler's point of view, it would be very boring, but Walt would seem like a total asshole.

According to Krehls, Skyler is used to build tension. She slows down the narrative development, making us ache to know what Walt and Jesse (his meth-cooking sidekick) are up to. Krehls: 'People hate on Skyler because she slows down the most exciting parts of the show. [Given] that the audience wants to see more of what Walt does when he's with Jessie, Skyler sometimes feels like the only thing holding us back.'

The fun of discussing Skyler from a savvy viewer perspective is in reverse engineering decisions made by the show's production team: how do they get us to be spellbound, involved or disgusted? For us viewers, these quotes suggest, there is then a second type of reward in understanding how we came to be immersed in the story in the first place. This makes savvy viewing self-reflexive viewing. It assumes a fair amount of critical and technical knowledge of television storytelling. It prides itself on being knowledgeable and cultured, and appreciative of the professionalism of writers, actors and producers.

Moral realism

The second way of talking about Skyler considers her as a mother and a partner and aims to evaluate her behaviour as morally good or bad. Specific views hinge on the commenter's position on femininity. Conservative gender notions regularly surface, as exemplified by remarks that imply that Skyler 'only thinks of herself,' which is not what mothers or good wives do (cf. MacDonald 1997: 135). Her smoking especially is felt to be a painful example of her badness, and of course, smoking in the presence of a lung cancer patient, at the very least, comes across as insensitive. Hughsie455 sees Skyler's smoking as proof she only thinks of herself: 'As if her husband with lung cancer, son with MS and infant daughter could use the extra second hand smoke.' Not only does she smoke around Walt, she smokes while pregnant. 'I just can't forgive a woman who smoked while she was pregnant (_Ofcourse). Others do defend Skyler, again in highly personalized terms: '[S]he's incredibly stressed out after finding out her husband is a murderer, and even more, so that he acts as though nothing happened and doesn't feel any guilt' (SarcasmForever).

Hating or defending Skyler becomes even more heated by the third episode of season three: 'I.F.T.' (2010), in which Skyler has sex with her boss Ted. Walt and Skyler may be living apart, but they have not divorced yet, so the question arises whether this constitutes cheating or not. BHarmony comments: '[S]he cheated. She was having sex with other men while maintaining their relationship.' Although others disagree, for those who want to hate Skyler, this provides the perfect justification. HolleringArepa simply says: 'She fucked Ted.' Zorium78 takes more words to condemn Skyler: 'Seriously she cheated in her marriage, thats a bfd bigger then lying. By doing that she declared herself a whore, so fuck her.' What is interesting here is that Skyler's infidelity is considered to be so much more important than Walt's lying. Whilst it can be taken as a given that those using the moral realism repertoire have intimate knowledge of the story development, it is remarkable that they do not connect Skyler's actions to how Walt's actions (he has finally owned up to her that he produces drugs) may have spurred her on. The savvy viewing speaking position is not used to analyze and understand what happens. Rather, Skyler's actions are taken out of context and put under a microscope to be held against her. The underlying reasoning is not merely geared towards moral condemnation; it also presents a classical patriarchal argument, upholding the idea that the integrity of the family needs to be maintained in order not to undercut the community (Donat & D'Emilio 1992: 10).

Other comments do defend Skyler, using the same speaking position, yet this time in a more positive way: 'She cheated on him because he was lying to her, and their relationship was in the shitter already anyway' (wtamar). ApexX_Advancer states that hating Skyler for her infidelity is wrong:

> [S]he finds out he's cooking meth, which was far worse than anything she imagined, so she tries to divorce him. [...] He continues the lying and manipulation, winds up putting his family in danger, and now Skylar knows her husband is a murderer who caused an explosion in a fucking retirement home. All within a year. Seeing people say they hate her for stupid shit like cheating on Ted makes me wonder if they're even watching the same show.

Fiction in these quotes is used to learn and to acquire insight into moral questions and categories: why do people do what they do, and how to understand and value their behaviour? This is a very different focus on *Breaking Bad* than in the savvy viewing repertoire. Rather than discuss the series from the perspective of its writers and producers, it takes the story as a realistic tale in its depiction of human emotions, relations and actions. Storytelling thus becomes an opportunity to learn and to sharpen people's reading and moral evaluation skills. A similar mechanism can be found in reading about celebrities in gossip magazines – a parallel which will return below.

Skyler and Walt are fictional characters who, in the discussion, can be taken for real people – for behaviour that also occurs in real life. 'Skyler did what she did only to hurt Walt' (Birnhill); 'Walt's motivation was always to provide for and protect his family' (Birnhill). Bezzie disagrees and feels that Skyler protects no one and is just 'a stupid person,' read: a morally flawed character. A minority of comments come to different conclusions. Fritzfriendzfan relates:

> You know what we call a lady who, when she finds out her husband has lied to her and that he has endangered the lives of their kids, does everything she can to leave and protect her kids, even to the point of endangering herself? Round my house we call her a good mother.

Breaking Bad is rich drama. It offers many more moments for commenters to ponder social relations in emotionally realist terms that are translated into moral evaluation. Lyricallion01 sums this up eloquently:

My problem with Skylar is that she decides on her moral code based on what is most comfortable for her, rather than have a strict line of right and wrong. [She] has a strict moral code that she feels everyone has to abide by [but when] she's given the opportunity to act in ways that she shouldn't deem moral (cheating, accounting fraud, helping Walt), suddenly that moral code disappears and she feels justified, and not even a little guilty, in what she is doing. tl;dr: her moral code is too subjective, and is based on her whims. She picks and chooses to whom and where her personal values apply.

Holding Skyler to account: public shaming

The third category of comments consists mainly of threats and swear words addressed to the character. Many more of these addressed to the actor herself can be found on the dedicated Facebook pages mentioned earlier. These posts are reminiscent of the hate speech found on right-wing populist web communities that seek to be provocative, suggesting it is all for the 'lulz' (just a joke). They are deeply disturbing in the violent suggestions made against individual persons. Only a small portion of the Reddit comments actually go this far, but throughout the 'public shaming' category of comments, a visceral emotion can be discerned that appears to stem from a sense of ownership of those who are 'publicly available,' for instance as a character or as an actor providing that character. This sense of ownership is deeply embedded in celebrity culture, as part and parcel of its democratic character that promises access but also a vote, whether this is a text message vote to oust a reality television candidate on a show, or a more personalized version on Facebook or Reddit.

Public shaming is not so much a substantial speaking position as it is a confirmation of the right of collectives to decide how their ideas and ideals are represented across public culture. As a perspective, it grants a speaker the right to be judge and jury of, in this case, a character/actor/celebrity. Through this 'holding to account' of individuals in the spotlight, we encounter the dark side of the empowerment entailed by celebrity culture that Marshall (1997) describes. The Reddit quotes below bear witness to a feeling of deception with a character that has come to feel like a real person. Although public shaming suggests a moral component, it is more akin to publicly confirming the falling short of expectations and standards of a given individual. The quotes in this category mostly bespeak unease with Skyler, for which the fictional character/actor is subsequently blamed. The implied message here is: who does she think she is for making me, as a viewer, feel uncomfortable?

Leap_of_faith's comment suggests a feeling of betrayal over a sexual fantasy. The comment is uncomfortable to read in its overly strong wording: 'I think she's the queen cunt. I fucking hate her. At first I liked her and even thought she was hot, now I just want her to die. I'd bang the hell out of her sister though.' Keeper of the Bell says: 'She's a Grade A shithead.' Whilst ThreeOverKnowledge states: 'I FUCKING hate Skyler! She's such a cunt every scene with her in it now just pisses me off and i want her dead!' An anonymous Redditter who deleted her name states: 'I'm a female, and I hate her everliving guts! When anything tragic happens in her life, I laugh inside. I don't know why my hatred for her is so deep ... ... I think it's her stupid face. >:I'. Different scenarios suggest themselves as a way to understand this quote, all highly hypothetical. Skyler may have come to embody what makes a woman vulnerable in a patriarchal family situation, even today. Such a reminder can be painful and unwelcome. Skyler may also simply stand in the way of identifying with the male characters and their deep self-absorption and need for recognition, or be hated for being an obstacle in Walter's narrative arc of self-realization, as pointed out in the savvy viewing quotes.

The obvious need felt to publicly shame Skyler and express hatred of her is part and parcel of the affordance of online social media communication. Here, what Mittell (2015) has called 'allegiance' (a strong feeling of connection and fidelity) may be carried over from fictional characters to living persons. Much of the hate speech in the public shaming category hovers between anger and abuse on the one hand, and pranking or trolling on the other. Pranking is usually associated with immature behaviour. In her ethnography of teenage life, *It's Complicated*, danah boyd (2014) includes pranking in a category named 'drama': 'performative, interpersonal conflict that takes place in front of an active, engaged audience, often on social media' (p. 138). The Redditters do not appear to be teenagers. The anger they voice, however, alludes to a similar powerlessness; an appetite for drama; and the gratification of seeing yourself assume the position of someone whose opinion matters.

The most outspoken of the shaming quotes suggest the type of prank played by trolls. In a review essay, Richard Seymour (2016) notes that for 'gendertrolls,' the goal is to 'silence publicly vocal women by swarm-like harassment, misogynistic insults (such epithets as "cunt" and "whore") [...] and threats of rape and murder' (ibid.). This fits the Skyler/Gunn insults and threats rather well, and explains them as outrage at this particular woman standing in the way of beloved anti-hero Walter. How dare she! Women need to know their place and should not upset a gender order some of us thought had changed. The public shaming of Skyler/Gunn is an amplified version of savvy viewing and moral realism. It positions both in a misogynist frame of threatened masculinity, with the sole purpose of bringing an erring woman back to heel. It appears to be born from what we might call 'counter-allegiance'.

Affect and allegiance

Affect is described by Wetherell (2015) as energy, as 'the ways in which bodies are pushed and pulled in contemporary social formations, in the "engineering" of affective responses, and in how workers and citizens become emotionally engaged and affectively interpellated' (2015: 140). Affect is what makes feelings translate into emotion. In relation to popular culture, it is a difficult-to-grasp but relevant term that addresses how for instance a tv series speaks to us as a form of insistence, as something that you feel you need to speak out about. When Mittell discusses Walter White, he writes about connecting with a person he never interacted with 'in real life' whom he came to love 'not as a person' but 'as a character':

> We might think of this engagement as operational allegiance – as viewers, we are engaged with the character's construction, attuned to how the performance is presented, fascinated by reading the mind of the inferred author, and rooting for Walt's triumph in storytelling, if not his actual triumph within the story.
>
> (Mittell 2015: 163)

Allegiance with Walter White is an energizing connection, built on the relative morality of the character. Walt, as Mittell calls him, does not start out as the amoral antihero he will become. He is a very ordinary guy, the antithesis of a sex object and a master rationalizer (ibid.: 154). He can also be overbearing and conceited, suggesting he is a man raised to understand himself as a pillar of society. Mittell is fascinated by how, throughout *Breaking Bad*'s seasons, we 'watch Walt convince himself that various immoral decisions are the right thing to do, given a lack of alternatives, leading to a descent into monstrous behaviour that is always presented as reasonable within Walt's own self-justification and immediate context' (ibid.: 155). Walter's self-rationalization rubs off on Mittell (ibid.: 162), the viewer:

> By the end of *Breaking Bad*'s fourth season, we have witnessed the remarkable transition of Walt from everyman schlub to amoral criminal kingpin, a gradual enough shift that we have still maintained a degree of allegiance to him – in part because we have invested so much time in following his exploits, an instance of 'sunken costs' of attention and engagement.

Walter's deeper goals – the real drama of the series – surface over the seasons. He needs to be seen, understood, recognized and appreciated for his talents and for his moral drive to take care of his family – irrespective of what he has to engage with in order to do so, and notwithstanding the fact that this is not what his family wants him to do.

As allegiance with Walter develops – as it did for most of those who loved the series – Skyler becomes a problematic figure. Walter develops the type of rugged masculinity that leaves little space for caring, consultation, or listening. Skyler suffers through it all, including two scenes of marital rape in seasons two and five (Wilder 2013). She neither fights back nor does she break. Her choices are painful and difficult to understand, and she is slow to take decisions. She is simply not a character for whom it is easy to care. To hate her and become angry with her is a much easier way to deal with her role as an obstacle than it is to root for her, although some viewers do. They understand Skyler as a tragic heroine, as a woman who tries to take responsibility under impossible circumstances. Moral realism and public shaming are very clearly interlinked forms of affect and discourse, of emotional and rational(ized) arguments. Savvy viewing is less clearly so but there too, the pleasure of control and ownership, in being the one that decides what is good and what is bad, is an affective response.

Celebrity gossip and the professional woman

The hating of Skyler as a form of 'counter allegiance' boils down to how gender ideology works across popular culture. It invites a tragic understanding of a strong woman as victim and an equally tragic misunderstanding in which the victim is blamed for not fighting back. These are the hallmarks of the logic of excess in melodrama in which emotions and feeling are given centre stage and the good are rarely rewarded. Interestingly, it suffuses gossip as well as contemporary quality television, according to Mittell (2015: 245). The very success of *Breaking Bad* is predicated on the fact that the series has made its viewers care about the drama. Melodrama has become a shared vocabulary that connects characters to actors – to 'live' celebrities. Melodrama also supplies much of the vocabulary of celebrity gossip: here we find how a professional actor unwittingly may become a 'composite' celebrity whose other half is the character she plays, and who is essentially hated as both.

Whilst melodrama might provide the generic rules for hating Skyler, gossip provides the vocabulary and the justification for vociferous online hatred. Gossip at heart is a process of inclusion and exclusion, and doubles as a *de facto* citizenship forum (cf. Meyer Spacks 1985; De Vries 1990; Dunbar 1998; Dunbar 2004; Hermes 2005, 1995). Judging others – especially celebrities – serves the dual purpose of showing oneself to be a discerning individual and a reminder to (especially young) women of the standards they need to aspire to (Edwards 2013: 28). In Reddit posts savvy viewing is a form of fan coauthorship, whilst moral realist viewing and public shaming are forms of bottom-up democratic control and holding to account. Read as forms of celebrity gossip, the moral realism and public shaming Reddit posts make sense as a terrain in which femininity is policed.

Celebrity gossip is a key social site on which gender is defined, discussed and reconstructed – often in a negative way (Vares & Jackson 2015). It builds a sense of community through its discussion of moral standards (even if by way of slut-shaming) and it reinforces neoliberal individualism by insisting it is important to be a subject of value (Allen & Mendick 2013: 77; cf. Gill & Scharff 2011: 5–7; see also Skeggs & Wood 2012). Typically, such demands are easiest made of others, and fuel a double pleasure of assuming control and holding someone else to account. In this way conservative notions of gender are reconfirmed. 'The world of celebrity, for the most part at least, tends to underline not undermine gender divisions' (Edwards 2013: 166). According to Edwards: 'it is precisely the machinery of celebrity itself that would seem to be the problem,' and the root cause of the hatred of 'demons of female fame' (Edwards 2013: 166). When women become public figures, they energize hatred.

That, surely, is not their own fault or responsibility. An important secondary role in these processes is played by the ongoing hollowing out of professionalism. Gunn's experience shows how the earlier protection offered by what John Ellis (1982) and Marshall (1997) describe as an 'aura of distance' no longer exists, not even for actors in high-quality dramas. Television's aura of intimacy grants intimidating liberties to audiences (Kavka 2016: 309), especially when it connects with the public accountability demanded of those who hold positions of status and power. Celebrity culture, including all public discussion of celebrities – whether positive or negative –, helps remind us that lives and bodies need to be shaped in certain ways, and that responsibilities have to be met. Whilst the rhetoric of neoliberalism speaks of choice, in reality, it is about discipline which is tested in markets (Fraser 2003). Under neoliberalism, the position of professionals as intermediaries who operate in and from sovereign fields – be they e.g., social care, the law or indeed the arts – has been very much eroded. Organizations such as a network or a studio are no longer a shield providing staff to deal with publicity, and if necessary, with media and audience attention if it were to get out of hand. Neither a professional nor a beloved character, Gunn becomes a celebrity and an object of hatred who finds herself at the receiving end of contemporary narratives of gender confusion.

Cultural citizenship and Skyler's culpability

Reddit conversation about Skyler White is easy to recognize as cultural citizenship. It literally inquires into the rights and responsibilities of women in relationships with men. It is also typically the cultural citizenship that popular culture gives us access to: it is not highly self-reflective but it feels spontaneous and, strange to say, honest. It is doubtful that face-to-face interviews would have resulted in similarly rich material. Beyond the shocking sexism in comments, there seems to be real confusion about gender and gender roles. The codes of melodrama embedded both in the series and in celebrity gossip clearly stacked the deck against Skyler and demonstrate how neoliberalism aligns with a conservative gender agenda.

Watching and discussing *Breaking Bad* functions as cultural citizenship in that the series allows for public, unforced reflection on traditional masculinity as much as it allows for attempts to re-inscribe traditional gender values via the misogyny directed at Skyler. However, it does not do so without contestation. Clearly, cultural citizenship can come in many different guises. Regretfully, neither reflection, politics, nor celebrity culture are by their nature progressive or geared to produce equal chances in life. Luckily, therefore, much more than hatred is voiced against White/Gunn. Witness the thread 'Skyler White Is Fucking Justified, Dammit!' in which GhostSacrifice lists Walt's selfish and criminal acts to conclude: 'I simply don't see why she gets so much damn hate. It's fucking bullshit, if you ask me.'

5
INNOCENCE

Raising children to be media literate and fear of popular culture

With Sarieke Hoeksma

Nowhere is 'modernist' apprehension about the possible effects of media consumption as strong as among parents of young children. 'Modernist' refers to the binary evaluation of media as either good: we learn from the media! The media help us maintain democratic control as citizens! Or bad: media (think games or currently TikTok) enslave us, turn us into couch potatoes and smartphone addicts, make children anxious or violent or lazy. The link between media literacy and citizenship is almost too close: keeping up with the news is our democratic duty; engaging with culture is building and maintaining the nation and its history. Entertainment and drama are okay when they make us wonder about other lifeworlds us and reflect on what we take for granted. They are bad when they seduce us to not follow scripts for safe living that avoid social condemnation.

This chapter will start with examples that underwrite the modernist structure of thinking about media literacy – which condemns television, screens and commercial culture as bad for children. It leads to short excerpts from conversations with children themselves who echo their parents' and teachers' positions but also take a more appreciative approach to media and media literacy. (With obvious tactical advantages of claiming 'the worst possible taste' as a position of their own, cf. Davies et al. 2000.) The second half of the chapter will be given to a case study of parents discussing television in a project on transgender characters in children's television. The example has been used in chapter 3 to discuss the importance of affect and intuition. As researchers we want to recognize it in others but we also want to take it seriously in self-reflective modus to check whether we understand what it is that our partners in conversation about media and media content are trying to tell us. All in all, from the perspective of cultural citizenship, it becomes clear that there might be more to discussion of media literacy than we hear, either in modernist or post-structuralist research modes.

Gender, it will also become clear, again, is especially important here. As the previous chapter has shown, media are an important civic space to rehearse where society stands when it comes to gender conventions and roles. While Skyler White fails to live up to the ideal of a wife and mother, parents in the second half of this chapter seem to fear the same of themselves, and that, as a result, their boys will not be boys. Girls are given more leeway to enjoy themselves outside the bounds of gender appropriateness. Young boys can forget about being given the little pink kitchen they yearn to have. 'Tomboyishness' on the other hand does not disqualify a woman, while being effeminate does disqualify a man. Other categories than male or female (whether non-binary, trans or queer identities) for most parents are even more painful to discuss. Why it is so important to (politically liberal) parents for their children to display cis-gender behaviour will become clear towards the end of the chapter. Gender confusion will return as a key element in doing cultural citizenship in the chapter after this one.

Concern

Parents of small children are almost always concerned about the time their children spend on media, and especially about watching television and playing games. In fact, experts agree. Recent Dutch research berates parents of 0–6 years olds for not taking World Health Organization guidelines for children's media use seriously enough and allowing their children far too much screen time (Netwerk Mediawijsheid & Nikken 2022). Especially higher educated parents use the argument that media use has positive effects (such as language learning) rather than negative effects when they use screens as babysitters to do chores or have time for themselves. Interestingly, at the same time, more than half of the parents surveyed do notice negative effects of media use in their children such as overly active and contrary behaviour, reticence and sleeping problems.

In the interviews this chapter is based on, conducted from the early 2010s to recently, parents tended to dutifully note the full array of detrimental effects the media might have: overusing the media will make children hyperactive, have nightmares, become cognizant of life lessons they are much too young for, make them overstep boundaries and engage in risky behaviour. There is a vast literature on children and media effects but that is not what this chapter is about. Rather, this chapter means to chart how using cultural citizenship as a lens in tandem with inquiring about media literacy, will help to heari what *further* conversations are afforded among the interviewed parents when they are invited to talk about their children and the media. What is it that they want for their children? A short interlude in which children themselves discuss media literacy will address how media literacy itself, as a concept, also allows for more divergent definitions than one usually comes across.

The triangular relationship of parents and caretakers, children and media provided the setting for Annika van den Berg, Marloes Mol and my own research on media literacy in the earlier 2010s (Hermes, Van den Berg, & Mol 2013). For an intercultural media literacy game in 2017, Christa de Graaf, Gijs van Beek, Karel Koch and I spoke and worked with teenagers, tweens, youth professionals and parents.[1] Sarieke Hoeksma, last but not least, turned to parents when inquiring into why there is relatively little gender diversity in Dutch children's television, otherwise lauded and progressive in many respects (Hoeksma 2016 and see chapter 3). Given their small size, none of these projects allow for generalizing conclusions about children, parents or professionals as populations in their own right. Together though, remarkably, they offer a strong pattern of how parents and professionals fear for what might befall children especially when it comes to media and media use and what kind of risk assessment they feel they have to do. In chapter 3, I discussed how important it is to attend to affect and sentiment and not only to discourse (as in the words spoken by informants). Attending to feeling and how we are oriented towards dominant interpretations and views of media, television, parenting allows access to what Richard Johnson called the 'unfinished business' that cultural studies research finds in its quest to reconstruct and understand everyday meaning making. The becoming more fluid of gender definitions ranks high on the 'unfinished business' agenda that is cultural citizenship.

Media education

Parents of young children and pedagogical staff in day-care centres

Without much ado, the long-running television programme *Sesame Street* disappeared in 2015 from Dutch public television and was relegated to one of public television's themed internet channels. It was still available but removed from easy and incidental access. In 2021 the theme channel too disappeared. It attracted too little viewers to merit the expenditure. For years no new Dutch material had been produced for the show. Its mix of education and friendly entertainment, according to the public broadcasters, had lost its appeal. It underlines how for a growing group of parents, there was little incentive to search for public television for their children. It might be that on-demand and commercial children's television offers the same (or more) benefits. Clearly, Nickelodeon's *Dora the Explorer* (8 seasons produced from 2000 onwards) is structured around learning. The deeply moralistic initially British Channel 5 series *Peppa Pig* (2004-) has been acquired by American toy merchant Hasbro. Perhaps *Sesame Street* simply 'hit the shark' (as a now defunct website called it) and stopped being fun. The small amount of discussion that its disappearance sparked, offers evaluations that refer to criteria that are reminiscent of the golden standard of media literacy education: reading a book.

Annika van den Berg (2010) researched the appeal of the book reading segment that *Sesame Street* offered as one of its returning items. It showed one of the presenters reading a book to a small group of children in the *Sesame Street* studio. She interviewed parents and day-care professionals, who were approached through two different day-care centres and a swimming pool (swimming lessons are obligatory in the Netherlands). They did not much like the show which at that time was still on television. They told her children found it boring and preferred other programmes. Interestingly, they insisted that they were very careful in the amount of time their children watched television and in controlling what was on. All underlined that reading a book was a much better way of spending time than watching television: for the child's development and well-being, and for themselves. Reading a book together was quality time. As a day-care professional and a mum said:

I think reading to a child this age [0–4 years old, jh] has many advantages: it is good for their language development ... the fantasy of the children is [triggered] and they learn to concentrate. That is really right for this age (children's day-care professional).

Of course, we read to our children! I mean reading to them is really really good for their development. And with Lamyae we found that she was really looking at things from a very early age onwards ... especially photos and pictures, so we read to her ... in my lap, looking at pictures ... that is all that is needed ... just leaf through a book (mother).

Parents and day-care centre staff were as unequivocally positive about reading to young children as they were dismissive of television. Not only were they critical of *Sesame Street,* but educational television in general was not part of their vocabularies, different though they were as a group in terms of class background, family size and, to a lesser extent, ethnic-cultural background. Television viewing needed to be limited as much as possible and was used mostly as a substitute babysitter when dinner needed to be prepared or when parents wanted to sleep in or start the day at their ease. These forms of ritual and unreflected-on use of television (or screens generally) were also noted in the recent Dutch research outcomes mentioned at the beginning of this chapter (Netwerk Mediawijsheid & Nikken 2022). As a father in Annika's research said:

As a family we'll watch in the early morning. She wakes up quite early, half past six, and then we tune to children's public service programming [Nederland 3] ... what is it called again?

Interviewer: *Zappelin?*

Yes! And we'll watch ... she'll watch until seven and we get a chance to wake up a little (father)

I prefer for them not to watch any television at all. That they do other things. Watching television is passive entertainment ... they just watch ... nothing else. ... I don't think it makes them more creative. (Another father)

In her study of *Television and New Media Audiences,* Ellen Seiter points to the discrepancy between how television is used and how it is talked about. Babysitting young children is one of the things television is felt to do really well. Television is undeniably handy for calming children down, confining them to one area, reducing noise in the classroom, and postponing demands for adult attention. Such uses of television however are widely condemned by the vast majority of early childhood professionals – or ignored in the publications and research of such groups as the National Association for the Education of Young Children (Seiter 1999: 61).

In the Netherlands, this is largely the same. Government initiatives that started in the early 2000s stress that television is a dangerous medium. *Kijkwijzer* (*Smart viewing*) e.g., provides a set of icons for audio-visual texts that by their nature signal the dangers of television to parents. Likewise, in early childhood education (for children from 2.5 years of age who can be expected to lag in their development), the exclusion of television as an educational tool is significant. This is a shame, concludes Van den Berg, who quotes Dutch and other sources that underline that paying positive attention to children's television experience can help children become more literate (see also Hodge and Tripp, 1986: 178; Buckingham 1993; Kellner & Share 2007). Interestingly, Van den Berg's results also identified a small group that held an oppositional position: while looking for ethnic diversity in her sample of parents and pedagogical staff, she also made contact with non-native speakers of Dutch. They felt that watching television was good for their (young) children's language acquisition. They saw none of the dangers that the other parents talked about at length.

Surprisingly, the book reading segment in *Sesame Street* had not, overall, endeared informants to watching television. While the expectation was to find a shared pleasure in both media, television was maligned and reading cherished. According to most of the interviewed parents and professionals, television viewing made children passive, diminished their world and offered only entertainment and a restrictive worldview. The medium stimulated aggressive behaviour, individualized and isolated children and lacked variety. Books and book reading, on the other hand, activated children, enriched their fantasy, educated them, offered them a world with no boundaries or borders, stimulated language acquisition, helped children and parents make contact, and was interactive and socializing. This may be true for 4–6 years old. Shortly after, of course, book reading becomes a solitary activity. What started as a simple interest in whether *Sesame Street* offered a good means to broaden children's media literacy turned into a portrait of a witch hunt directed at television. Such a perspective produces a hierarchical distinction between the literate and the non-literate. It reifies book culture in a way that Neil Postman (1982) and other culture pessimists would applaud. This is the propagation of literacy in its most conservative guise and a demonization of screen media that highly educated parents have learned to be less worried about going by the recent monitor research results. Unsurprisingly, children are less worried although certainly not immune to conservative media literacy talk.

From the mouths of... ... primary school pupils

Interested in gauging children's actual media literacy Marloes Mol (2011) approached 50 children through three primary schools in a large and a mid-sized city and a village. She asked them to make TV diaries for her. She taped her instructions on how to use these and discussed the diaries in small groups in the classroom. While the school environment was clearly slightly problematic and may have encouraged the children to stress what they felt they *learnt* from television, school is also a 'natural' environment for children aged between 4 and 16, in which they spend most of their week. A significant chunk of the time spent at school is leisure time, moreover: breaks, free hours and after-school care. Popular media and entertainment are certainly not absent in school environments. According to Duits' (2008) ethnographic research among girls in the same age group, it is discussed regularly.

Mol's first set of forms offered little that was useful in gauging whether and how her informants were media literate. The programmes they saw (a mixture across genres, and across children's and adult (mostly 'family' television) were deemed 'OK' and sometimes 'exciting' or 'funny.' A more extended version became the television diary. It included questions such as: If you could make a television programme, what would it be like? Or: What do you think is not good in television for children? Bad for your eyes, said one child, and it can make you asocial. Generally, however, the children felt that commercials and reruns were what was wrong with television. This is before Netflix arrived on Dutch screens. A slightly older audience group were moving from broadcast television to internet-based viewing according to national statistics at the time (Sikkema, 2009: 25). Good about television was that it offered fun, excitement, stories and drama. To learn new things was also valued highly. News and realism were mentioned on a par with funny and fake.

The understanding in the interview material that much of what television shows is not 'real' or happening that exact moment, but 'fake,' comes across as a mix between disappointment (a little) and a happy sense of superior insight in the workings of television: of being media literate. A 12-year-old boy said: 'And all those people, the presenters and so on, they read from a big video screen that says exactly what you have to say. It even has the jokes they make on it and all that.' Other children, too, had either witnessed or knew about the routines of television production, for example, that a programme can be live but that more often it is filmed in bits and pieces. Some of the girls were media literate in another way: they could explain how soaps might be fake, but also, in a way 'real.' Real versus fake is a theme the children liked to explore: there is the really real of the talent shows, although, even there, presenters use an autocue. The same is true for news programmes. 'What they say is never real, but the things that happened are of course.' An intriguing quote that suggests that media are always engaged in sleight-of-hand, even when they are well-respected and above-board sources of news. After real versus fake, which would seem to be a clear opposition but apparently is not, classical entertainment characteristics are valued in television: humour, suspense and action. These are balanced, in turn, by the wish to learn from television. 'Things that you can learn from' usually referred to facts and information rather than to understanding in a wider sense.

Interesting is how the interviewed children explain the value of humour. Humour is of overriding importance they said, and 'funny' was one of the most frequently given reasons for liking a programme. Jokes and humorous situations made it easy to concentrate and to be drawn into the world of the show. 'Television should be fun,' one girl said. 'With jokes, you keep focused. When you have a programme with a good story, I do think that it needs jokes, or I can't keep up and I don't get the story' (girl). 'Getting a joke' could well be a check for a 12-year-old viewer that she or he has a right to watch a programme because they understand what it is about. Davies et al. assume as much, based on interviews with both slightly younger and slightly older children:

> In cases like this, enthusiasm for the 'childish' and silly aspects of comedy were combined with a sense of exclusivity. In discussion, it was important for certain children to show that they could 'get' the joke (as it were), in order to show that they were grown up and sophisticated
>
> (Davies et al. 2000: 16)

While jokes, humour and 'funniness' keep you going as a television viewer, the children Mol interviewed also like to learn from television. The problem is that the slope from learning to boring is a steep one, as seen in a discussion about *The Children's News* (*het Jeugdjournaal*) and *News from Nature* (two programmes the children appreciated):

Girl: just talk, talk, talk, talk.
Interviewer: Too much talking?

Boy:	Yes, that is the news, they do show that a lot too, mind you.
Same girl:	That can also be boring

The problem of over-talkative and boring programmes, according to the children, could easily be solved by inserting more jokes. One of the boys summarized: 'Well, there are things that we children simply do not like. And if we don't like it, we don't learn from it either.' Overall, the children claimed that they do incidentally learn from television. In such cases they refer to small facts, news items and language acquisition (Dutch television subtitles rather than dubs). Although not very elaborate, they also claim to learn socially and emotionally from television. MTV's *Plain Jane*, for instance, was appreciated for giving the girl who gets a make-over more self-confidence (TV diary). In the group interview, the same girl explained: 'If you see someone making a mistake, and you watch it, you don't have to make that mistake.' Of course, learning is what you can expect children to talk about in a school environment but across these interviews it also became clear that television provided a forum for additional forms of learning: tips on how to live your life well, new words, interacting with others. News and quiz shows provided interesting facts, drama provided insight into social rules and the ability to recognize emotions.

If literacy is the ability to know what you like and why you like it, the interviewed children do well. Their definition certainly comes close to what Rita Felski (2015) defines as appreciative inquiry. Of course, the pleasure in knowing how deceptive television is, also points to appreciative inquiry's counterpart, suspicious reading. The children link funny to real and to learning. In drama, comedy and animated series they are happy to ignore the fact that these are fictional programmes (fake) if they have something funny or informative to offer. Generally, though, the obvious deception in how 'real' television may look but is not (presenters reading an autocue), pointed to a negative form of literacy that undermined their faith in any type of serious television. The references to humour and jokes implied a type of self-reflexivity and self-deprecation that they like: it suggested a shared sense of lack of control and overview. The unfortunate result is that this stopped them from acquiring the means to make full use of what television does have to offer. It is unlikely that this imbalance between suspicion and deception on the one hand and appreciation on the other will be righted in the future as parents are much more invested in cautiousness and awareness than in appreciation that is easily equalled to naive and uncritical.

It would have been good to get to know the children better and understand how specific programs became meaningful. It also would have been an ethical nightmare to do that well and a time-consuming one at that. Neither caveat made a grant proposal likely to be subsidized. The work of Duits (2009) and boyd (2015) suggests that it is important (and worthwhile) to spend time with tweens and teenagers, also in terms of charting how they use media for cultural citizenship. The next section discusses contact made with teenagers and youth workers and co-creating a game for intercultural media literacy that we called *Media Wizards*. The game was no big success (do email me if you are interested though) but making collage art works with teenagers, youth workers and a group of parents was.

Rolex watches and the online world of teenagers

The online life worlds of teenagers and young adults are notoriously difficult to gain access to. Occasionally patient and gifted researchers such as Linda Duits and danah boyd do manage to do so. Youth workers do too. Like parents, they distrust all media culture. Social networks and digital culture had generally replaced television as objects of suspicion and distrust when Christa de Graaf, Gijs van Beek, Karel Koch and I spoke separately with young people and parents about intercultural media literacy in order to see if we could develop a tool for young people and professionals to gain more of a foothold on how to navigate online lifeworlds. We hoped to address the concerns of parents and professionals and to gain the trust of young people to see where there might be an opening to discuss and establish intercultural forms of media literacy. That is to say, to attend, in addition to more conventional definitions, to representations of difference and diversity, whether in terms of class, gender, religion or sexuality to name some of the obvious candidates.

The interview material suggested three axes of evaluation for media and media use. The first related to *affect*: a game, a show or an app could be fun or not. The second is about *affordance*: the medium or your own behaviour can suit your goals (or not). And thirdly, there is *excess*: media use can feel safe or unsafe. The game addresses all three by asking participants to discuss questions in relation to fun (positive affect), suitability (technological affordance used well) and excess. In discussion the players can grant each other points. Discussing possible formats and prototypes, we learned about blocking and unfriending (to the point of simply moving to a new phone number and building new profiles and a new contact list). In collage art (in which informants were asked to depict the upside and downside of social media), we saw an amazing number of beautiful women and expensive watches to denote 'the good life.' Others associated the good life with pictures of families and symbols of 'happiness' (hearts, the colour pink). The watches especially we had not expected to come out of our newspapers and women's weeklies… … A returning grievance was the ongoing fight over access to telephones and enough credit to use it. Parents, we were assured, generally had no clue as to how quickly access was regained. 'Old-fashioned' tv met with great disdain but of course, it could be good fun to watch a show with your mum. Consistency, suffice it to say, was not felt to be important at all.

As for parents and professionals, media for young people are invasive presences that are also lifelines. They connect to others but in unwieldy and not always easy-to-control ways. I found myself greatly liking a teenager at a youth centre in Amsterdam-Noord who without at all feeling embarrassed declared that blocking individuals on her phone was too much work, she would simply take a new phone number to get rid of people who were a nuisance. These came in quite a variety ranging from pushy boys to girls 'cussing her out.' The group clearly greatly admired her force of character. When asked they conceded that blocking others was common practice as was finding out people's new numbers to taunt them. Maybe not a very friendly way of approaching others but clearly a fact of life.

Thinking about media and media literacy, affect, affordance and excess matter. While affect and affordance come as no surprise, excess is important to understand as relating to inclusion and exclusion (for the moment conflating *feeling* excluded or included and *being* excluded or included) (cf. Sheombar & Hermes 2022: 164). Definitions of media literacy, on the other hand, tend to be very aware of the possibility of excess and focus on skills, knowledge and competencies. Affect is not usually part of these definitions but would be extremely useful to incorporate. The young people we interviewed understood the media as a diffuse and gigantic assemblage of affect and effects. Fear and gaining a measure of control over their lives are points of entry for thinking about media literacy from their perspective. Not so much in a technical sense (as skills or competencies) but rather in terms of clarifying to themselves how they would want to live their lives and what that would take.

Before moving on to how difficult it is to recognize and respect the fear(s) of others, it is useful to summarize that across all these smaller studies and participative design projects, it becomes clear how much context matters (both in the experience of media texts and media use and in whether and how it is possible to have a conversation about either or both). It is also clear that media literacy tools need to have open formats and that a measure of co-creativity is useful, as is clarifying for what kind of context they have been developed (to use in school or at home). Educational games work much better if they are also fun. Openness is necessary because young people are different. Although this is stating the obvious, schools tend to want to diminish these differences (whether they are to do with gender, religion or class). They are in the business of producing well-behaved citizens after all. Conversation, last but not least allows for recognizing the tactical and practical media wisdom of younger people. Ideally, their wisdom meets with the life experience and wisdom of professionals and parents. Adults noticeably, tend to feel insecure about their digital skills. They are not sure they have enough of a sense of what is hip and happening in different kinds of media entertainment. Nor on what social media platforms you 'need to be' and what is going on there.

Understanding parents and accepting the importance of understanding fear

Children's television in the Netherlands, however lauded and progressive in many respects, could allow for far more gender diversity than it actually does. Could children have more space to develop regardless of authoritative gender definitions, Sarieke Hoeksma wondered. Boys should not have to be 'boys,' nor girls 'girls' and conform to what has come to be called cis-genderist culture, or the imperative to perform in accordance with conformist gender rules (Lennon & Mistler 2014: 63–64). Couldn't children's television be exactly the place where children are inspired to break such bounds? If, that is, their parents will allow them to watch a different kind of television. And, secondly, if media makers were to produce such audiovisual material? Chapter 3 introduced Sarieke's and later our collective work to understand how television viewing was such an issue for parents. It is not just the case that Dutch parents hold deeply culturally pessimistic views of the medium (Hermes 2013; Netwerk Mediawijsheid & Nikken 2022). Discussing children and media elicited a deep-seated gender-conservative discourse that contrasted sharply with other discourses referred to by the parents in the same interviews. If we want to champion inclusive and open-minded forms of media literacy that allow for appreciation as much as for critique, we need to learn how to understand and deal with the fears of others.

Gender conservatism from my perspective is a problem in its own right. Children's television typically supports and disseminates restrictive heterosexual cis-gender normativity. Exceptions to this rule are still a reason to celebrate, whether in children's or general audience television (Gray 2021; Halberstam 2012; Vanlee, Dhaenens & Van Bauwel 2020). Programs targeted at girls tend to sport pink and purple colours, are filled with hearts and butterflies while the behaviour of girl characters focuses on appearance and being popular with boys (Christensen 2011: 196). Boy-characters, on the other hand, are about force, speed, courage and power (Hofmann 2011: 210). There is little room for identities that do not conform to this norm.

The account below is a first step to how fear can be identified and understood. It is based on Sarieke's five long open conversations with six parents of young children who between them they raise 15 children. All informants had open-minded views on gender and on television (as estimated by our friends and acquaintances who asked them for us and as defined by themselves). There are no gay parents in the set of informants. Having been explained the purpose of the interviews and promised anonymity, parents were asked to talk about their children, their policies in television viewing, selection of toys and clothing and all other things they felt were relevant in relation to gender. All parents were happy to oblige and talked freely. A first validation of the material was the fact that individuals would contradict themselves without realising. When asked they would explain further, making clear that they often were trying to do justice to different points of view. Analyzing the interview material, we found three interpretative repertoires across the material. Below we have included a large number of quotes from the interviews to show how much this diverse group of informants held similar views. The progressive analytical iteration first identified keywords, which were clustered into themes. Using the available literature, the themes were condensed and contextualized to the three repertoires. (See chapter 3 for a visual representation of this process of condensation and interpretation.)

Be who you are, the first repertoire

All the parents passionately emphasized they will always love and respect their children, no matter what. Never mind whether their child behaves as a 'typical' boy or girl or not. Parents did not want to interfere; they only wanted to encourage their child to make its own decisions and to be who they are. Using this repertoire parents stressed being open-minded, respectful to their children, and on being a *good* parent. They seemed to want to convince themselves and the outer world of their best intentions and the absolute freedom they offer their children. (All names of parents are pseudonyms).

I liked [pink] for Feie too and I never limited him. (…) I'll just let him, he has to feel comfortable. (Fieke)

[Y]ou want your child to be happy with the thing she chooses. I won't tell her she can't [choose something pink] and that she has to pick something blue. If your child is happy with it, then you're happy as a parent too. So automatically you won't oppose it. (Jara)

They are allowed to look at everything (when we are in a toy store) (Kim)

I let them watch anything they like, really. Whether it's a girls' program or a boys' program, it's all fine with me. (Fatiha)

I don't feel like my son should play soccer and that my daughter should ride horses, or play hockey or something like that. No, they are allowed to make their own choices. …. (And later in the interview) …… And of course, one can stand up against it and try to change [the child], but that doesn't work. That's who you are. I think you'll get bigger problems when you don' support your children, you'll get huge problems. Self-confidence … . which those children won't develop because they are not accepted by the people they love.

> *Your self-confidence will be damaged thoroughly, I think. Everyone should be able to be who they are. That's what I believe. (Olivier)*

In these quotes, parents showcase their liberal colours whether it concerns choices in clothing, sports or watching television. Cisgender behaviour does not seem to be relevant. That is, a boy does not necessarily have to be boyish and a girl does not necessarily have to be girlish. Either way is fine, as long as the children are happy. In regard to children's television, they allow their sons and daughters to watch both 'girlish' and boyish' programs. A boy who wants to wear a pink sweater to school is not referred to as a problem at all.

The next repertoire shows how this is but one facet of how these parents deal with gender. When the boy who wanted to wear the pink sweater came home from school crying because other children laughed at him and told him that 'pink is for girls,' the sweater was retired from outside-the-home use. It could be worn at home but not to school. This is the precise point where parents stopped being liberal. Upon a risk of their children might get hurt, they feel the need to protect them by strictly adhering to hetero-normative gender codes and save them, beforehand, from being bullied or excluded. They know it is a nasty and difficult world out there. Better they felt safe at home and kept their head down out there.

Big, bad world, the second repertoire

All the parents feared that their boy children would be bullied. We found no examples of parents fearing their girls would meet with such a fate, while of course, this happens too. The boys were taught that it is better to conform than to be marked as an outsider. Both the 'be who you are' and the 'big bad world' repertoires have the same goal: to make sure children are happy. The underlying strategies though were very different. Instead of granting children their freedom, parents strongly limited their children in the hope of saving them from hurt and struggle. These two repertoires were clearly place-related. The home was a safe place, in which children could be who they wanted to be. The school, on the other hand, was a public space in which strong norms prevailed and where the danger of being excluded needed to be avoided. Typical statements within this repertoire were:

> *For almost a year he has worn the dress and we were like: 'Maybe not when we're picking up Michael from school.' We wanted to protect him from the reactions of the older children. (...) He wanted to wear it every day, really. But when we would pick up Michael ... look I just know, since I work with preschoolers myself, that even in grade 2, they can be very harsh and say things like: 'Ah look at that! You look like a girl!' You know. We don't think you have*

to expose him to those things and that after he hears such a thing he doesn't dare to wear that dress anymore. (Later in the interview): You know we don't choose the pink toy kitchen, a red wooden retro kitchen that also looks a bit tough. (…) 'Cause practically thinking, you want them to like it for a longer time and you just know that at some point they'll realize that pink is a colour for girls. And you don't want to give a present that isn't looked after anymore after half a year. And besides, I don't like pink at all and we also wanted to buy something that looked nice in the living room. (Kim)

'I wouldn't [let him wear a dress to school], 'cause you're making your child so different. And of course, you are allowed to be who you are, but with all the bullying, I would avoid that.' (Later in the interview) There are things in blue and in pink. And I did buy a little bike in blue after all, for her. (…) I thought if we would get another child and it would be a boy, I wouldn't put him on a pink bike. And a girl, it's totally fine for her to ride an aqua-coloured bike, it looks wonderful. But it's either pink or blue, that's how it is in such a store. (Jara)

And maybe – as a parent – you kind of want your daughter to be a girly girl and your son to be a boyish boy. Maybe that's something you partially bring about in your parenting. My son would never wear any make-up. That's just because I never taught him, you know, I never bought any make-up for him. (…) Yeah I think I would react like: 'Oh come one, you're a boy, you're not going to wear make-up, are you?' Yeah I think that I would … unconsciously, make such a comment. 'You are not really going to do that, are you?' (Fatiha)

Fatiha in all honesty described how she might guide her daughters into being girlish and her son into being a boyish person. The pressure on being cisgender clearly emerged here: girlishness followed 'logically' from being a girl and boyishness from being a boy. Fieke too had her ideas about what was appropriate for her daughter and son:

Well, it's more that I push Lotus to get a doll. But maybe that's against her natural will. (…) I think that it belongs to girls, but she is more the tough one who climbs the swing and races around (…) She should like [the doll]. But she doesn't do anything with it. Or maybe she is too young, that's a possibility. And I bought a soccer ball for Feie, but he doesn't do anything with that. So you know … (…) Because I believe that a soccer ball belongs to a boy and that I hope that he'll play soccer and becomes somewhat more masculine. Not that I … he has to be who he is, but I want to pass on a sort of toughness, like: 'Go for a run, race through that garden'. Instead of that very soft, introvert play, I try to make him go outside, to open him up. And he does, he climbs trees and he races and stuff. But uhm … even though I try to inspire him, it doesn't interest him at all. He is the one who prefers those dolls … (Fieke)

Boys were the more vulnerable gender in the interviewed parents' perception. They could not be seen in dresses or pink sweaters or on pink bicycles. The moment they are linked to girlishness, they could apparently expect to be bullied, jeered at and excluded. Girls face no such risks. In point of fact, while girls were spoken of despairingly at times for not wanting to behave as a girl, or for behaving too much like a girl, no one is really worried. Gender is not only organized dichotomously but with an implied acceptance of gender hierarchy. Who could blame a girl for doing boys' things? Likewise, being too much of a girl is not necessarily bad but may constrict a girl in later life. No active threats face girls, while for boys not to be a 'real' man remains the most serious of risks (Segal 1990).

Here too context was relevant. Depending on whether they talk about home, daycare or school – parents seem to make different decisions and have varying ideas concerning what is appropriate for their child. As the activity of watching television often takes place in the safe environment of the home, boys watching a 'girlish' program, is not necessarily a problem (the 'be who you are' repertoire). Parents chose not to engage in what they implicitly declared to be the hopeless battle for more open gender coding when that might deliver their children in the hands of bullies. They felt no control over the bad world out there, so they applauded openness and choice when and where they can. One of the mothers remarked that she felt that one of her sons might turn out to be gay. She is careful to underline to her children that you never know who you will fall in love with when you grow up:

> 'So I said: 'Well, you never know as a child who you will fall in love with when you're older. And if it's a boy or a girl, it doesn't matter at all and you don't have to be scared to tell anyone.' (Kim)

This reassurance given to the children, could well be directed at herself.

Do not hold me accountable, the third repertoire

Children are a force unto their own. They continually surprised and sometimes shocked parents with their behaviour and wishes. Parents underlined that while they had the very best intentions, this did not guarantee any form of control. When talking about raising children, they underlined – in contrast to the previous repertoires but simultaneously – that they cannot be expected to raise the perfect child. In fact, they seemed to want to make sure they cannot be blamed for any 'extreme' behaviour. The first repertoire shows how parents want to grant their children freedom of choice and preference. The second repertoire shows parents limiting their children in order to protect them from the big, bad world, and to guide them to age and context-adequate behaviour. They amount to a Fordist notion that a rationalized production process will guarantee the right outcomes. The 'right' parenting style will generate an ideal child (and the smooth functioning of the social in which all know their place, cf. Fraser 2003). In contrast, the third repertoire, underlined that parents could not be held accountable for their child's actions.

The 'do not hold me accountable' repertoire emphasized the idea that people have inner cores that are not amenable to change. While 'good' inner cores could be corrupted (bad friends, bullying) they were not open to other types of negotiation. All the parents believed that their children's behaviour could only be influenced to a limited extent. They argued that whatever they did – whether nothing at all or taking absolute control – did not matter: a child, in the end, is its own being. Parenting simply had its limits:

I think that girls fight less. And boys, it's their way to express themselves and girls will solve a quarrel differently. Boys just fight and then they're done. (…) I think it's also a bit in the genes. (…) It could originate from prehistory: the man hunts and the woman takes care of the food and the children. And that the testosterone of the man … with hunting and fighting … that came out physically of course. And with women it was the other way around. Maybe that's still continuing in people nowadays. (Fieke – who has a son she would have liked to be more sports-oriented and less into dolls)

Rachel is very girly (she prefers pink toys, authors). I am not like that though, so she didn't copy it from me. So I think that it's just something inside her. (-) (…) As a parent, you can prefer something, or do something, but it's just built-in. (-) It attracts her, like bees on honey. It really is a magnet. (Jara)

Did you read Dick Swaab[2]? […] Yeah, I am convinced [that girlish behaviour is all in the brains]. It is of course the opinion of one man only, but he did study for a long time on this subject and he conducted in-depth research. He is a sort of authority on this subject. I believe that he speaks the truth, when he argues you don't become gay, but you are born being gay. […] Well, I think that it's fixed in the brain. I think there certainly are primordial roles. That boys and girls, men and women are just different. [] [W]hen you go back a thousand years in time … . The mother just used to be there for the family and she would stay in the cave, so to say, with the children and uh … to cook. And the man would go out to drag the meat inside. That has always … in those times it was like that. And who knows, maybe the brains are just meant to work this way, it's how it's supposed to be and this way you function … it's the most efficient to act like that. Who knows, I don't know. (Olivier)

In my opinion (boys being more physical, jh/sh) that's just built-in, I don't know. (…) That's just in their nature. (Mark)

I remember that he already loved anything round as a baby. Not only balls, but also just an apple, everything that was round, he just loved it. That it could roll and that he could crawl towards it and had a lot of fun. So that is something that is just, yeah I really think it's in those genes that he has loved it all along. (Fatiha)

I don't think that [girls wanting to endlessly talk things through and not just have a fight and be done with it] is learnt behaviour. It's from somewhere inside… … (Kim. Below Kim argues the opposite, that children learn from their older siblings)

'Extreme' abnormal behaviour – whether deviant or deeply conformist – as well as simple preferences were explained as a result of either the child's genes or as caused by influences from the outside world. Both nature and nurture arguments are used: biological influences, genes and environmental influences such as daycare, peers, siblings and media may determine the child's essence.

I don't know where it comes from, yeah maybe because of Fara and Kate, his older sisters. Kate loves pink a lot and of course they are both girls, so he kind of grew up with them. They wanted their rooms to be pink, they wanted this and that pink… … So I think that has had something to do with it. (…) [I]n the past he always wanted to eat with a pink spoon. And oh dear, whenever he didn't have the pink spoon, he would go through the roof. You know, that sort of stuff. (Fieke)

A child's identity is fixed early on, with older siblings an important influence.

I wonder with June, she is a bit tougher, I think … But yeah … she sees all those things of Rachel, so it could be that she will want high heels because of Rachel.' (Jara)

No but with children it's extra dangerous, because they are still very green. They are relentlessly programmed. (…) When we … continuously see the same stereotypical uh … woman, or man … at a certain moment they will think like: 'Oh so that's how it supposed to be'. (Olivier)

I don't think that our children really, incorporate it, but you know they don't really watch it. So in that way they won't get, say, infected with it. That doesn't mean that they don't imitate it at school, since the other ones know how it works. [… …] We notice that the oldest one … he wasn't really aware of what was for boys or for girls, he played with everything. And at his nieces he played with dolls and he wanted to wear pink pyjamas as well, he didn't mind at all. And uh … I've noticed that the youngest one is very clear that pink is for girls. That is imprinted by his older brothers, really.' (Kim)

For my six years old girls, I do not think it's appropriate. I mean, they absorb these ideas; they are focused on it. And I hear them saying like 'Oh she's beautiful' and 'she's not beautiful.' (Fatiha)

Justin sometimes says: 'I'm not allowed to cry, I am a boy.' (...) I think that it has to be the daycare, that he has learnt it there. That would be the only place then. [... ...] They are taught gender distinction in several ways, at home, school, TV, everywhere you are. I think it's the sum of all those imprintings. (Mark)

How to read this abdication of responsibility? Feminist work on neo-liberal ideology made clear that gender is used as a toggle to switch from foregrounding freedom and individualism to underlining responsibility via moral imperatives of which women become the bearers (Gill & Scharff 2011). Here, parents identifying as women and as men deflected the assumption that carers can be held responsible for the gender performance of a child. They did not want to be held accountable. As parents, they felt a lack of control that translated into a fear of not succeeding in delivering a happy, successful child.

Gender as Achilles' heel

Gender, it seems, is our collective Achilles' heel. It makes us vulnerable. Embedded in hegemonic heteronormativity and its inherent promise of what a happy life looks like, adhering to gender codes has become a collective competition that comes with very strict standards that are repeated ad infinitum across all media. Trying to understand the importance of media, talking with parents, at first sight, offers a partial reflection of media pessimistic views that open up to a much more general fear of not being in control, especially when responsible for others. Parents fear that media use will undermine their children's chances in life when the children are fed ambiguous messages about gender identity. They fear that their children will exclude themselves and be bullied. In the Media Wizards game, children also consider being excluded a real risk. The teenagers bullied others and feared it. Like me, they admired the girl who did not feel dependent on the contacts in her phone. She was clearly an exception. Fear of exclusion, self-exclusion and bullying runs through all the material.

While a bit of a jump, this has enormous consequences for thinking about media literacy. At the very least it suggests that media literacy needs to be about being able to withstand the possible influence from outside sources, whether texts or people. If fear is a dominant emotion, there is little chance of a plea for appreciative media literacy to be taken up. Using cultural citizenship as a lens, a tool, it appears imperative to find friendly ways of discussing the fears and worries that keep us from allowing others the space to identify as whoever they want to be. We do not lack a repertoire for doing so but we do lack the skills to accept the contradictory challenges levelled at us, to understand when and how we might resist the pressure to conform. Whether as parents, as young people, as professionals or as media users.

Notes

1 The intercultural media literacy project was financed by the Dutch SIA Raak foundation.
2 In his scientific bestseller, *We Are Our Brains: A Neurobiography of the Brain, from the Womb to Alzheimer's* Dick Frans Swaab (2014) states that our brain – or in other words nature – is the crucial factor in determining one's identity. According to Swaab, homosexuality is already fixed in the womb.

6
CONFUSION

When the future (briefly) became female. Viewers discussing a woman being cast as Doctor Who

With Sophie Eeken

The fears of parents that steer their policing of the media use of their children, in the chapter before this one, suggest that attaining masculinity is a fragile and precarious process. Gender thus gets inscribed into how media education and literacy are understood. Understanding the nexus of gender, media and fear through the lens of cultural citizenship might prove useful as a first step to undoing the current often punitive system of gender performance. This chapter addresses discussion of the casting of the 'thirteenth doctor' in the BBC flagship television series *Doctor Who* that followed the BBC's reveal video of the new Doctor. Once the season started, discussion of the first casting of a woman as doctor soon died down. The shock wave following the reveal however was impressive. The emotions voiced online in comments on what are called YouTube response videos (the videos are mostly talking heads) provide insight and validity to the insight that coming to terms with fear is urgent. To wit, the online response to the Reveal video was huge: A YouTube search conducted in Spring 2018 netted over four million comments tagged 'Female Doctor Who' and over fifty thousand videos that included the tag 'Thirteenth Doctor.' Although the tone of the videos and comments is often deeply unpleasant, this chapter will argue that it is not so much misogyny or hatred of women that can be discerned but very real confusion about gender distinctions. Also, not all comments or response videos were negative. Emotions ranged from happiness to hatred.

Like other 'legacy' figures in popular media culture, Doctor Who, a shape-shifting alien, after 12 instalments as a guy, becomes a woman. The BBC online Reveal video in 2017 garnered a veritable storm of reactions, many of them deeply upset and hostile towards the idea of a woman playing the Doctor. Such reactions to women taking on established male roles are not

DOI: 10.4324/9781003288855-9

uncommon. Often, they are read as a symptom of the continuing underlying sexism and patriarchal structures in the societies studied. While this may be the case here as well, we want to offer a slightly different reading that suggests that the massive response may also indicate a moment of deep gender confusion. This argument is built on two observations. As soon as the actual season featuring Jodie Whittaker as the 13th Doctor started, the attack on the BBC, on 'social justice warriors' and other 'feminist traitors' died down. Secondly, in an online response to the Reveal itself, we found clear signs that more is going on than simple hatred and disgust at a world that is taking away male privilege and thereby 'destroying tradition.' What Emma Jane (2014) calls 'e-bile' (vicious online hate speech) makes up a relatively small proportion of the reactions. This chapter goes back to our analysis of the 2017 material, and compares it to the much smaller volume of responses to among others Jodie Whittaker's (humorous) YouTube reply to the outraged and sometimes vicious comments and reaction videos to the seasons in which she plays the Doctor. Beyond the knee-jerk e-bile comments that by now almost customarily come the way of women actors, we can see media texts facilitating a conversation, however uncouth and uneasy, that may benefit cultural citizenship in the sense of reflection on how we belong, what we need and want from society and how we want to contribute to it.

In hindsight and with actor Jodie Whittaker almost coming to the end of her stint as the 13th Doctor, it feels almost ridiculous to go back to the avalanche of heated reactions to the BBC's Reveal of the new Doctor in 2017. Looking back, it seems little more than a flash in a pan, your everyday outbreak of misogyny, painful to behold but soon over. But was it a mere moment of disgust at men losing some of their privileges to women? Or was it something completely different? It all started on 16 July 2017 with a video. Shock, horror: the next actor to play the eponymous protagonist in *Doctor Who*, the BBC's long-running science fiction television series, turned out to be a woman (BBC 1963–1989, and 2005-present). Despite 12 actors playing the Doctor, a humanoid alien who travels through time and space, none of the Doctor's embodiments had until then been female. Earlier we inquired how the Reveal video was interpreted and made meaningful in comments posted on YouTube by a variety of fans and viewers (Eeken & Hermes 2019). Here, we would like to continue discussion of how legacy figures have the power to activate broadly shared gender anxieties.

In the first part of this chapter, we will focus on the reactions to the Reveal, collected for 2017 and 2018 in the comments below YouTube reaction videos. They show an amazing gamut of emotions and especially a surprising amount of anger and disgust. We then move to an online discussion of Jodie Whittaker's seasons as the Doctor. This is not a huge volume of reactions, on the contrary. We conclude by asking ourselves what exactly was at issue in the discussion of a female Doctor? Beyond male disenfranchisement hovers transphobia as much as deep distrust of the BBC. It makes us wonder whether we need to reconsider how we understand gender in media representation and how it is threaded into the understanding of institutional governance. If the two are intertwined, discussion of legacy figures in media entertainment needs to be less about role models and more about how they have imprisoned our notions of social justice.

For those unfamiliar with the series (and with apologies to its fans), Doctor Who feels nicely old-fashioned. For those of a certain age, it is reminiscent of the children's television of the late 1960s and 1970s, the period in which the first seasons were made. Although the Doctor's look and dress code have clearly changed, they still use a 'sonic' screwdriver as their main weapon and generally are not into fighting and what Yvonne Tasker (2012) somewhat jokingly called 'musculinity.' The Doctor is a rebellious time lord who has fled Gallifrey, their species' home planet, in the TARDIS, a space and time machine. A curious being, the Doctor finds themselves in the midst of adventure after adventure. These usually begin with the investigation of some intriguing event or phenomenon and turn into the Doctor having to protect innocent beings from evil forces. In doing so, the Doctor relies largely on ingenuity and wit. Throughout his incarnations, he has mostly been aided by female companions. A rich literature discusses the Doctor and their fans (Britton 2011; Butler (ed) 2007; Chapman 2013; Cordone & Cordone 2010; Hills 2010a&b 2015; Nicol 2018). Aronoff (2017), Cherry (2010), Jowett (2014, 2017, 2018), Melzer (2010), Wallace (2016) and Williams (2010) discuss the Doctor, their companions and fans, from the perspective of gender.

2017: The Reveal

The Reveal was posted on YouTube and Facebook as well on the BBC site. In one year, the Reveal had been viewed 3,214,641 times on the BBC's own website and prompted 31,691 written comments. The video was also posted on Facebook, where it was viewed 11,000,000 times and garnered 44,900 comments. As the BBC moderates its own website, we chose to focus on videos posted by fans on YouTube in which they commented on the casting decision and the comments that were left by their viewers. In Spring 2018, there were over fifty thousand videos tagged 'Thirteenth Doctor' on YouTube and over four million comments tagged 'Female Doctor Who.'

Such a large volume of spontaneously offered material was irresistible and much easier to retrieve than Facebook posts that are dispersed over groups and pages. YouTube's user comments do have a bad reputation. Indeed, *The New York Times* typifies them as 'juvenile,' 'aggressive,' 'misspelled,' and 'sexist' (Schultes et al. 2013, 660). Possibly, this decision meant that we headed for the most sexist and negative comments. A random check of open-group Facebook comments, however, suggests that this was not the case.

On the open Facebook Doctor Who page comments and their tone correspond to those we found (see https://www.facebook.com/DoctorWho/). Also, while generally, both on YouTube and Facebook, the comments posted beneath the Reveal video and reaction videos were negative in tone, there were also those who defended the choice of a woman as the new Doctor.

Analyzing such a huge volume of material needs a strategy. Having decided to focus on YouTube, we turned to the first three YouTube videos with lengthy comment sections to appear that put forward a critical (negative), a positive and a (relatively) neutral or undecided perspective on the Doctor's casting as a woman. These three fan videos each had high viewing rates (over 30,000 views), generating around a thousand or more reactions per video. They are titled: 'The Female Doctor: Why People are ACTUALLY Pissed,' posted by Denying Sexism (a pseudonym) (critical); 'THE 13TH DOCTOR REACTION!! A Female Doctor Who' by Clara Foxley (positive); and 'A female Doctor Who … …a pandering risk or righteous move?' by Commonkarl (undecided).[1] Our grounded theory analysis was based on the 4,230 responses to the three fan YouTube videos as well as the 31,691 responses to the official BBC Reveal video (Corbin & Strauss 1990; Glaser & Strauss 1967).[2]

Starting from a comment-by-comment analysis, we moved to analyzing every second comment, then every third comment and so on, while attending to 'saturation': we started jumping comments after no new arguments, threats, emotions and forms of abuse were found. The material was coded in three rounds, in which we undertook open, axial and selective coding (Strauss and Corbin 1990). The open codes consist of the sentiments and literal expressions presented in the comments. In the phase of axial coding, we grouped sentiments and expressions into thematic clusters. We named these clusters: praise, patience, love, conspiracy, hostility, treason and trauma. Then, in undertaking selective coding, we theorized these clusters as speaking to three affective practices (Wetherell 2012, 22–24) in which television drama comes to intersect with feminist ideology, women's emancipation and a sense that public service television has lost status, importance and sufficient funding. In two of these three practices (*emancipation* and *gender anxiety*) gender is defined in binary categories and linked to nostalgia versus progress. *Patience* is built around the suggestion that gender may not be as important as it is made out to be by the other discussants.

The 2017 comments

In the comments to the Reveal reaction videos, a clear majority disapproved of the casting and perceived it as a means of aggressively pushing a progressive political agenda. 'This feminist takeover is a joke, everything they touch, they kill' (Bill Markham). A much heard argument was that the BBC was busy achieving diversity quotas – with which not all commentators agreed (all misspellings in original texts[3]):

> The change wasnt made for diversity sake, it was mad to replace yet another 'white male character' with a 'minority' (which to feminism, women are classified as minorities …… somehow). This whole thing is to take men and specifically white men, and replace them as much as they can. Which is the main reason I hate the decision. (Crennshaw)

> Yup. The first commandment of Feminism is 'Vagina gud, penis bahahahaaad.' If wonder woman ever did anything that made men not look like inferior subhumans, Feminists would go amok (My Awesome Hero Deserves Respect).

Casting a woman was regularly seen as posing an extremist threat: 'Those followers of feminism that act to suppress and silence those of the male gender, classic fascist tactics, are perfectly reasonably compared to Nazis, hence the portmanteau feminazi' (Kevin Parks). The logic here is that the BBC has been taken over by a left-wing elite minority, and secondly that this minority, despite its progressives posturing, is of an extreme, right-wing variety.

Another line of thought, which runs throughout the comment sections, blame the former showrunner Steven Moffat (2010–2017) ('Moffat killed the show,' according to Thedogg02645). The last couple of seasons were 'proof' of bad writing, driven by 'SJW (social justice warrior) motives.' The casting of a female Doctor, by a new showrunner, is seen as a final blow to the show's earlier entertainment value. The casting of Jodie Whittaker thus came to stand for feminism as such and the perceived ways in which it disturbs what Sara Ahmed calls 'the promise of happiness, or the social pressure to maintain signs of getting along' (Ahmed 2010, 584). In this context, women generally – and feminists specifically – are typecast as 'killjoys.'

A small number of commenters (most of them responding to Tessa Netting's positive reaction video) were optimistic about the gender change. Their posts characterized the move as bringing something 'fresh' to the series. A female Doctor, some suggested, signalled possibilities for new storylines in an exceptionally long-running series: 'Honestly I am so excited to see all the areas of the show it can open up. It gives them so much they can explore' (Edenish Idylls).

Patience!

The 'withholding judgement' comments solicited patience by appealing to others' loyalty and trust in the series' legacy. Nostalgia here surfaces as a responsibility and respect for a long-standing relationship.

> So, there's some reasons, but time will tell. With reservations, will give it a chance, hoping it will prove us wrong. I've contemplated, same as you, but I think we owe that to The Doctor) (MK).
>
> Why wouldn't you [watch the new season]? Because it's a woman? You have no idea how she's going to be as the Doctor and the fact that you don't even want to give her a chance because of her gender means you're not a real fan of the series anyways (PotHead).

The argument put forward here is that ideologically gender should not be the issue: 'It shouldn't matter whether the Doctor is a man, women, black, white, ginger, or blonde' (Oshnier Price). Pointing forward to how gender comes to fully block nostalgic bonding, one commenter wondered: 'If gender doesn't matter to people then why are they making such a fuss over it? Give her a chance she may be fantastic!' (Kevin Peters).

Comments advocating patience conveyed both hope and worry. The new female Doctor need not necessarily fail. Success, however, would require a production team able to handle a female lead character. Of this, users were not so sure: 'As for the Doctor being female, I'm OK with the idea. However, it will depend on the way the story is told' (Rodney Allport). Apparently, a female lead was a more difficult and risky choice than the 'usual' male casting. There is a sense of solidity in tradition and that tradition happens to be that doctors are men.

Emancipation

There is no nostalgia in the comments that celebrate the casting of a woman as the Doctor as part of a wider move toward inclusive media representation: 'it's a small step that feels more like a giant leap for equality and inclusion on television' (Doc Trower). Rather, Doctor Who as a woman signified social progress:

> I feel like it's really important to introduce, like a different gender. I think that BBC introduced a female doctor to make a change. An actual change (Earlybeans).

Dreamfaller63 was moved to tears and felt that now s/he was allowed to assume 'her place. I don't have to be the companion anymore, the sidekick. I can be the smart sexy space lady. All I've ever wanted. Thank you Doctor Who for taking this long overdue step' (Hopecatcher53). Proof, finally, that women amount to something:

> I love that the doctor is a female because now I feel like I can actually be the doctor not just pretend to be her. 😍 🙌 🎉 (Clara Johnson).

I'm anxious for her season to begin! Yay!! Finally a woman! (Anna Janson Kerman).

I cant wait for the female doctor!!!! How can we effect change in the world when only half of it is invited or feel welcome to participate in the conversation. – Emma Watson (MariaKC098).

SOOOO happy the new doctor is Female! Have been waiting for a role model like that in this show for ever, and I expect great things from her:D (Dolce Hobart).

Compared with #metoo activism and the increasing awareness of male domination in media industries, it is not particularly radical to applaud the casting of a woman as Doctor. Nonetheless, it is a distinct and happy moment in the formation of emancipation and equality. As Hopecatcher53 puts it: 'Boys had 54 years of the doctor. ... It's time the other half of the population gets their share.' This type of political reasoning can be traced back through both socialist and liberal feminism to first-wave Suffragette activism (Van Zoonen 1994). We note that emancipatory politics such as these can easily fall prey to either essentialism, which equates bodies with an innate gender (Butler 2011), or forms of reasoning that discount intersectional logic in the functioning of social power relations at the expense of people of colour (Wekker 2016).

Gender anxiety

While crucial to understanding how reactions to the Reveal are structured, the themes of patience and emancipation accounted for only a tiny portion of the comments as compared to those that we grouped under grief, trauma, conspiracy, hostility and treason. Here the gender of the Doctor matters because changing it (de)stabilizes identity and community. Up until the twelfth Doctor, they had offered structure and the promise of continuity – a form of what Roger Silverstone, quoting Giddens, termed 'ontological security' (1994, 5–8). Changing the Doctor's gender for a considerable number of viewers and fans exposed the fragility of the social order. It was not the specific actor playing the Doctor that mattered so much as the instability of gender as a category, the power of the BBC over how we can imagine the world and our future and the powerlessness individuals may feel in a fast-changing world. A deep nostalgia colours feelings of grief and loss that are voiced often:

There is no bright side to this situation for many of the Doctor's longtime classic and nuwho fans. We see this as a time of mourning, as indeed, #TheDoctorIsDead (Swertov TRR).

Rip ... ... and i thought that he would just regenerate (BlackHoundDog).

Commenters grieving the loss of their now really dead beloved Doctor were not unaware of emancipatory arguments:

> The doctor was a non-stereotypical role model for boys. Not a fighter, but an intellectual. Yet someone who could still be 'cool'. Taking this away we're left with a load of GI Joe's unless the trend keeps shifting and we get male heroes who aren't sleeping with every second girl and picking up mass murder with weapons within 5 minutes (Nick Carter).

How the Doctor's gender matters is important: is it the character's *becoming* a woman or *being* a woman that is so problematic?

In the most negative comments, gender was endowed with a mythic status and masculinity served as a guarantee against everything falling apart.

> This was my problem with Ghostbusters [another recent popular film to cast women in men's roles, jh, se] but people need to understand that you can just take a character and change its sex and say it works but they do not realize that men and women have very different characteristics and writers dont realize this that women dont like seeing their female characters act like men. The only people that are happy are a small group that is really loud or bata males for a lack of a better word. Women want men to be manly and women to be feminine. The average woman hates SFC and love their men like men (RainFallHunter).

The fact that Doctor Who, the tv show was resurrected in 2005 after cancellation in 1989, adds to commenters' worries. A similar demise is cynically predicted:

> [B]e prepared for a 10 year cancellation folks, with a bit of luck in 2027 we'll have the same effect the 2005 reboot had, great stories, great actors and actresses but above all the Doctor being who he always was and always should be, a Man (Cranes36).

The idea that the Doctor's regeneration as a woman was a conspiracy appeared to provide users with an outlet for their grief and trauma. Comments adhering to this view described feminism as a radical anti-male movement. In television and film, the theory goes, (white) males are targeted for elimination. Feminism is a fight not for 'actual' diversity, but rather for female domination.

> This was blatant misandry and pandering to feminists in the name of 'diversity'. The more male characters they can remove from lead roles, the happier they seem to get (Esssex2099).

Commenters found it astounding that the BBC would adhere to new diversity norms: 'It is certainly concerning, BBC is drinking the Social Justice kool aid' (Trey Toliver). The world has gone off-kilter. Balance and reason have been lost. There is no respect for established 'dynamics':

> The doctor we know was always a man, he always had female companions, and its a theme that the show is known for, it is the dynamic of the show, a man taking a woman around the universe and back again. For me this is breaking the concept of the show, it is now not a lonely man showing ladies round the universe, but a Feminist... ... . (Sean Beard).

Reactions that offer blatant misogyny, transphobia and homophobia, are sometimes aired through jokes: 'Nurse who?' (Stork Testa). At other times they take the form of disgust:

> Basically, in brief terms – Now that Dr Who is morphed into TRANNY gay married Charles Manson SUPERGAY child Abductor & possible molester, the morons at BBC cant understand why this kids show is failing... ... . The show is dead (Manfred Dunst).

> Is he now trans? Conveniently right at the height of all this far left, ultra feminist transgender crap? It was a calculated decision, and Chriss Chibnall [the new showrunner in 2017] knew exactly what he was doing (Pete Lake).

In fairness, statements as overtly hostile as these were limited in number. They represent the most outspoken criticisms of the new Doctor. They read like 'geek fragility' (Blodgett & Salter 2018, 194). Geek fragility is reminiscent of 'white fragility,' that is, the hostility expressed by white subjects in the face of racial stress:

> [A] state in which even a minimum amount of racial stress becomes intolerable, triggering a range of defensive moves. These moves include the outward display of emotions such as anger, fear and guilt and behaviors such as argumentation, silence and leaving the stress-inducing situation. These behaviors, in turn, function to reinstate white racial equilibrium.
> (DiAngelo 2011, 57)

Likewise, geek fragility 'is a constructed fantasy, a world in which young white men outside the traditional definitions of masculinity are victims turned heroes, entitled to their rewards' (Blodgett & Salter 2018, 195). Cult texts such as *Ghostbusters* in Blodgett and Salter's research, or *Doctor Who*, are particularly proprietary for Geek subcultures, for whom a television series can become something of a Bible (Hadas 2013, 330). The most negative of the comments on the Reveal video, despite being in the minority, showed 'geek' culture of Doctor Who fandom deploying rhetorics of betrayal in the face of their key text being mainstreamed. Their sense of treason, however, is echoed in a multitude of milder comments that combined gender conservatism, fear of change and populist distrust of elite institutions, in this case, the BBC.

Rearguard battles

We read the comments as invoking cultural citizenship, as a performance of the right and responsibility to engage with others in conversation about our worries, hopes and dreams, and what might be the best world for most of us. They bespeak a diverse community that uses the series to reflect upon social and political conundrums while revering the Doctor. In all but the most extreme comments, it does not appear that the outpouring of distress was especially meant to relegate women to defined spaces or roles. The problem was the act of *changing* the Doctor's given gender more than her femininity. Gender mattered to *Doctor Who* viewers and fans in different ways. We cannot say whether it was the fans and viewers' sense of common ownership over the series that started the debate, or whether the Reveal simply served as an opportunity for venting existing gender anxiety, or indeed both.

Whichever the case, the Reveal functioned as the kind of 'incitement to discourse' through which gender and race emerge as today's contested social categories (Foucault 1976, 17–18). In such debates, expectations of peace and happiness become tied to the privilege accorded to some and the oppression suffered by others. Given that transgenderism and gender-neutral toilets in workplaces and public buildings are also engendering enormous discussion, it seems that the Reveal was made meaningful, at least in part, as a symbol of the loss of a well-ordered, recognizable world in which men are men and women do not attain the status of the Doctor. For the vocal majority of the fanbase, the instability of gender was supremely upsetting. It became intertwined with feelings of injustice, powerlessness and dependence in the face of unaccountable institutions.

Five years later, the ferocious energy of the reactions to the Reveal has all but dissipated. Checking YouTube again for reaction videos, now to the seasons that featured Jodie Whittaker (or '13' as she is referred to), we do not find much. There are fans who declare their love for the new Doctor and quote from the series or who leave comments underneath Jodie Whittaker making fun of all the negative reactions that have come her way. There are themes however that do return such as that the showrunner is not doing a good job and 'did her dirty' (Naomi Trent). Online commenters reiterate that the show 'has failed' (its ratings were not very good) and there are some who reiterate attacks on the idea of a female Doctor (clearly ridiculous) and wokeness. Sorting comments we again encounter the themes of grief and betrayal and the theme of love. Betrayal quotes still use 'lesbian' and 'trans,' 'woke' and social justice warrior as insults while the feeling of having been betrayed by the BBC is as strong as it was. There is a group to whom Whittaker has proven herself as an actress, notwithstanding the 'bad writing.' As crokey tb says: 'Jodie is so great here im sorry for her for bad writing two seasons:' Roderick Priestley adds that: 'It's a shame that the first female doctor had to be ruined by the writing of this series.'

It seems to us that there is less e-bile. Negative videos and comments are clearly a minority. Having clicked on one negative video, the YouTube algorithm generally offers you another one but it did not manage to come up with much. Videos from the same channels kept returning even though we clicked comments and manifested ourselves as in the market for nasty comments. We could not find traces of the earlier really strong link between negative comments and gender and diversity either. Opposite groups seemed to have decamped to their own bit of internet and were not bothering to engage much.

The Jodie Whittaker fanbase

Jodie Whittaker has a fan base who have her back. Eyelam long writes: 'She was wasted imo. She's a great actress and had hardly any good episodes.' Margaret Angel Herald replies to a remark by Dark Horse:

> 'She can act. The problem is, due to the writing, her character feels a bit off and forced. Same thing happened to prequel Anakin Skywalker. George Lucas wasn't very good at making dialogue. In this example though, Chibnall's just not cut right.'

> Jo Banks concurs: 'Completely agree. We've seen that she can do the crazy/ witty side of the Doctor and we've seen glimpses of her being able to do the serious aspects but I feel she needs more grand scenes to really show us she's the Doctor, scenes like Capaldi's War Speech or Smith's stonehenge speech.'

Five years past the Reveal there are far more conversations between commenters. Read Tarda Wish's reply to Silentpartner BM:Hint

> @Silentpartner BM:Hint: 'You're right, and I can see that happening. Though this type of situation happens so much in fandoms that one can only flip a coin at this point for how the fans will turn. Which is too bad, as I love this Doctor. I don't have a problem much with this doctor as I have a writer's brain, as my mom calls it, and understand what the show

was going for. I don't focus too much on the commentary of the story for real-world things, as I do for the story itself in the show. That's why I love doctor who. And so many people write for doctor who, in books and audios, and create a story within the universe that it is amazing. I just hope that the fandom doesn't give up on this show, just because of this doctor.'

@Tarda Hope yeah. though with some those youtubers spreading negativity it may be hard (Silentpartner BM:Hint).

@ Silentpartner BM:Hint Yep …

Weaponized sarcasm

One of the YouTuber's spreading negativity is The Serious Eater. In 2020 The Serious Eater posts a 4.49 minute video 'Fugitive of the Judoon, Doctor Who's most stunning and brave episode ever' on YouTube that sarcastically comments on the show's attempt to be inclusive. It underlines the bad ratings and serves up misogyny as humour. In sarcasm, commenters bond with the Drinker.

> K.L. Jansenz remarks: 'Now we know why the Doctor has never settled down with anyone. He's a strong, independent black woman who don't need no man.'

This inspires Mate Noname and a number of other commenters:

She left Gallifrey for cigarettes 60 years ago and never looked back. (Guy Incognito)
AND she's 'body-positive' (Happybiker!).
D. P. Robertz This is the best comment, sistah!! (Alpha Timepiece).
You meant transgender (Busted Doorway).
Uhhh huuuuh honey. (Click my fingers in a sideways motion) (Greenjoy).
Witch Doctor are we talking about? Get it? Witch Doctor!!! (EarlyUp).
I'm so proud of Chibnall, he's so brave and revolutionary! For so long i've wanted an overweight, butch, middle aged black lesbian doctor and they've finally delivered on that dream. I think this is what we all wanted, deep in our hearts. Such a brave (IronBerth641).

Replacing the shock horror of the early reactions, sarcasm has become the weapon of those who feel betrayed by television history and bemoan the erosion of an era they felt was theirs. In addition to comments that simply repeat that '(t)he show ended' (Corbin G. Grantwoord, Peter V..) or 'died' (Hansome Bugger) with earlier showrunners, other commenters turn to sarcasm to suggest that the 'death' of Doctor Who is part of the entire collapse of culture as they knew it: 'What a decade it has been for cinema. SW, GoT, Dr Who, Ghostbusters, MIB, Terminator, ... What's next? Indiana Jones? Oh yeah, 007 too' (parmihaa_parmihaa). Sarcasm in psychology and language literature is associated with fun and friendship. Generally, it is understood to be a form of irony. Only in the older literature sarcasm is related to social power inequality. Thus, in a cross-cultural study Blasko et al (2011: 118) conclude that: '(f)or all countries, the most common reasons for using sarcasm were "to be funny" and "have fun with friends."' They do note that men are more likely to use sarcasm than women. Drucker et al (2014: 552) surveying sarcasm literature note that '(d)uring the 1970s and 1980s, several studies found evidence showing an anti-female bias in the appreciation of humor. Humor deriding women was considered funnier than humor deriding men, among both female and male participants.' While generally sarcasm may be more widely used by women and against men today (to keep to an overgeneralized and flat gender distinction for now), it seems safe to say that sarcasm is further weaponized in these discussions for bonding among the gender-conservative. These are most certainly not only men, some identify or are identified as women.

'Filking' the Doctor

Fortunately, and as in 2017, gender-conservative disenchantment is not the reported experience of all fans. There are those who simply disregard the bemoaning of the soon-to-be-expected or actual death of the Doctor to claim her (rather than him or them) for themselves.

> 13 is great, love almost every episode of hers 'Are you two seeing each other?' 'I don't think so. Are we?' Doctor being a lesbian (and me here loving it) (Lesbian Loveboat).
>
> '13 being 13 for 13 minutes straight' there is absolutely nothing 'straight' about Thirteen (The Millay is driving the Seven Mile Meatvan).
>
> I just realized the 13 doctor is me if I was the doctor (Partylover Pony).

We offer these comments as a counterpoint. Filking and romantic fantasies have long been part of fan culture. They were a welcome sight among the sarcasm and negative feedback we also found.

Discussing hopes and dreams through the Reveal

The initial wave of public feeling over the new gender of the Doctor after the Reveal, showed how a woman cast as the Doctor became what Ahmed calls a 'blockage point.' She 'disturb[ed] the promise of happiness,' which Ahmed suggests she would 'redescribe as the social pressure to maintain signs of getting along' (2010, 584). As in an earlier study (Müller & Hermes 2010) we find that an argument can be made for how the fight over ownership over the Doctor and over the gender identity of the Doctor can be understood as the performance of cultural citizenship which shows itself as fierce discussion. In the comments, the Reveal became a political platform, a space for cultural citizenship that linked affect, emotion and discursive practice.

Grasping this entanglement of affect and discourse poses a significant methodological challenge (Hill 2019, 61). Our only access to all these connections and mediations is through language, and language that is regularly doubly or triply coded through humour, sarcasm and implicit references which we will not have picked up on. Ideally, a discourse-analytical approach such as this, is followed by 'live' contact with Doctor Who viewers and fans. We would love to talk with them about nostalgia and the world they see going asunder. We are also curious about the 'stickiness' of binary gender definitions in both the gender-conservative comments and in the women's emancipation comments. Only for those who declare their lesbian romantic interest in the Doctor, we expect the insult 'tranny' would be something of a joke but that too needs checking.

Taking a bird's eye view, three positions suggest themselves in the discussion of the Doctor: most prominent is the one that objects to women being cast for legacy male roles; far less prominent is the second position that such 'recasting' does not undermine the social order. The third position 'filks' the Doctor. By implication, these comments take their faith in the social order further and undo the hetero-normative contract by turning the Doctor into a lesbian love object. It seems then that the minor shift in cultural power associated with being represented as a legacy figure, has a seismic effect. At issue in discussion of a female Doctor is more than male disenfranchisement or even transphobia. The deep distrust of the BBC and of the showrunners are surely also a sign of how the formal mission of public institutions has been regarded as mere camouflage. To see such institutions become accountable to new gender politics can only be a shock if they were felt to be embedded in older systems of social relations that provided well-defined and safe spaces for classes, regions, genders and cultures.

Gender seems to be a remarkably strong activator of anxiety. The BBC has just announced that *Sex Education*'s Ncuti Gadwa (who plays the lovely Eric, an attractive and outspoken gay character) and none of the early comments let rip the way they did when Whittaker was announced. If black men who happily embrace a gay identity on screen are so much less a problem than white women, it is the gender of legacy figures in media entertainment that matters. It is as gendered role models that they have imprisoned our notions of social change and justice. Notably the first commenters on YouTube reacting to a fan compilation of earlier Doctors introducing Gadwa mostly worry about the writing and of course about the BBC.

Looks interesting, the actor seems to have charisma, no I just hope the writing doesn't let him down (leo stuttgart).

Great trailer! Concerning though that fans on YouTube are putting more effort into advertising the new doctor than the BBC! (Sam Gorse).

Trying to learn from the earlier flash-in-the-pan outbreak to the conversations within isolated camps five years later, we need to wonder whether provoking discussion is a good route forward for those interested in a more open, diverse and equal gender order. In 2022 after all, YouTube calculates there is no profit to be made by bringing sarcastic and lesbian romance reaction videos and comments together. Also understanding the performance of cultural citizenship and putting it to use for a constructive discussion, we need to master the use of sarcasm while respecting nostalgic investment. Or we might take up the suggestion in the earlier comments to really hold the media industry accountable for new gender arrangements and representation, and to put their money where allegedly their mouth is.

Notes

1 The names of these makers are not their real names but pseudonyms with a 'feel' that is similar to the original names. Although YouTube is a self-publishing platform, these makers have not been asked for consent and have a right to their privacy. One of them changed their name between the moment of research and writing. Videos are often removed. Likewise, commenters' names have been replaced with pseudonyms similar in style.
2 Our focus on YouTube entails that we have no 'feedback from those who did not post comments' (Chung 2015 in Thelwall 2018: 313) or who do not use social media. Nor could we check commenters' gender as unlike Facebook YouTube uses screen names. In defense of our choice, we want to point out that comments are the main way in which videos are discussed and an essential part of YouTube as a cultural form (Schultes et al. 2013: 660; Snickars and Vondereau 2009).
3 All quotes are verbatim. We have neither corrected language nor added anything to the cited quotes. We have used (long) excerpts. Where sentences have been left out of a running quote, this is indicated by an ellipsis (...). We choose not to mark passages with sic, for misspelling is the norm rather than the exception in the YouTube comments we studied.

PART III
Listening with generosity
Another three case studies that take a broader intersectional approach and a conclusion

Chapter 7 Patriarchy: Good guys (or not). Feminism, auto-ethnography and *the Mentalist*

Chapter 8 Responsibility: Content analysis with the help of fan-viewers: Sorting through the appeal of a decade of *RuPaul's Drag Race* With Michael Kardolus

Chapter 9 Storytelling: Meanwhile in the real world: Popular culture and cultural citizenship politicize online on social media platforms

Conclusion: Democracy II: *(Searching for)* cultural citizenship as *(attending to)* worldbuilding in action

7
PATRIARCHY

Good guys (or not). Feminism, auto-ethnography and *the Mentalist*

Going by the three chapters in the section before this last one, hatred, concern and fear define the ongoing public conversation I suggest we understand as cultural citizenship. As the focus is on popular media culture which at least historically we have understood as providing us with pleasure, it makes sense to also think about how we might stimulate our collective emotional intelligence and media wisdom to find out how we can hold on to what makes us like popular texts. This chapter wants to offer a route to appreciative inquiry. It will not suggest that we give up a critical mindset but that we put the means at our disposal for using and discussing popular media texts to better use. The reason this chapter uses the crime drama series *the Mentalist* is simple: it is one of my all-time favourites.

Writing about *the Mentalist* was not simple at all; it took an incredibly long time. As behoves a 'mentalist,' according to the Oxford dictionary, 'a magician who performs feats that apparently demonstrate extraordinary mental powers, such as mind-reading,' whether a series or a live performer, it kept slipping through my fingers. Or rather, translating what *the Mentalist* did for me as a viewer would not shape itself as a single story, which is still what academic writing is all about. In its current form, this chapter talks about how understanding and using cultural citizenship benefits from listening. Focusing as it does on my own viewer experience, it makes clear how my private enjoyment of the series affords a highly particular and partial view. Reflecting on the series as an academic and as a feminist produces wholly different narratives and judgements. Instead of judging the series, I would like to understand it through what Rita Felski (2020) calls 'attachments' or enduring ties. Following and respecting attachments requires letting go of a more traditional critical mindset. In an earlier book, Felski suggested

DOI: 10.4324/9781003288855-11

we opt for appreciative inquiry. Rather than practice suspicion and expose 'what texts are really about,' we might want to try and combine critique and credit and link the idiosyncratic entanglements that invite us into a text or, as the case might be, exclude us. Before using these insights to listen to others, I might as well see where such a strategy will take me.

It is part of the magic of popular television that there are series that seem to require that you watch them again and again. Is it possible to go back to them, without psychologizing why they do so? Can a close look at *the Mentalist* help a cultural understanding of how this series helps think through nagging questions and intractable connections, habits and dependencies that ultimately point to how popular culture feeds cultural citizenship as an ongoing conversation? This chapter will use the tools of textual criticism. Generally, in doing audience research, the close reading of texts is a tricky move. It easily reads as arrogance and a form of condescension, implying that as an academic, one knows better. Textual analysis is useful though. It is offered here as a critique that hopes to serve collective knowledge building and reflexivity, the training of future professionals and 'maker knowledge.' Textual analysis and analysis of the experience of viewers each bring their own strengths to media and cultural studies. Bringing them in close proximity here is both a test and an exploration of whether and how they can connect.

Watching *the Mentalist*

The Mentalist was initially screened on Dutch television in the first half of the 2010s. Produced and broadcast by CBS (2008–2015) and then available on Netflix, it was a globally popular police procedural centred around former psychic and 'mentalist' Patrick Jane. Jane, the series' main character, is a self-made entertainer who manages to insert himself into a team of police detectives. Using his wits and exceptional talent for 'reading' people, he helps the California Bureau of Investigation (CBI) apprehend perpetrators while patiently working to trap serial killer Red John to avenge the murder of his wife and daughter (five years before the narrative of the series starts). You could like Patrick Jane and the series for his charm and wits, for his tragic backstory or for his lack of conventional male accoutrements such as the use of muscle, weaponry and sheer force to intimidate. Referencing an old and not very woke feminist joke: he is a guy who often acts like a girl. The series never met with much critical acclaim but did score high ratings, usually attributed to actor Simon Baker's exceptional and highly sympathetic performance of Patrick Jane.

I liked the series for its characters and actors rather than for the Red John series' storyline in which violence, fear and paranoia were prominent elements. The lack of academic interest in *The Mentalist* (bar the occasional reference) continues to mystify me. It is surely the kind of non-highbrow popular television that would be enormously useful when teaching paradoxes in gender construction in media studies or media literacy as appreciative inquiry (to which I will return below). Jane as a character and *The Mentalist* as a series speak to feminist legacy in many ways by offering what might be called post-feminist masculinity that takes its distance from traditional ways of being a man, including typically 'masculine' poses and mannerisms, while retaining its position of superiority and male privilege.

My own partiality to *the Mentalist* and Jane came as a bit of a surprise. Wearing a three-piece suit and setting out to avenge the death of his wife, surely I should have caught on to the patriarchal imprint of the overarching narrative? If I did, I managed to convince myself it was just another series, which became a bit more difficult to do once I had watched all of its seasons several times. While I watched my first episode by chance, I quickly moved into a making-sure-I-would-see-new-episodes mode, and then to chartering one of my children to download entire seasons via torrent sites. The family joke soon was that I was preparing to write a paper to be called 'Jane and feminism.'

Watching the series with different members of my family, we enjoyed the plot twists to do with the main character's clever reasoning, pulling the wool over his colleagues' and superiors' eyes while catching out evil doers. We all liked actor Simon Baker's sympathetic portrayal and winning smile. The jokes about my Jane and feminism paper must have been in the fact that we were all apparently also fully convinced that he was not a feminist. The always being right, the tricking of his police superior and later love interest, Teresa Lisbon, and the subtle hint of condescension, however friendly and magnanimous in appearance, must always have been perfectly clear to all of us. Nonetheless, when tackling Jane and feminism, I did not want to do the usual thing and find fault with the series. Belgian colleagues suggested I read Rita Felski and her argument in favour of appreciative inquiry.

Appreciative inquiry

Looking at myself watching and puzzling over *the Mentalist*, I can see how, when you discuss careful listening, you also need to trace and map what it is you are able to hear. Part of the discussion about what cultural citizenship is has to do with alignment, appreciation and attachment. As a researcher, a cultural critic and a feminist, cultural citizenship is as much my means of critique as a means to capture and translate ongoing discussion in the world out there. Merging the different kinds of critique at my disposal means moving from a more formal and deconstructive approach to what Rita Felski (2015) would call appreciative inquiry. In a nutshell, that is bypassing a 'hermeutics of suspicion' (2015: 31). Although there is great pleasure in catching a text in the act of befuddling us (Jane may seem a 'new,' anti-macho man but *actually* this is male supremacy in a new guise!), there may be even more pleasure in charting the attachments that bind me to the text, to cultural criticism, to reflection on who I am, and what the goal of (occasionally) close reading a text for an audience researcher might be. The project of this book does rather betray the answer to this question (textual analysis is best applied in small dosages). However predictable the outcome, can I suggest you read for process?

For starters: will taking apart a series not spoil the fun? As with literature and art, I think the opposite can be true. Speaking for myself, popular culture teaches me about the world as much as I think it does others when allowing us to speak about what concerns us. 'Jane and feminism' is a point of entry into debate of masculinity and femininity and of privilege. 'Jane and Black Lives Matter' doesn't sound as good but that too would be a good project. The careful orchestration of ethnicities in the show leaves white privilege intact which made it an easy worldwide sell of a friendly melting-pot Americanism. 'Jane and LGBTQi+ politics' could only be a project for a fanfiction writer. There is a disconcerting lack of non-straight characters.

Time to unpack the series using the usual array of instruments of the media critic: narrative analysis, a keen eye for meaningful signs as per a semiotic analysis and a decoding of the ideology that permeates the show. Undoing the tangle of attachment, of which enchantment and deception are both a part, points me to the dialectic of listening, hearing and cultural citizenship. It will point me to another dialectic as well, that of hypocrisy and sincerity that Judith Shklar (1984) unmasked so beautifully in her book *Ordinary Vices*. I aim to overcome my disappointment in Jane's charm. Friendly, everyday hypocrisies should be defended from an ideological critique of acting in 'bad faith,' however true.

Enchantment

Whether to Simon Baker or the script writers' credit: Patrick Jane, the mentalist is a dreamboat. He has the looks, the easy smile and the charm; he is a man who is happy not to be a macho which he offers with a lovely sense of somewhat sarcastic humour:

Cheryl Meade: No. Rick didn't believe in guns.
Patrick Jane: He didn't think guns existed?
Cheryl Meade: He didn't like them.
Patrick Jane: Me neither. Terribly dangerous. Have you seen the statistics on Police shootings? One bullet out of every ten hits a bad guy, and that's the trained people.
[to Hightower, his police chief]
Patrick Jane: No offense
(*The Mentalist* 3: 15 'Red Gold')

Teresa Lisbon:	You coming or what?
Patrick Jane:	Are those bulletproof vests?
Teresa Lisbon:	Yeah
Patrick Jane:	I don't think so, good luck
	(*The Mentalist* 3: 20 'Redacted')

Born in a travelling circus family as what the series calls 'a carnie,' Jane uses his extensive experience as a performer who claims to be able to 'read' people in accompanying the police detectives to crime scenes. While reading clues rather than 'people,' he indeed helps the investigative team he has infiltrated to solve their cases, often by charming others into following his cues or disclosing themselves. Going out on a limb, it could be argued that what is enchanting about *The Mentalist* is that it offers a male feminist hero: a caring man who relies on his wits. He does not mind being seen as a coward. His very presence in a police team – taking a nap on a couch, drinking a cup of tea – in addition demythologizes the idea that weaponizing small groups of professionals will keep us safe. *The Mentalist* is a police series that in no way celebrates law and order.

That seems a good starting point to reflect on 'the distinctive qualities' of a television series, as Rita Felski suggests in *The Limits of critique* (2015: 192) to understand works of art starting from appreciation rather than the suspicious mindset of a classically formal critique. It comes closer, I think, to what others do using 'affect' as a key term. To be sure, studying *the Mentalist* aesthetically would also probably not be a long story. While the series seemed to reach for innovative storytelling, it did not do so well. The seasonal and the series' story arcs (the bringing to justice of serial killer Red John) contrasted awkwardly with its episode storylines which often came with a comedic twist: Jane identifying a killer with a trick or pulling a fast one on his boss Teresa Lisbon to pursue his own agenda.[1] Around a quarter of the episodes focused on (the hunt for) Red John and stayed away from comedy and humour, offering only sarcastic observations by Jane as a form of relief. They were darker, sometimes verging on the decidedly sombre. When re-watching episodes, I would often skip them. Jacobs argues (2001: 429) that 'success or failure in the patterning of its drama, its character development and its rendering of a credible and coherent story world' is a useful first step in analyzing a television series. For me, this immediately also points to the kind of energy and emotion that is generated by the series. How, as a viewer, you are allowed to relate to it and make the series' world your own, if only temporarily.

A combination of co-owning and 'path finding' is how Annette Hill (2019: 59–61) understands affect when writing about media experiences as energizing internal force and embodied meaning making. She also points to how affective activity poses methodological challenges not easily met in empirical research (2019: 61). Rather than a deconstruction, a demythologizing or an unravelling (or any of the other ways Felski identifies as the practices of a hermeneutics of suspicion), I intend to use Hill's example through an associative and an appreciative logic. While discourse may be all that we have in a technical sense – as means of communication – we know that the senses extend beyond language. Sean Redmond discusses this as 'celebrity affect,' spotted in 'the ecstasy that greets live performance (as) testimony to the power of emotional outpouring and the way it questions the "fixedness" of subjectivity and routinized life' (2019: 16). Similar, if less strong, forms of affect are experienced in 'ordinary,' everyday media experiences too and deserve to be paid close attention. Personal and powerful as that response was, when it comes to my *Mentalist* fandom, it deserves a detailed analysis, says Sarah Cardwell (2006: 74).

There is a great range of options to do so. Geragthy suggests using such aesthetic tools of the trade as attending to narrative, audio, visual organization, writing, dialogue, performance, characterization and innovation (2003: 41/2). In this case, the visual presentation of its key character, writing, dialogue and narrative all stand out. They feel connected with what Redmond calls 'texturality' (2019: 171) and Cardwell (2014: 17) the signature 'texture' of television as both medium and art. The 'design' of the series is as important as its tactility, Jane's charm, his colleague Cho's managing to be superbly efficient and lovable at the same time or team leader Lisbon's awkwardness. Such elements allow us to feel the texture of the series as if it were made of material fibres that are woven together.

To set the scene, in the following section, I discuss generic conventions and storytelling in crime drama; the figure of Patrick Jane, a mentalist, and why and how he moves me (using analysis of narrative, dialogue, semiotics and texture); and thirdly, what led to the loss of affective energy in the last two seasons and my disengagement. Disengagement after all, as Annette Hill argues, is too often ignored while it is a routine feature of our media experiences, whether it is 'sudden, a brusque disconnect with a series, or (-) happen(s) gradually, (as) an increasing awareness that the presence of a series in your life is gradually becoming an absence' (2019: 62).

The appeal of the Mentalist *as a police series*

Generically, *The Mentalist* is a mixed police procedural and drama series, combining episode-long storylines with season and a series story arc. Jane works with Teresa Lisbon, a senior detective in charge of detectives Kimball Cho, Wayne Rigsby and Grace van Pelt after he becomes a consultant with the CBI. The team deals with criminal cases, usually murder. The Red John serial killer case is on their dock when Jane infiltrates the team after wandering into the police station and asking to see the Red John files. In the mayhem of an unfolding case, Jane makes himself useful and manages to secure further access as an apology for having become involved in police work as a civilian. Over the following five seasons (spoiler alert for what follows), the team will chase and identify Red John. Underdefined as a character (the reveal is a bit disappointing), he will turn out to have an extensive network of accomplices in law enforcement. Per episode, a case will be solved. In the last two seasons, Jane, Lisbon and Cho work for the FBI as part of a deal Jane has made with the federal government not to be prosecuted for killing Red John (in season 6). The new quest is to dismantle the still partially intact Red John network, called the Blake Association. The series ends with Jane and Lisbon's wedding, providing the background for a final reckoning with this network of law enforcers gone bad.

For a fan of police series, *The Mentalist* is interesting for the contrast it offers between the friendly interaction within its team of central characters and the suggestion of gruesome crimes committed by the serial killer they hunt. It is far less serious than *Criminal Minds* or any of the versions of *CSI*. Like *White Collar* (USA Network 2009–2014) or *Suits* (USA Network 2011), it allows for the occasional light touch: Patrick Jane outwitting a wrongdoer or offering sarcastic commentary. Given its prolonged hunt for Red John, it binds us the way all police series do, by making present what threatens us and by suggesting how such dangers might be slain. In seasons 6 and 7, the series loses its unique energy: the original team is no longer a given, although all of its original members make appearances.

Fear, according to Fiona Jeffries (2014), is the defining emotion of Late Modernity. The shredding of the 20th-century social safety net under neoliberal rule and the decline in solidarity are, she contends, expressed and experienced in subjective ways that have lost their social context. Surveys, she says, report that we fear the loss of a loved one, illness and death. This is exactly *The Mentalist*'s backstory. The series portrays a man who has lost his wife and child to a serial killer whom he taunted on a television talk show. Clearly, *The Mentalist*'s overarching storyline suggests that fear is a reasonable emotion in today's world but this is not a sentiment shared by Patrick Jane or the CBI team. On the contrary, the series foregrounds a fearless team that unflinchingly stands up against the forces of evil (Red John) and corruption (the Red John network in law enforcement agencies). Jeffries argues convincingly (2014: 253) that social (as opposed to natural) fear produces subjectivities in which human solidarity becomes increasingly illusive and exclusive. The *Mentalist* offers hope that solidarity is not lost to us altogether, given the loyalty between its team members.

Jeffries also suggests that our insecurities are exploited in increasing authoritarianism (2014: 254). While crudely, this provides a link to what is to be liked in action and police series as well as feared. With pleasure, I see series such as *The Mentalist* (or *24* or *Bosch*) hark back to the lone fighter against incompetent bureaucracies or corruption in law enforcement, an old popular cultural archetype (Neale 2000: 223; Tasker 1993: 114). Jane, Bauer and Bosch are in many ways critical of the law enforcement agencies in which they work. They uphold romantic and nostalgic notions of the individual as saviour of the morality and integrity of bureaucratic organizations. While police procedurals can be read as suggesting that we should count ourselves happy to have the force of the law to shield us from what threatens us, most depend on portraying quirky and headstrong individuals going against bureaucracy and its endemic corrupting mechanisms, which serves the needs of entertaining storytelling and a politics of hope well, both for the viewer as a citizen and for a feminist raised on the fantasy identification of strength with masculinity (whether performed by men or women – of whom we have far too little in tv crime fiction).

As an experienced viewer, I expect a credible and worrying threat as well as resolution: fear and hope. I would like more clever women to be in the lead but not when the threat is directed against them or their loved ones. Easier perhaps to not have to identify too directly with being threatened. Or a perverse feminist reckoning that men have it easier anyway and are welcome to deal with a little of what women deal with a lot. Then again, I did not like the Red John storyline in *the Mentalist* and would have been happy to do without it. An impossible scenario, of course, which would have removed the narrative urgency for Jane to be part of a police team and thus made the entire story collapse.

Noteworthy is that I am apparently happy with clever white males as protagonists. There are many more of those than any other kind. While tv crime drama has long had its share of interesting non-white and female characters (Luther, Jane Tennyson), this is a field in which masculinity and femininity are written in traditional and conservative terms, even in series that are otherwise highly innovative (Brunsdon 1987; Buonanno 2017; Lavik 2011). I interpret this as one of the many ways in which modernity's politics of fear extend deeply into constructions of identity by insisting that we define masculinity and femininity as a dichotomy. This entails that men have to fear feminization (Huyssen 1986; Segal 1990). Bauer, Bosch or a book and movie character such as Reacher appear explicitly written to escape such a threat. Not so Patrick Jane: *The Mentalist's* central character is even more a feminized friendly creature than *White Collar*'s con man main character Neil Caffrey or *Sneaky Pete*'s Marius Josipovic (Prime, 2017–2019). He is not a tall guy; he never fights but wins his battles via subterfuge and 'reading' other people, typically qualities associated with women rather than men. If he is to be faulted for being a guy who does not measure up to 'real' man standards because he was unable to protect his wife and child from evil, the wide viewership for the series did not do so.

Patrick Jane, the character

Patrick Jane is a 'mentalist.' The opening credits imitate a dictionary-style text to tell us that a mentalist is someone who uses mental acuity, hypnosis or suggestion. A master manipulator of thought and behaviour. Jane is funny and, when afraid, sarcastic. When in the episode called 'Red Sauce' (1:20), he has a gun pulled on him, he cowers but says: 'There's three reasons I'm not scared. Well, okay, I'm scared, but there's three reasons I'm not terrified.' In 'Red Bulls' (2:7), Jane and Lisbon following a lead in the dead of night find themselves in a somewhat scary house. Another team of police officers suddenly storms it. Everybody shouts, there is mayhem and Lisbon asks angrily: 'What are you doing here?' Jane answers, hiding behind her: 'You're waving guns around is what you're doing. Can you just put your guns away!' And then, in disgust: 'Cowboys.' Hiding behind chief Madeline Hightower, in an episode called 'Red Gold' (3:15). Jane says right after she has shot a man:

Patrick Jane:	You know I should applaud your bravery, but I gotta say - practically speaking I-I-I -what were you thinking? You could've killed me.
Madeleine Hightower:	Sorry. I got mad. I didn't know what I was thinking.
Patrick Jane:	That's some good shooting though. That - leg shot that took him down was very precise.
Madeleine Hightower:	I was aiming for his head.
Patrick Jane:	Oh fantastic.

Jane, a mentalist and con artist, is the picture of innocence. Blond curls and an easy smile, always conveying friendly interest, detract from the sleights of hand he tends to play. He always wears a suit: in the earlier seasons with a light-coloured shirt, without a tie. Later, he will wear a dark blue suit and blend in with the FBI team, whom he then consults with. The suits are always worn with brown shoes, apart from one episode ('Not one red cent,' 5.03) where he has them resoled and borrows a pair of enormous ugly white trainers. The aberration underlines how Jane otherwise is the picture of a gentleman. Not coincidentally, this is the tagline for an advertising campaign Simon Baker does for Givenchy's 'Gentlemen only' perfume. There is also one episode where he does not wear the suit and carries the brown shoes. Here he wears a man's skirt, a sarong, topped with an elegant looking and (we learn from the narrative) locally tailored flowery patterned dress shirt ('My blue heaven,' 6:9), looking, if possible, even more elegant. He is in exile at that point outside of USA jurisdiction on what appears to be a Pacific Island. The 'texture' of Jane, the well-worn suits and the man's stylishness are carefully designed to feed viewer affect and it works.

Jane's 'texturality' also makes him a bit of a nerd: he is often seen reading a book, either lying down on the office couch or walking around. He drinks tea, dunking a tea bag in a cup, signalling Britishness. In the earlier seasons, he drives a baby blue vintage Citroen DS (phonetically 'goddess' in French: déesse). In the later seasons, he uses a silver Airstream camper in which he also lives. Jane's attachment to the couch and tea cup is open to other interpretations than European nerdiness or dandyism. His' is not a strong work ethic; the couch also signifies psychoanalysis or therapy: a connection to the unconscious and the invisible, an echo of the psychic Jane denies he is. Jane's love of snacks belies this ethereal link. He often brings in street food to share (ice cream, roasted nuts). It hardly ever gets eaten, signalling that there is no time for real crime fighters to leisurely have a snack. Unless it is pizza, of course, to celebrate the end of a case with booze provided by Lisbon which Jane does not drink.

These are all examples where *the Mentalist* gets to be an enjoyable puzzle and the Red John-related drama becomes background. The suit, the book reading, the car – they are a set of signs that allow for at least three different frames to read the series and Jane as a character. This is also where critical reading and appreciative inquiry part ways. While two of the three frames spoke to me, as did Simon Baker acting Patrick Jane, the third frame did not. The first is a comedic frame in which Jane comes across as a modern-day Charlie Chaplin. This is especially the case in the episodes where he is both a sad and funny figure in a suit who challenges norms and is a court jester. The gender frame offers an unsettling mix of feminist and patriarchal elements. The third frame understands Jane's cons, his reading of people and his sarcasm as signs of genius. Reconstructing my viewer engagement, I find I am uncomfortable with the third frame and its implications. I prefer to stick with the first two and will return to query why that is.

Suspicion and disenchantment

The *comedic frame* allows for a friendly interpretation of the con man. Even if Jane does break all the rules, there is no need to take him too seriously. His is never a violent intervention. Until, of course, at the end of season 3, when Jane thinks he has located Red John and kills an innocent man in 'Strawberries and cream. Part II' (3:24), for which he is acquitted in court after pleading his own case in the first episode of season 4 ('Scarlet Ribbons,' 4:1). Halfway through season 6 (6:8 'Red John'), Jane kills the real Red John and flees the country (to return two years later in episode 6:9 'My Blue Heaven').

His friendly and innocent looks suggest *a feminist man* in the second frame who is comfortable having a woman to answer to at work. Indeed, Jane hardly ever outright crosses Lisbon but he will manipulate her by indicating he may know 'who did it.' He often 'plays' her (which Lisbon recognizes but only half-heartedly protests against). Jane's fear of guns and projected innocence signal someone who needs protection rather than someone who provides it. His tendency to offer comfort food around makes him a bit of a mum, someone providing care: classically feminine qualities but also the mark of the impossible combination of the manly and caring romantic hero Janice Radway (1984) found romance readers favour. Narrative development eventually closes down a feminist interpretation of *the Mentalist* much to my regret. Along the way, Jane is moulded into a more conventionally paternalist figure. During an attempt to capture Red John, he abandons Lisbon to keep her away from danger (thereby deeply angering her). He also becomes less of a coward, holding his own against an armed group that Lisbon has infiltrated by, to my relief, playing the coward and the trickster rather than being one ('The Greybar hotel,' 7:2). Changing Jane provided a route to closure for the production team and an end to the series. Rather than prove that Jane never was a feminist, it suggests to me that paradoxical identities are hard to sustain.

The alternative interpretation, and *third* frame, is that Jane is unambiguously saved for modern masculinity. While he may at first feign to be a friendly bumbling idiot, a passive and thus feminine figure, this will turn out to be the decoy of a man obsessed with revenge for his wife and daughter. If that is how you want to read Jane, *the frame of the genius* provides a useful arsenal. It is precisely the fault line for my appreciative inquiry. I so enjoyed the comedic and the feminist gender frames that I have tried hard to discount the frame of genius. A suspicious reading of *The Mentalist* could take this further and hone in on how Jane ultimately betrays the possibility of men being feminists.

The frame of genius recognizes Jane as one of a considerable group of nerd characters that abound in today's popular culture, especially in police procedurals and medical series (*Sherlock* BBC 2010–2017, *Elementary* CBS 2012–, *House MD* Fox 2004–2012, *Criminal Minds* CBS 2005-2021). These hyper intellects are easily read as lacking in empathy. Stratton (2016) notes that television shows such as *Dexter* (Showtime 2006–2013) endorse neoliberalism by holding up for our inspection and amusement a set of characters who are unbothered by compassion for fellow human beings and fully taken up by their own quests. Their individualism is characteristic of neoliberal ideology and rule (2016: 278). They also appear to suffer from autism spectrum disorder. Sidore adds that television programmes like to make use of the symptoms of mental illness (2015: 18) which disguise how the

> various incarnations of Holmes, including Gregory House and Patrick Jane from *the Mentalist* (2008), are fully aware of how the real world works and feel no need to be bound by the normal laws. They know better

and choose to encounter the world on their terms. In fact, many of these characters use odd and inappropriate behaviour as a means of provoking actions and reactions, often getting others to reveal secrets to their keen observational skills. ... Dr Cal Lightmen (*Lie to me*, 2011) and Patrick Jane are walking lie detectors. ... The spectacle of their social ignorance thus serves to display rather than undercut their abilities

(Sidore 2015: 22).

JZ Long takes this pathologization of the characteristics of genius to be the consequence of a long-standing myth of anti-intellectualism in the USA, which under recent conditions of populist politics has been strengthened. The argument is a two-step one: first, ... 'the positioning of the genius as tragically flawed allows the viewer to celebrate specific characterizations of intellectuality while maintaining an anti-intellectual stance of detached (anti)enlightenment' (2015: 33). The 'fictionalized representations of genius,' Long continues, 'rather than improving our intelligence, provide us with both the means and the ends for anti-intellectualizing our own alienation from everyday life' (Long 2015: 34). Secondly, dominant anti-intellectualism decrees that '[t]he truly intelligent person translates ideas into practical solutions to real problems, lives "off" ideas instead of "for" them and recognizes that human identity is found essentially in the heart, not the mind.' (Long 2015: 35/6). In the case of Jane, such reasoning suggests that it is not Jane's considerable intellect that is to be emulated but his uncontrollable need for revenge, which will turn into vigilante justice being meted out. Via the frame of genius, Jane's intellectual prowess is but a decoy while his far more practical pursuit of Red John is given precedence as what is really to be admired about him. This changes the interpretation of the character dramatically, from the friendly guy who shares nuts and fruit and abhors guns and violence to a guy who shows us that justice at times needs to be taken into one's own hands. As a viewer commenting on a YouTube fragment entitled 'the best Mentalist episode ever,' says: 'No, this guy wasn't a villain, he's like Patrick, he just wanted revenge!'.[2] Well, I disagree. My Patrick Jane was about closure, not revenge.

Criticism cast as distrust would stop here. Suspicion confirmed. The deep truth of *the Mentalist* has been uncovered. Seemingly a nice guy, but in truth Patrick Jane is a vigilante avenger. It would fit the unsatisfactory feeling of the last two seasons: after killing Red John, Jane's need for revenge should have been sated. The scriptwriting recognizes this and portrays Jane as hardly willing to come home to the USA. He works with the FBI under duress. Appreciative inquiry is much milder on Jane. It urges us to take seriously that Jane can be seen from three angles rather than just one. Reducing him through the frame of genius does not do him justice. Attending to affect, it makes sense to give the earlier seasons their due. I, at least, wanted to hang on to what made Jane such a likable character. The fear of guns and generally cowardly behaviour are part of his charm and not, to me, trickery or a form of hypocrisy. In contrast to Sherlock Holmes or Gregory House (who, full disclosure, I like to watch too), Jane does a far more sincere line in empathy. Ultimately, this is also exactly where my close reading will connect with what needs discussing when you have seen (or are watching) *the Mentalist*.

In defence of **the Mentalist**

The eagle-eyed reader will have noted that I said I was not much of a fan of the Red John episodes. However, I have quoted a fair number of them. All episodes have a colour code in their title; the ones with 'red' in them refer to Red John. My three frames (comedy, feminism, genius) can also be faulted e.g., for not taking on Jane's grief. It is part of the frame of sadness, showing Jane lying on the bed his daughter was murdered in, in the otherwise empty and abandoned family home. Or Jane secretly living in the attic over the police station bare but for a camp bed and his Red John investigation files and notes. Then there is my forgiveness of Jane ultimately being a hypocrite. Of feigning feminist respect for his female superiors while acting like a paternalistic male when he keeps Lisbon away from a hunt to keep her safe. Judith Shklar shows hypocrisy to be the counterpart of sincerity, a defining trait in modernity when we start depending on individuals rather than traditions and conventions. The series invites me to reflect on my own attachments, if not exactly in the Actor Network Theory 'ANT-ish' manner Rita Felski searches for in *Hooked*, as well as on my own hypocrisies. There is a 'bad faith' quality to textual criticism that is not open to what drives it – then again, it would be utterly patronizing and hypocritical to denounce the textual critique of others. I propose that with Shklar, we give hypocrisy the benefit of the doubt. That we employ self-reflexivity in a friendly and open manner that leaves intact what we like and enjoy, that we forgive the intellectual for not always being a hard-nosed activist. Much as I think cultural citizenship can be understood by moving from careful listening into the mode of hearing – predicated as that is on taking in the ensemble of sounds and sensations, an open mode rather than a targeted, precision tool.

It helps me in any case to understand that it is not just Jane, his stylishness, his jokes and his sleights of hand that 'make' *the Mentalist*. It is as much the way the cast of characters work as a team. It is the hero and helpers who go up against the villain together (cf. Kozloff 1992) that tip the balance towards hope and away from fear. It may well be why I like the last two seasons so much less, even though the serial killer line has been completed. When *the Mentalist* shifts to dismantling the Blake Association network across law enforcement agencies, its definition of evil changes. More than individual pathology, evil becomes invasive, located not merely and therefore addressable in individuals but a network constellation, a virus that infects entire organizations and society as a whole. For me, against this portrayal of evil as infectious and close at hand, I want *the Mentalist* to tell me the story of how its five closely linked key characters come to act as one in finding, capturing and neutralizing Red John. I want family and peace and happiness for it. And that is how the team, from the beginning, functions: Wayne Rigsby, brawny, somewhat naïve as a younger brother; Grace van Pelt, his love interest who will become the resident computer specialist and more of a nerd than Jane, the quintessential daughter; Kimball Cho, with his deadpan humour and carefully guarded emotions as an older brother; and Teresa Lisbon, their mother – of the tough-but-just kind. Lisbon raised her brothers and keeps helping them, together with Jane, when they are in trouble – suggesting Jane's father's status to the team. There is a shift here in gender definitions, allowing for attractive straight male effeminacy and equally attractive female professional strength and bossiness, that is well worth talking more about.

Not only are the key team members configured as a (work) family much along lines noted decades earlier by Ella Taylor (1989), but their qualities are also a comment on how Jane deals with life and loss and with fear. While Lisbon thinks she does old-fashioned police work by the book, her quality, when mirrored in Jane as a character, is that she takes charge. Cho's unemotionality and independent moral reasoning strengthen Jane's relentless pursuit of Red John to right grave wrongs. Van Pelt is a defence of Jane's nerdiness: she will develop from a shy, naïve and religious girl into a researcher who dares read between the lines. Together they enact and portray a solidarity that is not swayed or moved by fear. Several key moments show this: when, for instance, they decide to help their former and suspended boss, Hightower; or in the last season, when they come together after having gone their separate ways after the killing of Red John, to help Jane and Lisbon, who are now with the FBI. Jane's unique and constant contribution meanwhile to the law enforcement team is in not feeling bound to rules, to understand that a rule-bound organization also needs its free-thinkers. It is Jane who sees there is a mole in the CBI, for instance. Although the family is held together by Lisbon as boss and surrogate mum, as a team they perform spectacularly with Jane in their midst. Not just in terms of their apprehension statistics but also in clearing the force itself of malicious elements.

In their togetherness, they prove resistant to sexist stereotype (with Van Pelt a nerd, Lisbon an efficient law enforcer and Wayne Rigsby a caring father when out of an ended relationship there is a child). Although care and comfort are not abundantly present, these are given at key moments. The professional respect the team members have for one another is another way the team combats fear and provides safety: as far as control can be had, they trust one another to both have it and use it. Tellingly, when Grace's boyfriend and later fiancée fails to cover for her in a shooting, the truly clever viewer (not me) should have known that he is not just outside the family but that he is a bad guy. He turns out to be a Red John accomplice. Rigsby, in love with Grace, saves her and will later be in a relationship with her. Solidarity in *the Mentalist* merges with hope and with love.

It seems, then, that my personal preference to not engage with the evil fought by Jane and team, nor with Jane as a genius/vigilante-taking justice in his own hands fighter, makes me blind to the logic of the series while I do enjoy what I only come to see late in the day. This tells me that reading as an academic, there is more to be said and possibly a milder judgement to be made as there will be more than what immediately meets the eye, whether for me or for other viewers. Reading as a feminist, Jane disappoints as much as the series in allowing it to move into 'happy end' equals 'Lisbon no longer pursuing a career' as both apparently stop working. Reading as a fan, I simply stop short of watching the last episode, much as in earlier seasons I bypassed much of the darker Red John episodes. I don't need evil or fear to engage with crime as a puzzle. I would love for a feminist agenda to also be one that promotes fun and friendly flirting, strong women and men who do not invest in masculinity as the need to protect vulnerable others which, it seems to me, is the counterpart of using and abusing others. If strength, authority and vulnerability are organized along a strict divide, there is no escape from the different forms that toxic masculinity takes.

These would be my talking points when discussing men, masculinity or *the Mentalist*. When offering Jane as an example of a better kind of guy, others might well point out the episodes I don't like or the ending of the series. This makes it abundantly clear that it is impossible to 'do' cultural citizenship on one's own. It does also suggest that it pays to use the honesty of auto-ethnography to understand investments.[3] If I have them, others will have them too, and they might lead in fully different directions. And finally: appreciative inquiry as per Rita Felski's suggestion here traces the links between viewing practice, the television series as text, biography and circumstance.

And yes, textual analysis has helped me understand that for me *The Mentalist* is attractive television for its team chemistry, allowing both Jane and the team members to grow their strengths regardless of gender ideology. Appreciative inquiry allowed me to *attend to empowerment*, to recognize how the particular types of pleasure and engagement a text offers are important in their own right and are not, in everyday viewing, negated by how it might also be ideologically or otherwise 'wrong.' Applied to popular television, there seems little need to value epistemologies of evidence over those of experience. Here the two have been combined. If anything, it proves how the core quality of media criticism is to establish for specific contexts and audiences how a text is meaningful. Evidence in media interpretation can be compelling but it is hardly ever conclusive. That is to say that popular television can be a training ground – whether in media education or in everyday life – for understanding how all media texts can be understood via multiple frames which we may not value equally but need to be able to recognize with a degree of respect. Recognizing engagement and investment against suspicion and distrust can then provide a road to new forms of solidarity and the bridging cultural capital that today seems in such short supply. More on that in the next chapters.

Notes

1 In a review, James Hibberd suggests that the quality of storytelling might have been better had *The Mentalist* not been a CBS series but a serial (rather than a procedural) such as Fox's *24*. https://ew.com/article/2013/11/24/the-mentalist-red-john-review/.
2 Chris Coto, viewer in discussion of Tommy episode https://www.youtube.com/watch?v=cAxEQYqo7no, best Mentalist episode ever video posted by Comicpencil. Misspelling in original corrected.
3 In auto-ethnography, the researcher draws on and analyzes their own experience in relation to a broader social, cultural and political *context*.

8
RESPONSIBILITY

Content analysis with the help of fan-viewers: Sorting through the appeal of a decade of *RuPaul's Drag Race*

With Michael Kardolus

Political philosophy offers the concept of 'agonistic dialogue.' It suggests that we can remain in a conversation even when we fight. 'Agonistic' is an adjective derived from the Greek ἀγών (agon) or 'struggle.' When debating the (de)merits of popular cultural texts, disagreement is likely to be part of such a conversation. Sometimes only for the fun of it and to sharpen what exactly makes a particular programme, book, song or show particularly good (or bad). Sometimes there is more at stake, for instance, when it comes to how popular texts address identities, representation and community. That makes agonistic dialogue a useful term in relation to cultural citizenship. To collectively determine what the best possible world for most of us would look like, strong examples need to come to the fore that allow for differences and disagreements. They void consensus becoming too general or abstract to be of use. The agonistic dialogue in this chapter is between a fan community and their hero. My co-author, Michael, and I represent the fan community; our hero is RuPaul. The fight is over who is included and who gets excluded from *RuPaul's Drag Race*. For us, the show represents the queer community and needs to stand up to the discrimination of any of its members. As season 5 contender Detox put it: 'And to @RuPaulsDragRace: Enough with the feigned inclusivity. Time to start putting your money where your mouth is. #AllDragIsValid' (published on Twitter, 23 January 2020).

The chapter follows in Chantal Mouffe's footsteps when she is critical of how Habermas and other philosophers have tried to exclude 'irrational claims' ('inappropriate emotions' really) from the public sphere (Mouffe 2000, 2019). As Matthew Jones argues, we need to include a diverse body of subject positions to come to a truly representative polity and inclusive democracy. Jones is worried that Mouffe does not make clear why

DOI: 10.4324/9781003288855-12

participants would want to act democratically and adhere to 'the requirements of agonal respect, nor what should happen when the ethicopolitical principles of liberty and equality are not accepted' (Jones 2014: 14). Well, in the case of passionate debate in the *RuPaul's Drag Race* fan community, that becomes abundantly clear.

Participants, fans and viewers in and of this competition reality tv show deeply love it as a space to rewrite dominant heteronormative gender coding. Materially, there are beautiful outfits and the magic of turning literally any kind of body and body shape into a sexy creature. Politically, it is a space of exchange, whether on social media, such as Reddit or Twitter, where all involved make themselves heard, as in the quote from drag queen Detox above, or in real life in the cafes and venues where *RuPaul's Drag Race* is watched and drag competitions are staged. It is the kind of lively ongoing conversation that qualifies as cultural citizenship for even the most skeptical of the concept. Intriguingly, in (online) discussion, fans and viewers come very close to textual criticism. Its passionate engagement does not always present as the appreciative inquiry discussed in the chapter before this one (and based on Rita Felski's work, Felski 2015, 2020) and that is putting it mildly. There is attachment here though which travels across the boundaries of the television text into a range of practices, however agonistic in nature. This chapter will use viewer and fan discussion to reconstruct what it is that connects their deep commitment to speaking back to the show and its host.

The initial success of *RuPaul's Drag Race* on television from 2009 onwards was predicated not just on RuPaul Charles' exceptional qualities as a drag queen and reality show host but on the show's backing by the queer community (*RuPaul's Drag Race* Logo, VH1, MTV 2009 – today and available on Netflix). Backing, recognition and warmth do not rule out critical engagement or agonistic dialogue. Ongoing discussion of new seasons (as well as of *All Stars*, a spin-off, and *Untucked!* the backstage sister programme to *Drag Race*) shows both the continued support of a broad queer community and outspoken criticism of 'Mama Ru' who is clearly understood to be owned by the community. This chapter investigates recurring themes in discussion of the show by reading it through the eyes of two fan-viewers: myself and my friend Michael Kardolus, who these days teaches art. We had much fun working together on this project; the mode of address from here on will therefore change from 'I' to 'we,' with many thanks to Michael. As part of this book, the chapter will engage in audience-led textual analysis to show what that might look like and how it could be part of the tooling of cultural citizenship for media literacy.

RuPaul's Drag Race is a competitive reality television show in which drag queens compete to become America's next drag superstar. Not only does the show 'queer' gender and sexuality – as drag will – it is also a space of ethnic and cultural diversity. The show is a typical example of 'after broadcast' 'post-television' in its remix of genre rules, its intertextual referencing, its cross-media presence, its outrageous and sexualized performativity (unthinkable in earlier broadcast times) and in its allowing for an important role for audiences in defining the (de)merits and meanings of the show. It is from an audience-led perspective that *Drag Race* will be discussed in this chapter: taking double-edged sentiments about the show and its host in the gay community as a point of departure, its policing of gender, race and (national) culture will be focused on.

In a way, *Drag Race* would seem to run counter to the 1990s drag club scene of which the show and its host are direct descendants. RuPaul made their name in the 1990s. The drag culture of that decade signified emancipation and liberation of enduring and stifling definitions of gender and sexuality. The subsequent uptake of drag and camp in mainstream culture was felt by many to usher in an era of gender freedom, coinciding with a new appreciation for popular cultural forms. A quarter century on, popular culture no longer connotes bad taste. The realignment of taste and cultural capital has not coincided with decreased social inequality, however, and popular media culture appears to have remained the training ground for what Miller (1993) called 'the daily organization of fealty to the cultural-capitalist state.' Today's neoliberal governmentality and its defining form of offering freedom and stricture at the same time appear to be exemplified by the show hosted by drag queen, singer and television presenter RuPaul. Taking as our point of departure double-edged sentiments about the show and its host in the gay community and the ways queens are divided into role models versus underperformers, we will discuss how race, gender and national culture are policed. Below camp and drag will be introduced as distinctive cultural phenomena, then *RuPaul's Drag Race* and the discussion the show gives rise to.

Camp, drag culture and *Drag Race*

In almost all discussions of camp, Susan Sontag's famous 1964 essay is the point of departure. Sontag identifies camp as a 'sensibility' that revels in artifice, stylization, theatricalization, irony, playfulness and exaggeration rather than content (1983 [1964]: 105, 107, 115). Hutcheon underscores that for some '(c)amp sensibility is disengaged, depoliticized – or at least apolitical.' For others, though, she continues, such as postmodernists, feminists and queer theorists, camp can trouble the belief that gender is 'natural' or inherent and therefore work against heteronormativity (Hutcheon 2002: 9). As a style and a distinct form of cultural appreciation, camp is usually dated to the popular culture of the 1960s. In the 1980s, it gained popularity with the advent of postmodernism and its celebration of popular cultural forms. In the 1990s, drag culture is taken up as a form of camp that is not solely an underground or gay phenomenon. This decade also marks the start of RuPaul

Charles' career as a singer, drag star and television presenter with *Supermodel (of the World)*, the first song by a drag queen to hit the Billboard Hot 100 in 1993. Her/his[1] first television programme, *The Rupaul Show*, had its short run from 1997 to 1998.

Drag culture is the subject of an extensive literature (Goodwin 1989; Hermes & Kardolus 2019; Newton 1972; Warren 1974; Zervignon 2009). While RuPaul would say that 'we're all born naked and the rest is drag' (Charles 1996: Foreword), drag is generally understood as a tradition of men dressing up and performing as women. Drag has often been accused of sexism for its exaggeration of codes of femininity. Less well-known, women also perform in drag as drag kings or faux queens, likewise contesting gender as a category (Taylor & Rupp 2004). Most recently transgender performers have further upset the troubling of heteronormative gender categories in this popular art form (Dougherty 2017). Detox's tweet that opens this chapter underlines how 'all drag is valid.'

The uptake of drag and camp in mainstream culture was part of a new 'permissive populism' that others situate even earlier (cf. Hunt 2013). For those, like us, who follow *RuPaul's Drag Race* (Logo, VH1 2009 – today and available on Netflix), this is a show that offers a mixture of nostalgic pleasure, new political energy and occasionally, unease. These are predicated on a continuing sense that drag, like all camps, protests the stifling conventions of a male-dominated society (as RuPaul puts it) and in that sense is a liberating practice (in Aitkenhead 2018, *Guardian*). At the same time, Ru's politics, or more to the point Ru's lack of a political presence, has been a bone of contention among viewers, fans and the gay community.

In a collaborative auto-ethnography project, Michael and I hoped to find out what happened to the promise of drag culture as camp and its potential to rewrite heteronormative gender coding.[2] Is *RuPaul's Drag Race* despite its massive global success still drag culture, only now on television? Or does the logic of television (of genre, formats, celebrity as a brand, ratings) undo the potential freedom of drag? As viewers and fans, we have mixed feelings: sometimes because of how the show sets up contestants against each other, sometimes because of the reactions of other 'fans.' Intense viewer discussion directs us to key moments in the past 13 seasons of *Drag Race*. They are all about specific queens. This does not come as a surprise, as Sontag writes: 'Camp is the glorification of "character." (-) What the Camp eye appreciates is the unity, the force of the person.' (Sontag 1983 [1964]: 114). Before we discuss how we compared and contextualized what, according to fan comments and our own viewer experience, were moments of racist and transphobic exclusion against instances of emulation and celebration of the power of drag culture, we will turn to why it is important to understand *RuPaul's Drag Race* as competition reality television.

Drag Race as competition reality television

In the global North, culture is understood as a domain of freedom, whether as artistic freedom or as freedom of speech. Liberal democracies however also rule in and through cultural policy (Miller 1992, Yudice 2003). Policing through culture can be a long shot. When it works, culture, and especially popular culture, becomes a terrain of training but it can also be a domain of revolt, raucousness and energy (Cohen & Taylor 1992; Hermes & Hill 2020; Stallybrass & White 1986, 1997). Traditionally, in cultural studies, it has been argued to be a domain of multi-dimensional, multi-arena struggle where hegemony is established (Hall 1996: 424). Fiske goes as far as to suggest that television can be a domain of semiotic democracy and resistance against the hegemonic social order (Fiske 1987). From the perspective of its users, (popular) culture can thus, paradoxically, be a domain of freedom through contestation or through being rewarded for obedience and abiding by the rules (cf. Tally 1999).

Reality television, according to Ouellette and Hay (2008), provides a key example of this particular paradox. They argue that different reality television formats are at the heart of the 'reinvention' of government in neoliberal capitalist democracies such as the United States (2008: 471). They see distinctly neoliberal reasoning in how the spirit of personal reinvention is endemic to makeover reality television (idem: 472). Citizens are called upon 'to govern themselves through freedom, not control' (idem: 473). More even than makeover television, competition reality tv requires successful and savvy self-management in order to 'sell' the self. Miller, discussing cultural citizenship, finds the call to self-government in '(f)our types of cultural subject produced by public policy under the sign of civility' that are united in being ethically or politically incomplete: they are in need of training, of a mirror to come to self-recognition, or to align their consumption with political goals (Miller 1993: xi-ii).

While 'civility' is not the term that immediately comes to mind for *Drag Race*, the show accords with the fourth type of policy: contestants are in need of self-completion by taking on challenges and performing their best selves. They need to rid themselves of their cumbersome 'inner-saboteur' and release a free, authentic persona, reminiscent of how Foucault described the confession and the will to knowledge in *the History of Sexuality, part I* (Foucault 1976). Entering *Drag Race* as a contestant may be a free choice, but otherwise, it is a treacherous road to a 'freedom' that is far from guaranteed. It comes at the very least at the cost of subjecting oneself to judging and the evaluation by co-contestants, both of which can take extreme forms. The entrepreneurial self is made to work hard, and the meritocratic myth that everybody can 'make' something of themselves is a decidedly minor solace (Littler 2017).

The format of *RuPaul's Drag Race* is to pitch 10–13 (and recently 15) professional drag queens against each other to become America's Next Drag Superstar (Collins 2017). It is competition reality tv at its most outspoken, a camp superlative of the genre. By taking on talent- and supermodel reality show conventions with the twist that drag is about female illusion and fashion sense, the talent the contestants try to 'sell' to the judges and audience is their personality as much as their talents in singing or sewing (Berns 2014: 101–102). Like *The Voice* (2010–present), *Next Top Model* (2003–present) or *Next in Fashion* (2020), *Drag Race* features talented contestants who have careers and are hoping to boost their professional success by participating. All these shows are closely tied to celebrity culture and its business models (Kavka 2016). Its contestants are dancers, performers, make-up artists, designers or 'influencers' on social media. They come to the competition with very different sets of experiences and resources. In the sister series *RPDR: All Stars* (VH1, 2012–present), we see the contestants who have become professional performers and celebrate their success by showing off their designer garments and discussing their newfound wealth. Some contestants find mainstream success, such as Trixie Mattel and Katya, who are now *New York Times* bestselling authors with their *Guide to Modern Womanhood* (Mattel & Zamolodchikova 2020, 2022) and Bob the Drag Queen, Shangela and Eureka O'Hara who host the Emmy-awarded HBO-series *We're Here* (2020–present). *Drag Race* should not be underestimated. It has become an international phenomenon and Ru's empire continues to expand with shows across the world doing well.[3]

Aca fans

We speak as 'aca fans': academics and fans, an identity in media and cultural studies that needs careful attention for its unique power constellation and (methodological) responsibilities (Hills 2002, 2012: 33). Here that responsibility entails underlining, first of all, that we have no wish to appropriate the politics or diminish the multi-ethnic appeal of *Drag Race* or its viewers as it provides a mainstream platform for queens of colour. Our own viewer experiences entangle with the viewer comments of others (through our use of Reddit and YouTube and in conversation with friends). We cherish a sense of co-ownership and the personal and political engagement that it entails. *RuPaul's Drag Race* feels like 'our' show. That includes declaring upfront that we know we are limited in gauging its importance and that we will doubtlessly misread codes and jokes because of our location (in Europe), our age and our ethnicity. We do hope our writing is energized (and not just hindered) by the aca-fan logic. As academics, we do not want or need a final say; we hope for discussion and exchange. As fans, we are affectively involved and find ourselves moved, and sometimes mad, with Ru. While trying to keep these two voices apart, we apologize in advance for doubtlessly overstepping boundaries.

As authors, we are very different, even if both of us are white people who love television. One of us is an older cisgender straight woman, the other a younger non-binary gay man. One of us watches *Drag Race* incidentally and likes to hear gossip about the contenders, using YouTube as the preferred site to re-watch bits and pieces and the running commentary on the fashion choices of other queens. This is where Raven and Raja 'toot' or 'boot' fashion and where Trixie Mattel and Katya operated as a duo – well before they wrote the book. The other watches first thing in the morning after a new episode arrives and has an indexical knowledge of each queen, challenge and episode. In addition to following all available spin-offs, he also closely follows *Drag Race* threads on Reddit. Both of us, as fans, are deeply critical of the new mainstream route the show seems to be taking, even if we both greatly appreciate that *RuPaul's Drag Race* brought queer culture to mainstream contemporary television.

Discussing *Drag Race* and Ru by pooling our stories and 'wrestling with these stories to discover (their meaning) in relation to their sociocultural contexts' is what Chang, Ngunjiri and Hernandez call 'collaborative autoethnography' (2013: 17). How drag 'leans' towards sexism and unfair treatment of queens are key talking points for us, as is simply exchanging our pleasure when watching favourite contenders. Talking about Ru and *Drag Race* therefore combined well with Mittell's suggestion in *Complex TV* to focus on allegiance with specific characters (Mittell 2015). While we could have chosen to document and share conversations or to systematically analyze discussion on Reddit and in YouTube comments, a focus on characters allowed us to understand how complicated it can be to mould one's appreciation of *Drag Race* to an inclusive form of camp while the show is elimination-race television and therefore has a natural affinity with exclusive and caustic jokes.

Where Mittell points to the 'varying degrees of creative authority and collaborative ownership of their ongoing characters' for actors, the queens in *Drag Race* are under strict regimes of performing to type (2015: 119). *Drag Race* is invested in building complex story worlds by switching between biographical inserts and the challenges the contenders have to perform, much like the added value of paratextual frameworks for television drama (idem: 121). While in drama, we would fear for the safety of beloved characters, there is no need here – as there is none. The strength of reality television's post-scripting of unfolding interaction among contestants means we focus on praying that our favourites make it to the next round. As Mittell observes, '(t)elevision's character consistency is more than just an industrial convenience, as one of the primary ways that viewers engage with programming is to develop long-term relationships with characters. (...) (W)e temporarily give part of ourselves over to a fiction to produce intense emotional affect' (Mittell 2015: 127). *Drag Race*, its spin-offs and its accompanying YouTube and Instagram presence moreover enable a long-term relationship far beyond the limitations of traditional tv forms.

As viewers, we root for queens who speak to us, which makes us co-dependent on Ru's ruthless authority. The analysis as follows focuses on a small number of queens, whose treatment by the show also met with outrage and critique from viewers. While hardly a very objective course to follow, Michael and I claim the space of participant observation and how we embody feminist and queer politics differently to suggest that fans will easily recognize the selection of queens and incidents we focus on, even if they may differently analyze and evaluate them. The examples we discuss are moments in which we felt authority was abused to police race, gender and national identity. They show a paradoxical logic. Policing takes the form of praising specific queens for behaviour or style choices that others are criticized for or ridiculing queens for their lack of language proficiency or presentation by disregarding their backgrounds. The examples show how *Drag Race* undercuts the freedom that is promised by drag culture generally. In 'speaking back' to the programme as fans, we documented our performance of cultural citizenship, literally, in discussion of inclusion and exclusion, of who may belong and who cannot, and also how our critical commentary is not at odds with cherishing the show and its host.

All examples come from the two interconnected series that are at the heart of RuPaul's empire: *RuPaul's Drag Race* and *RuPaul's Drag Race: Untucked!*. Although separate programmes, they are the front and back stages of the same series and refer to one another. While *Drag Race* has the singing and dancing and the jokes, *Untucked* has the behind-the-scenes tears, laughter and drama. As RuPaul said in the intro of the earlier seasons of *Untucked*: 'Girl, if you're not watching Untucked, you're only getting half the story.' The twin shows spark the most online controversy out of all the affiliated series, have the biggest audience internationally and give us the most source material to work with. Ru believes in the power of hard work and entrepreneurship; he is often less than sensitive to social inequality. The show however will feature backstories of oppression, poverty, health struggles, racism, homophobia, etc. *Drag Race* thus has its cake and eats it: it seems produced to exploit this tension between Ru's neoliberal attitude and a more communitarian and compassionate outlook that invites us as viewers to appreciate the hardship that comes with specific intersectional identity combinations, such as to be black and queer and a drag queen.

One such intersectional identity deserves special attention, which is that of the trans women who are queens. Checking back through the Reddit pages we follow as fans (r/rupaulsdragrace and r/rpdrdrama), we see that racism, representation, race, appropriation, controversial, black, Latino and trans are key words when indignation and controversy over the show are shared. More than anything, specific forms of exclusion versus practice and the promise of inclusion come up in the comments. Notably, the exclusion of trans women as contestants in the show has been a long-running source of discontent. For long, it was unclear whether and in what capacity trans women were allowed to compete. While Ru has been quoted as saying that including trans contestants is unfair competition, there have been some trans contestants on the show. In earlier seasons, Carmen Carrera (s3), Kenya Michaels (s3) and Jiggly Caliente (s4) had to stop their transitions to be allowed to compete. Monica Beverly Hills (s5) and Peppermint (s9) came out as transgender women during their run of the show. In season 13, GottMik was allowed to compete as a trans man. Seasons 14 and 15 had trans women, under pressure from the community we think. It is only relatively recently that Ru changed her opening line. It used to be: 'Gentlemen, start your engines, and may the best woman win.' From the 13th season onwards, it became: 'Racers, start your engines, and may the best drag queen win!' The website *PinkNews* (2020) considered this '(a)n important change to an iconic Drag Race catchphrase to be more inclusive of trans and non-binary contestants.'

With fellow Redditors, we share that the message of *Drag Race* is that queens are free to do whatever they want, as long as they do it Ru's way. In addition, online discussion, like our own in real life, tends to start in reference to specific examples and incidents and thus to specific queens. Reflecting on our viewer experience, checked against Reddit comments, we found three routes in how the show produces the exemplary drag subject: *teaching femininity, policing blackness* and *making fun of non-native speakers of English.*

Policing to perfection

In Drag Race, it turns out, particular body types are judged (or admired); embodying one's ethnicity comes with strict rules; and good manners, cultural knowledge and speaking one's languages are made prescriptive. Those who 'underperform' on femininity, ethnic representation and language-cultural knowledgeability are ridiculed and dismissed. Going back to older Reddit discussion and reconstructing when we felt deeply uncomfortable, there was a choice of focusing on more general discussion about, e.g., Black Lives Matter and RuPaul's silence, or the way trans contestants have been treated. (Carmen Carrera [S3], Kenya Michaels [S4] and Peppermint [S9], who had started transitioning before their appearance on the show, had to put their transition on hold to be able to compete. They were also required to have a male-presenting body during their appearance on the show.) Instead, we have chosen to focus on bounded examples to show how the fan community has always done 'lay' forms of textual analysis and paid attention to mechanisms of inclusion and exclusion. Following in the community's footsteps, here is a selection of key examples that were discussed heatedly.

The teaching of femininity

Throughout its history, contestants, the jury and RuPaul have made claims about femininity and drag. The choice in the show's sexist parlance is to be a 'camp queen' or a 'fish queen,'[4] i.e., look like a real woman (fish, the derogatory label attests to drag's misogyny) or use your femininity as a clown costume (camp). While the show presents femininity generally as an artistic choice to be made by an individual contestant, femininity-as-drag is scrutinized for style, aesthetics and upsetting of what to some would be seen as naturally given. The 'Drag Con Panel Extravaganza' episode in season 10 is almost a tutorial. The critical reception by Ru and the judges of Nina West, Milk and transwoman contestants makes clear that *Drag Race* may appear to offer inclusion by showing how you do it while actually practicing exclusion. There is clearly a 'correct' way to do drag, and there is a correct body to have while doing so.

Underlying the easy-to-recognize instruction in femininity and disciplining of wayward and quirky queens is the animosity between 'fish queens' and 'camp queens,' a classic narrative in *RuPaul's Drag Race*. The fish queens have big hips, breasts and asses, female-presenting make-up and human hair wigs. The camp queens perform a more artistic style of drag in which the classic notion of femininity is up for discussion. Discussing how the candidates do drag, combined with the jury commentary and the elimination order of contestants, it became clear that there is a 'natural' ideal: wigs had to look like real hair and could not be removed unless there was another wig underneath; make-up had to make the contestant look like a woman and be applied flawlessly; the male body had to be altered (with padding and/or plastic surgery) to represent the ideal female hourglass figure; the quality of the tuck of male genitalia is often commented on. Candidates who are able to do conventional femininity well received high praise for their performance.

The show's teacherly mode became painfully clear for Nina West in season 11. She is one of the unfortunate queens who falls short of the standards of the judges: her shoulders were too wide, her hips not wide enough and her overall proportions didn't fit into the beauty standards the judges perceived as feminine. Although Nina made it to the final five, she was held up as an example of what queens should not look like throughout the season. Similarly, Milk in season 6, a courageous performer, was criticized during her entire run. Neither her make-up nor her look passed scrutiny. A non-conventional queen, Milk sported facial hair, pants and a bald cap. While deemed 'creative,' this was also wrong. She had to turn herself into a pained artist who had to conform to beauty ideals to fit into the show. She did not manage to do this and was eliminated.

The policing of blackness

Ru is not only strict on a feminine appearance; how to be a black performer is also vigilantly policed. In the few interviews that he has given, Ru will underline his blackness and how that has shaped him. In 'I'm 55, always been Black, always been gay. I don't fuck with the police' (Reynolds 2020). It makes fans wonder how making the right use of stereotypes and preconceptions is so important to the show. Commenters note how, when practiced for comedic reasons and 'controlled' by the performer, stereotypical black behaviour is celebrated. Anyone, however, who invites others to laugh at her by being awkward and out of control will have Ru and the jury come down on them hard. It seems to be the upside-down version of how, as a black person in a white society, you always have to do twice as well. It is, in a way, social censure.

An example that gets talked about is the comedic 'ghetto' black woman stereotype, a favourite in *Drag Race*. She is represented as an African-American vernacular English speaker, overtly sexual and/or a sex worker, poor and/or cheap and most of all an aggressive woman. In contrast to the more common negative connotation of this stereotype, candidates are praised when they use this stereotype in comedic challenges where it has become a drag staple. Shangela wins the stand-up comedy challenge season 3 (episode 8) for her performance as a self-employed 'post-modern-pimp-ho.' It is noted that the judges do not especially praise her for the use of this stereotype but she is told that her set was hilarious and that the act could make her money (yes, *double entendre*). She also wins the episode. Likewise, a comedic 'ghetto' black woman act is also praised in *RuCo's Empire* challenge in season 8, episode 3. Bob The Drag Queen, who wins the challenge, follows a pre-written script that spoofs the HBO-series *Empire* while doing a comedic impression of the original characters. Clearly, the 'ghetto' black woman is part of the show's repertoire. How curious then that African-American contestants tend to do best when they erase their blackness in other parts of the competition. We see how, in backstage conversation, contestants of colour regularly discuss whether they should use this denigrating stereotype. They are allowed is the consensus among contestants and the fans, because they are part of the minority discriminated by the stereotype and they use it in a comedic way. However, outside of these stereotypical comedic performances, we also see how they underplay their blackness and how it cannot be a theme in any other way. Such depoliticization sits uneasily with many.

Season 10 showed this exceptionally clear and was discussed heatedly. It is the season that The Vixen's season-long narrative arc kept casting her as the stereotype of the angry black woman: unreasonably confrontational and always angry.[5] During *Drag Race* season ten's episodes (2, 5, 6, 7, 8 and 13) and in the *Untucked!* season nine episodes 1, 3, 4 and 7, The Vixen kept having arguments with other contestants, almost all of which she appeared to have instigated. Ru castigating her made for good tv. The *New York Times* fan reviewer Amanda Duarte wrote:

> Showing-not-telling just how important acting skills are to the art of drag, Ru faux-innocently asked The Vixen about her 'history of conflicts here,' as if he had not spent the previous seven weeks violently crunching Tic-Tacs over the shoulders of the story-editing team and shaping her 'villain' narrative. The Vixen theorized, 'I think they know that I keep it real and they can't play phony around me,' at which even the Miss Congeniality front-runner Monét rolled her eyes. Drag Oprah Ru advised Vixen, 'You can fight, but ultimately the biggest fight you have in this life is with yourself, you know?' Vixen reacted as most people her age react to a bitch-slap from an older person, and did not visibly snap out of anything.
>
> (Duarte 2018)

Not as much fun as you'd think, this putting down of The Vixen when, in *Untucked* episode four of that year, Eureka O'Hara and The Vixen clashed badly. Here too, The Vixen seemed unreasonably confrontational and angry. However, not five minutes after the fight, Eureka O'Hara was shown admitting that *she* started the row to 'test' The Vixen. What to think of a white instigator taunting and playing an African-American contestant?

In the last episode of the season *(13)*, which is always retrospective, the actions of The Vixen and her angry black woman storyline are discussed in detail. First Ru and the other contestants criticize The Vixen for acting hostile and aggressive. The Vixen defends herself by saying she didn't start arguments. While there is some evidence to support this claim, she is still criticized for *reacting* the way she did, upon which The Vixen walks off. RuPaul's speech after she leaves is instructive. The Vixen, he said, does not know how to act correctly (as a black person) because she does not want to learn how to, which means she cannot become a successful, non-confrontational (we fear: appealing to white people) person. When challenged, a rare occurrence indeed, by Asia O'Hara, Ru even lost his cool and says: 'Look at me, damn it, I come from the same place she does' (*Drag Race*, season 10's Reunion episode). Clearly, politics do not come easy to Ru who has been criticized often for not speaking out against racism and for gay rights. Inserting this bit of dialogue by the producers, we suspect, may have been meant as an explanation of sorts for Ru not standing up politically.

Ridiculing low proficiency in English and a lack of cultural capital

Ru is not only a neoliberal who believes in pulling yourself up by your bootstraps but also a schoolmistress/master of the kind that does not believe in grading for diligence. Only the final results count. This makes her uncomfortably unliberal when it comes to stereotyping Latin-American queens. Latin-American contestants tend to fall victim most to the show's policing of 'not being a cultured person' when they act like the slightly silly Latin-American queen. Their Spanish-accented English nets them easy laughs and becomes a comedic crutch. In season 3 (episode 3), Yara Sofia does a 'sassy, crazy Latin' stereotype, main-challenge performance and runway look. RuPaul and the guest judge are shown cackling while overseeing the performance and later commend her for her use of the stereotype and 'using that whole Latin-thing and that sexy swoosh.' The condescension in the comments becomes clear when she is also warned not to overplay the 'funny but dumb' stereotype. RuPaul comments, 'you took a potential liability, which is your accent, and made it work for you.' A Spanish accent is a risk then and only works when presented as a joke.

When Cynthia Lee Fontaine in episode 3 of season 8 is struggling with her lines, the talking head that is shown to make clear that she does not understand what she is saying or why she is being funny is not so very funny. Sound effects and laughter from the other contestants and the judges ridicule and deride her. Rather than act a part, she *is* a 'funny but dumb Latin queen.' Jessica Wilde's failure in the maxi challenge of episode 7 in the second season was even more unsettling. She had to come up with a book title, do a satellite interview and dress for the launch party of this book on the runway. She clearly has no clue about what it is she needs to do. Talking headshots of other contestants, the facial expressions of the interviewer and the sound effects played during the interview make merciless fun of her. The judges say her interview was a 'trainwreck,' but that they wouldn't change a thing. It was 'so bad it becomes good again.' While a liability for her, her accent is a source of fun for others. Then, when she does not understand 'golden shower' as a reference to a sexual act, the judges laugh at her and call her 'naïve.' She is cast as dim-witted without allowing leeway for English not being her first language. Watching this, you wish someone had protected this woman from herself.

Ru's 'right' kind of queen can perform femininity and ridicule it. Ethnic stereotyping underscores the ridicule and is encouraged by the show. Racialized caricatures give a performance 'personality,' according to Ru (Strings & Bui 2014: 824). However, at the same time, a queen should always be in control of her performance: she should be able to do an accent or a stock character and step away from it. *RuPaul's Drag Race* thus favours a particular form of being cultured: speak your languages, recognize innuendo and trash talk as much as high cultural etiquette, fashion and customs, such as the codes of the book launch. Ru combines his 'you have to work hard to make it' neoliberalism with being deeply referent of distinction (Bourdieu 1980), which in turn is predicated on exclusion and knowing you are above the common folk. Ru's dislike of trans women participating might be explained exactly by her insistence on the value of performance and not conflating practice with identity. There is no need to be who you are as a performer. Drag after all is about illusion and show; it is a craft. Similarly, (identity) politics may come too close to defining and nailing down who you are for Ru to be comfortable engaging with it.

Why do we love this show?

Looking at all the examples we collected, you would think we would be disgusted or at least severely disappointed but apparently, we are not. Watching *RuPaul's Drag Race* is to step into a dream world *and* to support a politics of difference, even when Ru takes long to speak out on grave and urgent political matters. Watching *Drag Race* is to come to understand how breaking away from gender normativity needs performing to rigorous codes, the necessary paradox that makes drag a political statement. More than in any other reality show, politics are part of the popularity of *Drag Race,* which allows us and other fan-viewers to discuss citizenship in an almost classical form as inclusion, merit, opportunity and justice. *Drag Race* is reality television. Its format decrees that there need to be winners and losers from one episode to another, habituating us to exclusivity and competition rather than inclusion and community. As we resist this neoliberal logic, the television programme engages us as audiences not only in political questions of gender, identity and sexuality and the complexities of a wish to 'be ourselves' but also in thinking about what solidarity should mean and in practicing the art of fighting well for what is worth fighting for.

Of course, appreciative inquiry is also possible when it comes to *RuPaul's Drag Race*. In such a case, I would write about the clothes and the make-up and the creativity of the contenders (and have done so elsewhere, see Hermes 2018). Michael would focus on the performers and the glitter and glamour. When focusing only on the agonistic appeal of the show (and however more fitting agonistic conversation is then 'discussion' or 'debate' for how the viewer and fan community use the show to discuss identity, representation and community), the pleasure *RuPaul's Drag Race* affords would be ill-served and that may be a real downside to foregrounding it. Then again, it is fun to go where discussion leads you, especially when discussion among fans and viewers is so close to textual analysis. While it needs to be wielded with care, audience-led textual analysis by 'aca' and lay fans and viewers feels like a collaborative enterprise. It turns the tooling of cultural citizenship into the collaborative effort it needs to be. Which also means that understanding cultural citizenship needs to be able to contain anger, disappointment, fear and other negative emotions as much as pleasure. Whether that pleasure is escapist or passionate, and whether it is about being moved or feeling included.

Notes

1 RuPaul says:'You can call me he. You can call me she. You can call me Regis & Cathy Lee; I don't care! Just as long as you call me' (RuPaul's Drag Race Twitter, twitter post, September 2013, 6:35 P.M). As RuPaul does not care about their pronouns, we have chosen to mostly call them 'her,' as this is the general way drag queens address each other and we feel most comfortable calling Ru and the contestants with that pronoun. The occasional 'he' denotes the deliberate doubling of gender options in Ru's self-presentation as both a queen and a male presenter on *RuPaul's Drag Race*.
2 Our research was published as a commentary in *Critical Studies in Television* and as a research article in a themed special issue of *Javnost/The Public* on freedom. Joke Hermes and Michael Kardolus (2019), 'Occupying the Intersection: RuPaul's Celebration of Meritocracy,' and Joke Hermes & Michael Kardolus (2022): 'The RuPaul paradox: Freedom and stricture in a competition reality TV show.' Collaborative auto-ethnography refers to researchers questioning each others' reflections on their experiences and interpretations of social, cultural or political or cultural phenomena. Cf. Chang, Ngunjiri and Hernandez 2013.
3 In 2021, the original (American) version of the show is starting its 13th season, which brings the number of queens featured on the show to 166. The 48 of these original contestants appeared on the wildly successful *All Stars* (*RuPaul's Drag Race: All Stars* VH1 2012–present), 30 on the less successful spin-offs *RuPaul's Drag U* (LogoTV 2010–2012) and *RuPaul's Celebrity Drag Race* (VH1 2020, Real n.pag.). Beyond these American successes, *Drag Race* has two spin-off seasons of *The Switch: Drag Race* (Chile, Mega 2015–present), three seasons of *Drag Race: Thailand* (LINE TV 2018–present), two seasons of *RuPaul's Drag Race UK* (BBC3 2019–present), one season of *Drag Race Canada* (TMN 2020–present), one season of *Drag Race Holland* (Videoland 2020–present) and *Drag Race Brazil* and *Drag Race Down Under* (Sim 2019, n.pag., Street 2021, n.pag.) have been announced. In season 13, episode 3, RuPaul had contestants sing her 2020 song 'Phenomenon': 'Drag is all over the world, it's a phenomenon, it will live on and on.' That phenomenon is currently driven by the *Drag Race* franchise, even if drag as a phenomenon and *Drag Race* the tv show should not be conflated, as will become clear below.
4 This term has become highly controversial in recent online discussions due to its reference to the smell of a vagina. However, as the term is used on the show, we decided to mirror the language use of the show, begrudgingly.
5 The Vixen prefers her name spelled with a capital T.

9
STORYTELLING

Meanwhile in the real world: Popular culture and cultural citizenship politicize online on social media platforms

This too is a chapter on non-fiction, like the reality tv chapter berore this one in which agonistic conversation is suggested as a form of and for cultural citizenship. It will make clear that agonistic conversation requires a willingness to engage and at least minimal respect for one another. As we now know, this is not what the online world has to offer. However, not all is lost, even if a bleak conclusion is warranted. In a mere 15 years, online storytelling changed dramatically in the Netherlands and elsewhere. The populist right and generally the conservative forces that dominate today's platform capitalism have gained a monopoly on affective speech. Sensational stories have all of us in their stranglehold. This suggests we need to invest in empathy and emotional intelligence and new forms of media 'wisdom' (the Dutch expression for media literacy). Although reactionary social movements are today's 'key activists of affect,' as Toby Miller pointed out when reading an earlier version of this book, there are counterstories as well. We need to pick up on both types of stories: the hurtful and the hopeful ones.

I have defined cultural citizenship as querying belonging, identity and representation in and through popular cultural storytelling. This chapter will take the lessons learned from studying popular entertainment (across fiction and non-fiction genres) to two cases of real-life online storytelling by ordinary citizens. That too is popular culture, even if it is to be found at a remove from the media industry's polished versions. The first case comes out of over five years of working with the Marokko.nl web community as an outside advisor from 2005 to 2010. The second is a very different story of participant observation and online ethnography. It concerns the Black Pete turmoil in the Netherlands in 2015 around a Facebook page called Pietietie where support was pledged to a contested racist stereotype 'because he is part of a children's feast.' The two examples span a crucial decade, in which the script for feeling rooted in the Netherlands was voided. They will set the stage for how, today, cultural citizenship can be thought of, tooled and used, to which I will return in the last chapter.

In 2005, the Marokko.nl team saw real potential in a separate news website, inviting its community to engage in classic political citizenship. Five years later, in 2010, I had to stop an online 'telenovela' project with young writers from the community about a young journalist called Faysal who starts a blog. As the project threatened to become successful, it was taken over by community members. Although not from the writers' group, there was increasing hostility in the community towards my presence and that of my co-researchers. In the real world, two competing blogs had started, called De Joop (socialists) and De Jaap (a collaboration of progressive and conservative liberals), signifying a brief and unique moment of collaboration between unlikely partners. Another five years later, De Jaap had made way for the ultra-conservative PostOnline (online from 2012 onwards), while two million Dutch liked the Pietietie page.

The overlap between political and cultural citizenship matters, as does ongoing polarization in the Netherlands and how popular culture became an arena of an ugly struggle. As the examples in this chapter move out of the realm of entertainment and become openly political, they offer less and less space for open discussion. Listening in on what is said would hardly seem to require the tools of the media and cultural studies trade. Meanings are hardly hidden, and feelings show themselves as hurt, anger and pain. Looking back, it does seem there is traction in looking for cultural citizenship through participant design using collective storytelling and inviting others to co-create images of that better world that commercial popular culture manages to suggest with such apparent ease. As the one but last chapter of this book, it will reflect on the ethnographic and participant design methods used and gauge the reach of cultural citizenship as a concept.

There seems to be widespread agreement that the outpouring of emotions made possible by social media is co-shaping contemporary history. A quarter-century ago, a qualitative audience researcher would have looked at the meanings and pleasures of popular media (Ang 1985; Radway 1984). This would involve speaking with audience members about everyday routines, about the series or novels they felt strongly about as much as about genres they enjoyed only incidentally or in habitual, off-hand ways (Gillespie 1995; Gray 1992; Morley 1986). Whether or not they were popular, the vast majority of media texts referenced, ranging from news programmes to drama, popular fiction, game shows and other forms of 'ordinary television' (Bonner 2003), would have been made by professionals. Fan fiction is a notable exception. Before the internet, it was exchanged at conventions (Bacon-Smith 1992; Jenkins 1993).

The job at hand was to understand the meaningfulness of media-related everyday practices and to deconstruct them. The relevant parts of such a deconstruction were suggested by Stuart Hall's 1973 encoding–decoding model, which recommended looking at the frameworks of knowledge (of both producers and audiences) and the relations of production and technical infrastructures (Hall 1980). Done well, such work informs its readers about how unequal power structures are lived, reproduced and resisted in and via the use of popular media. It assumed that media representations are negotiated in order to construct identities. While all such practices are suffused with emotion and affect, neither feature was specifically focused on.

Today's media audience research is faced with a decidedly different challenge. It is clear that the emotions, and especially the anger that social media allow their users to express, cannot be reduced to meaning making, even if making sense of the world is part of it. Neither can a 'media text' be considered a given – that is to say, as something produced by professional organizations for consumption by audiences. Today's media landscape is a hybrid mixture of what John Fiske (1987) presciently described as secondary and tertiary texts that are intertextually related to primary texts. Unforeseen by Fiske, such primary texts today are also produced by 'amateurs.' Unhindered by codes of professional conduct, individuals today produce all sorts of content, including mash-up videos and memes that blatantly disregard copyright as well as original materials (vlogs, music videos). Occasionally, such content finds its way back into newspapers and tv shows made by media organizations, but mostly it is used directly by followers and friends of the new makers. The result is a hybrid media sphere. Variety rather than accountability or verifiability is its strong suit, as is the open invitation to rage and vent.

Rather than look at single issues, moments in history, media platforms, media(ted) art or activism (Kraidy 2016; Papacharissi 2016; Postill 2014), however necessary and urgent, this chapter will continue my search for 'cultural citizenship': that is to say, the ways in which we frame sociality and negotiate a sense of belonging and of identity in today's world in unreflected-on, everyday media use (Hermes 2005; Postill & Pink 2012: 130). We know that 'professionally produced' popular fiction and non-fiction media have been and remain important. Social media today however enable cultural citizenship in much more public and heated ways (see also the chapters in part II of this book). While initially YouTube could be called a platform of cultural citizenship expressed via vernacular creativity (Burgess 2006) and evaluated positively, today's social media platforms carry increasingly worrying amounts of excited anger and hatred (Coe et al. 2014; Seta 2018) as well as unpleasant forms of humour that are meant to cause pain rather than to encourage reflection on what might make the world a better place for most of us. Are those cultural citizenship too? I think yes, which begs the question of how to contextualize and separate perverse effects and tragic outcomes from the urge to blame and hold to account.

Social media have reshaped public discussion (Bucher & Helmond 2018; Papacharissi & Trevey 2018). How and what emotion and forms of affect are allowed has seen a sea change. In the initial years of web communities in the early 2000s, there was little reason to suspect that, partly as a result of these new codes, the internet would become a stronghold of discrimination, hatred, anger and right-wing conspiracy thinking (Boeschoten & Ven 2019; Dagnes 2019). Today, this seems to be exactly what has happened. Rather than a new arena for democracy and emancipation, it is a media field in which polarization is fuelled, even if it is not where it started, as e.g., Arlie Russell Hochschild's incredible portrait of Tea Party sympathizers in *Strangers in their own Land* shows (Hochschild 2016).

This chapter stays close to (my) home and will focus on the social position and media representation of the Moroccan-Dutch, which is intertwined with fear of Islam; the second is the ongoing debate, or rather quarrel, about the yearly Dutch Sinterklaas festivities and especially the figure of Black Pete. Pete is supposed to be a helper of Sinterklaas, who is a Santa-like prelate. Petes are kitted out in a stereotypically racist manner. They wear blackface and black wigs. They tend to be silly if not outright stupid. The figure of Pete has occasioned protest since the mid-20th century (and possibly even before; the figure itself is a 19th-century invention; Boer-Dirks 1993; Helsloot 2012), but heated debate, hate speech and riots coincided with the rise and establishment of social media platforms, roughly between 2005 and 2015, and continue to this day. As a major newspaper reported in early September 2019: 'good idea to discuss Pete in peace time' (*NRC*, 5 September 2019). At the moment of writing, members of Kick Out Black Pete were not given any protection on their way to a demonstration. Police officials looked on (NOS 2022). Questions asked in parliament in January 2023 were referred back to the local authorities. Earlier, court cases started by Kick Out Black Pete took very long to be resolved. The expectation is that this will again be the case.

The Pete controversy needs to be read in counterpoint to how Dutch society has turned more and more towards overt racism and Islamophobia. Between 2001 (911) and 2010, Moroccan-Dutch were increasingly its target. More recently, refugee groups, e.g., from Syria, have met with the same fate. Apparently, Ukrainians coming in because of the Russian war against their homeland are given a slightly warmer welcome. It is early days to say whether this will remain the case. The Moroccan-Dutch case is of special interest because it coincides with the coming of social media and the change from earlier and arguably more defensible democratic uses of the internet to a logic of bubbles, rabbit holes, hatred and paranoia. On social media, ordinary people discuss what occupies them. Surely it is a domain in which to look for cultural citizenship. As in the earlier chapters, I will do so using a specific case based on the work I undertook with two co-researchers and the Marokko Media web community which in turn will provide background for the impact protests against the racist figure of Piet, Sinterklaas' helper, have had.

A little background

Moroccans came to the Netherlands as migrant workers in the late 1960s (Haas 2007). While they lived precariously, their families were reunited and lives were built. Dutch society prided itself on being liberal and welcoming until well into the mid-1990s. An essay in the Dutch quality newspaper *NRC* called 'The multicultural drama' by publicist and social-democrat Paul Scheffer (2000) marks the turn to increasingly open hostility towards migrant groups. Prins and Saharso (2008) reckon that Dutch pride taken in vertical segregation or 'pillarization' (Christians, Catholics, socialists and liberals each had their own autonomous social circles) had long given way to heated debates over integration and immigration before '9/11,' the 2001 attack on the Twin Towers in New York and before Scheffer's article was published. According to Prins and Saharso: 'in September 1991, the then leader of the Conservative Liberals (VVD) initiated what was called the "national minorities debate" (...). European civilization, as party leader Frits Bolkestein argued, is sustained by the values of rationality, humanism and Christianity' (Prins & Saharso 2008: 366). All of these Bolkestein depict as antithetical to Islam. Usually, the position of women was the argument to point to what was considered to be the backwardness of Islamic culture (idem).

Interestingly, these same young Muslim women are early social media adopters who turned to Yasmina.nl, the forerunner of the immensely successful Marokko.nl web community which today mostly operates as closed Facebook groups. My contact with the manager-producers of Marokko.nl dates back to 2004, a period in which Marokko.nl was seeking to ward off trolling and hate speech by training moderators. They also wanted to empower the community by providing its 200,000 members with a news website, a project on which they asked us – as media audience experts – for advice.

The Pete discussion came later, in reaction to both real-life and online reactions in defence of Pete in blackface. What seemed to me a reasonable request to slightly update a folkloric ritual by refashioning Pete and doing away with the ear-rings, the blackface paint and the exaggerated lips (but maintaining the costume) was met with breathtaking hostility, and not just from groups at the far-right end of the political spectrum. A significant number of friends of my daughter signed Pietitie, an online action in 2013, a 'petition' demanding that Pete not be changed. When asked, they explained it was not something they had given much thought, it had just 'felt right' that this particular tradition should continue to be honoured.

To be accepted as Dutch and non-white, or as Dutch and Muslim, is not easy in the Netherlands, and the process is compromised by what initially were the trolling and hate-speech practices of small minorities. Pietitie, which gathered over two million signatures at a moment when the Netherlands had only five million Facebook users, revealed otherwise. Over the last decade and a half, social media platforms transformed into a safe haven for alt-right and alt-light emotions. They have become a gateway for anger as part of the public sphere. Before that, the internet felt like a safe space for marginalized communities caught between two worlds.

Of course, neither social media platforms nor professional media sites can be understood as adhering to single logic or single stories. Messiness characterizes the mediated public sphere as much as the ongoing creation and bursting of 'filter bubbles' (Parisher 2011). Media ethnography, with its commitment to broad contextualization and a polylogue of the voices of members of different social groups, is perfectly equipped to help understand the broad and continuing unease with diversity and multiculturalism which is a shared characteristic of societies across the globe today (Steger & James 2019). Three social-media-related moments in the early and late 2000s and in the mid-2010s will help identify how emotion became a key element in digital media culture. These three moments show the ongoing relevance of understanding representation and identity when looking at how media are used, whether these media are 'legacy' or 'digital native.'

Understanding everyday digital media culture

There is a strange split between qualitative audience research and media ethnography. Both found their own way of taking the digitalization of media practices on board. While 'media ethnography' as a term is widely used in media and cultural studies, there are not that many studies that rely on the forms of fieldwork we find in anthropological work (Mankekar 1999, 2015). Marie Gillespie's *Television, Ethnicity and Social Change* is a unique exception (Gillespie 1995) for which she used her vast network among the South Asian community in Southall, London, which she built as a schoolteacher. Long open interviews rather than fieldwork became the method of choice in media and cultural studies in the 1980s and 1990s.

'Virtual' or 'digital' ethnographies appear later, from 2000 onwards (Baym 2000; Hine 2000). They use exchanges on discussion lists (message boards and discussion fora) to reconstruct underlying patterns and logics in the communications of communities that routinely use the internet to connect. Jumping another decade, Miller and Horst (2012: 3) speak of understanding 'particularity and difference' in digital communication in order to better understand 'the framed nature of analogue [...] life as culture' (idem 4). Field sites, says Hine, have multiplied and come in various forms (2017: 24).

Miller and Horst understand digital anthropology as a holistic and culturally relativistic undertaking that accepts the ambiguity of the digital with regard to its 'increasing openness and closure.' The digital has become part of material culture, including, as Miller and Horst point out, its remarkable capacity to (re-)impose normativity (Miller & Horst 2012: 4). While they do not link normativity explicitly to affect and emotion, this connection marks precisely what digital communication has added to existing forms of media and mediation in the public sphere.

The advantage of doing media ethnography, as it was developed in the cultural studies tradition and backed up by digital anthropology, is that it not only underlines the importance of attending to emotion but that it offers new means to do so. In addition, it helps to recognize that the shift from personal to mediated interaction via social media demands following 'negotiations inherent in knowledge production and forms of knowing' across different field sites, actual and virtual (Horst 2016: 154). Too strong a focus on text(s), whether interview transcripts, online discussion or other media content, would leave precious little space to appreciate what has changed. Discourse analysis can become overly technical and lose its link with materiality, with bodies and with feelings, as early discussions of affect pointed out (Gregg & Seigworth 2010). The visceral qualities of online discussion as well as its entanglement with everyday experience matter. It is important to therefore undertake the kind of affective-discursive approach to meaning making that was propagated in chapter 3. It will allow for tracing and theorizing how meaning making, emotion and bodily affect become interlinked with the coming of the digital media age.

Three interlinked moments

Difficult though it is to fathom now, early internet-facilitated communication and community-building were very different from social media use today. Interaction and identity construction in the Marokko.nl web community in the early 2000s was predicated on a 'hard' rather than a fluid sense of identity, on shared history, everyday life challenges and ways of being in the world. The Dutch blog site *GeenStijl* (*BadForm*, founded in 2003) shared an anti-ideological outlook with other liberal sites and offered deadpan and funny comments that seem far removed from the sexist and racist hate speech it spouts today. Although a less serious news medium and far less successful than its contemporary, the North American site *Breitbart*, by the early 2010s, *GeenStijl* was firmly on its way to establishing itself as a Dutch alt-light domain in its turn espousing hard identity politics. The open Facebook page Pietitie which came online in 2013 showed the alarming degree of polarization in the formerly pillarized and consensus-oriented Netherlands.

Summer 2005

In 2005, my co-researcher Robert and I were in the offices of the ethno-marketing bureau Marokko Media in Amsterdam-West. Also present were Gijs, Khalid and Annebregt. Khalid, Said, Redouan and Otman had worked for a competing website (Maroc.nl) which they left to start Yasmina.nl (in 2002) and later to build Marokko.nl. Gijs was their fundraiser and a social activist. Annebregt became editor-in-chief of the news website that Marokko Media wanted to create and on which we were asked to consult (cf. Hermes 2009). The massive success of Marokko Media as a community website depended partly on its early use of 'hard' rather than soft identity definitions. Moroccan-Dutch youngsters, unlike other groups with recent migration histories, had the handicap of not reading Arabic. They had no access to the media in their parents' countries of origin. Also, they preferred keeping a bit of distance between the traditions of their parents (which they respect) and the new lives they were hoping to build for themselves in the Netherlands. Rather than a space defined by long-distance nationalism or religion, it celebrated the flair associated with Moroccan youth culture: epitomized by great fashion sense, especially in shoes (Dibbits 2007).

In retrospect, 'soft identity' definitions describe the Marokko Media team in 2005 much better than the harder, essentialist ones that carry the identity of the web community. Though they identify as Muslims, they talk about enjoying an occasional glass of alcohol, referring to the likewise looser form of religious observance in Turkey at that time (in contrast to today) as a bit of a self-deprecating joke. (The Dutch have a problem distinguishing between ethnic Moroccans and Turks and tend to lump the two groups together). The general sense in 2005 was that right-wing populism would surely fade away again, even if Geert Wilders, the Dutch parliamentarian who made islamophobia his main issue, was felt to be a threat. Of course, at that time, 9/11, the murder of the early populist Dutch politician Pim Fortuyn in 2002 (by an animal-rights activist), the murder of filmmaker Theo Van Gogh in 2004 by a religious fanatic and the terrorist attack on commuter trains in Madrid had left everyone weary of the hatred faced by those suspected of being Muslim. (The London public transport attacks of 2005 were yet to happen).

The dual problem we discussed was that of trolling and training moderators and of how to get Marokko.nl users to be interested in the news. With trained moderators, discussion threads would not need to be closed in their entirety when trolls tried to take over. The news site is meant to further empower and connect urban youth, to free them from a sense of being caught between two worlds in neither of which they fully belong. With the benefit of hindsight, it is interesting to see that *emotion* needed to be controlled: discussions should not become rants or fights; being well informed (the goal of the news project) will counter fear and anger.

To interest Marokko.nl users in the news, we worked with community members who were active as writers in the much-loved 'story corner' of the web community to make a 'telenovela' about a young Moroccan-Dutch journalist-to-be. Even though, eventually, the telenovela died in the offices of the coordinator of one of the three national public television broadcasting channels, it was special to spend time with a group that generally found it difficult to trust white middle-class researchers. Our link to a polytechnic defined us as teachers, which helped us to come across as reliable and as beneficial authorities (even if that was the last thing we wanted to be).

We learned how identity construction is negotiated and with whom. Respect for one's parents was important as well as the careful marking of personal space against outsiders (such as us). Eventually, barriers were thrown up by male moderators and technicians (groups with influence and standing who also hung around the Marokko Media offices where we met with our mostly female group of writers). By the time we started planning the making of pilot episodes, over two years later, the third researcher on our team, Christa, and I encountered overt hostility that we had not had to face before. 'That is not how we do things around here,' I was told in a meeting. Christa was admonished for being ignorant about Ramadan (which she was not).

Alongside doing fieldwork memos, we recorded a series of interviews with the writers. Conventional methods of discourse analysis (interpretative repertoire analysis inspired by Wetherell & Potter 1988 and see chapter 3) delivered three central themes: 'confusion,' 'safety' and 'fight or flight.' All three pertain to identity politics and are a mix of emotion, affect and cognitive reasoning (Hermes & de Graaf 2015). 'Confusion' referred to not fully belonging. Typically, our writers told us that, especially in the summer, when visiting family in Morocco with their parents, they would feel very Dutch, while in the Netherlands, their being Moroccan was always a defining trait. Religion provided a much-needed sense of safety, as did their parents' homes – no matter that those same parents would force them to come on boring family-visiting holidays. 'Fight or flight' describes the frustration that was an undercurrent in all the interviews. Mostly, we found flight in fantasies of travelling and going to faraway places, for instance. Not a likely prospect for most of the young women we worked with. Their parents would object, they said; the necessary funds would not be easy to find. 'Fight' was never voiced directly. References were always indirect, if hard to miss, and alluded to the growing numbers of adherents of Jihad and Islamic terrorism.

When seen in terms of cultural citizenship, the three repertoires need to be contextualized against the high emotions of the much-beloved story corner on the site or the best Moroccan weddings, another well-visited page, that bespeak a pleasure in togetherness and being a community through thick and thin. Clearly, the more emotional the storytelling became, the stronger the sense of connection and bonding. Where politics and Islam are discussed on the website, it became important to bring about the exact opposite and temper emotions running high. Moderators made sure that discussions did not get out of hand, especially when outsiders started trolling but also when exchanges became fights among members. Their go-to solution was to cut discussion threads. It worked. Marokko.nl was kept safe against early outbursts of right-wing populism. A sense of community and belonging was safeguarded by favouring rational argument over emotion when politics and religion were discussed while allowing emotion in matters of the heart: a 20th-century solution of separating the personal and the political on a 21st-century digital platform.

In the interviews, our writers were very critical of the negative representation of Dutch Moroccans in the national media, reminiscent of another 20th-century trope: the sensationalism and commercialism of the mass media, always out to attract viewers over the heads of vulnerable groups. The telenovela they were writing was to redress this situation. However, when the possibility of seeing the series on national broadcast television gained a life of its own, our writers became enthralled with the machinery and the magic of the mass media. Their initial disdain and criticism of national broadcast media receded and became much milder, the main character of the series their hero. He had been devised as a journalist-to-be, an ambitious truth-seeker whose blog, called *Faysal's News*, was the way in which the series would address social and political topics that were in the news. 'The thing with Faysal is that he has aspirations. And that is what I see in myself. I would not mind becoming a journalist' (Marukh -a pseudonym- was one of the writers, winter 2008/9).

Tracing cultural citizenship in this project pointed to a set of paradoxical feelings. Our informants had a strongly felt need to have a taken-for-granted social presence and for being represented in the media, literally, to be visible in the public sphere without fear of being vilified. In our fieldwork notes and interviews, there are numerous references to the villainous mass media and to celebrities who despite everything manage to survive there. One favourite example is of the comedian and actor Najib Amhali, whose jokes poke fun at Dutch Islamophobia. 'There isn't a Moroccan home in the Netherlands where Najib Amhali would not be welcome,' said Achraf, another of our writers. However critical of legacy media, our writers also, paradoxically, wanted to be part of them. Repertoire analysis allowed us to chart their contradictory emotions. How feeling vulnerable made the Marokko.nl writers and personnel angry and in need of recognition at the same time, caught between the worlds of their parents and their own, between ambitions and imagined solutions on the one hand and first- and second-hand everyday experience of discrimination on the other, between trust and distrust.

The really amazing feat, in retrospect, is how well Marokko.nl managed to contain hate speech, trolling and discrimination and redirected emotion among users. Its managers mobilized the community to deliver moderators (hand-picked community members who spent much time online and were felt to be dependable), and these moderators kept cool heads. Even though populism in politics was gaining strength, Marokko.nl literally remained a safe space from which we too would disappear. As older, white, middle-class professionals, we were less and less welcome. We witnessed how religious rules were observed more and more strictly, while anger and distrust gained ground. After 2010, we lost contact.

Autumn 2009 (Intermezzo)

Our writers' fictional *Faysal's News* was inspired by what was happening in the actual online world. Blogging, vlogging and Twitter had become new forms of public exchange. Instead of the older, inward-looking web communities, these sites/platforms operated completely differently. In due course, there would be blog sites not unlike *Faysal's News* that credit recent migrant histories (such as *Wij blijven hier* – We Are Staying Here – or *Republiek Allochtonië*). The real eye-catchers however are the sites that initially simply intended to provoke. They became forerunners of the misogynistic hatred, painful joking and aggression that are a central part of Gamergate (Mortensen 2018) and sites such as Reddit, 4Chan and 8Chan, where, for instance, the 2019 Christchurch killer left his ultra-right-wing and racist manifesto (Massanari 2017). Asserting themselves against the political correctness and 'ideologism' of a site announced by the Dutch socialist broadcasting organization called *the Joop* (the Joe), a band of unlikely co-conspirators established *the Jaap* (the Jake). Coming from very different parts of the political spectrum, *the Jaap* intended to promote open discussion beyond fixed political or identity positions.

Looking back, its deputy editor-in-chief, Linda Duits, a self-identified feminist, academic and influencer, emphasized in an interview that making *the Jaap* was fun (Ven 2019). It undercut an overly serious approach to the world. 'The idea was to be a platform where everybody was welcome to discuss whatever issue. That was the then democratic notion of the internet: as a place where people meet to exchange ideas, not to confirm one another' (Ven, idem). As a result, *the Jaap* had headers such as 'Let's discuss n******,'[1] or 'Black Pete needs to be abolished' (Ven, idem). After three years, the site was renamed *the Post Online*, still headed by Bert Brusse, its initial editor-in-chief. Gone, though, is the sentiment that 'public debate needs to be rescued' (Duits in Ven 2019); all optimism has disappeared. The platform has hardened and embraced right-wing populism. Duits can count on being called 'the driver of the totalitarian gender nag-train' or a 'spreader of propaganda.' Ven (2019) concludes that despite the initial good intentions, instead of online debate, we now have echo chambers. Algorithms reward harsh language and strong statements. Debaters are forced back onto their own patch. Brusse (in Ven's reconstruction) says: 'It isn't as if we used to agree, but we laughed about it. Now it is war online. The gap is a very deep one.' Duits would find it difficult today to work with her then colleagues. From libertarians, they turned into right-wing ideologues whose sites feed on anger and outrage, resentment and conspiracy theory.

While it is tempting to understand the development of social media platforms as intrinsically linked to populism, it is doubtful whether this is actually true. Making *the Jaap* bespeaks the privilege of education and journalistic savvy that will spread to Twitter, a platform that small elite groups of public intellectuals initially shared with teenagers making a sport of tweeting about the most mundane of everyday activities. The algorithms driving social media platforms, however, reward intensity. Rather than zooming out or contextualizing, suggestions for further browsing (Bahara et al. 2019) point users 'down the rabbit hole,' as insiders call it. The alt-right and alt-light have profited most from this logic of amplification. Venting on Twitter, they have effectively changed public debate (Boeschoten & Ven 2019).

2013

In the mid-2000s, Khalid, one of the Marokko Media directors, was joking when he said in the period just before Sinterklaas (5 December): 'I can't believe how the Surinamese allow the Dutch to persist with their Black Petes. We would not stand for it.' Other 'outsiders' too, such as the writer David Sedaris (2002), have commented on the oddity, to put it mildly, of having a Santa-type figure with black 'helpers.' In 2009, *the Jaap* felt that the suggestion to abolish Black Pete was a perfect challenge to get a heated discussion going. By 2013, the figure Pete divides Dutch society.

Anti-Black Pete activism in 2011 is met with harsh police counter-measures including the arrest of two protesters wearing a t-shirt that says 'Black Pete is racism.' It was the first of many 'incidents' at the yearly Sinterklaas events, culminating in 90 arrests for rioting in Gouda in 2014, with ongoing riots, incidents and threatening situations to this day. While it can be argued that the riots involve activists, Pietitie in 2013 was 'liked' by almost two million ordinary Dutch people. Pietitie is a Facebook group for everybody who feels that Pete has to stay exactly the way he is: including the black hair, the blackface, the thick lips and the general silliness.

Comparing two studies of pro-Pete protest that appeared almost simultaneously but are based on different sets of material, it appears that it is not so much emotion and uncouth language in and of itself that defines social media practices. The much more remarkable thing is that apparently on Facebook you can speak your heart. Whatever you say will have no consequences. It is a domain of entitlement, a populist dream space and a prime example of appropriation of the public sphere for and by 'ordinary people.' Turner (2010) called this 'the demotic' turn. This is where any ordinary person can say what they like ('demos' means people), a domain of free speech where sentiments can be voiced, where spelling does not matter but feelings and allegiances do. It is a fully new public logic in a new type of (semi)public sphere.

Aware of Pietitie and reactions against 'Black Pete is racism' activism, Wekker (2016) goes back to the (mostly anonymous) hate mail sent to two museum curators in 2008 who were preparing an exhibition for the Dutch Van Abbe museum. When a Dutch populist newspaper wrote about their plans for a protest march against Black Pete, the curators were bombarded with messages. Going through these, Wekker found ten themes that share a remarkable overlap with themes Van Dijk found in 1998 in similar protests against criticism of 'Zwarte Piet,' well before 'Black Pete is racism' – activism and well before social media platforms were set up and became a new public sphere (Dijk quoted in Wekker 2016: 158). Even more remarkable is that a second 2016 study by Sacha Hilhorst and myself found the same themes again in the messages posted on the Facebook Pietitie page in 2013, five years later. Wekker identifies aggression and deep feelings of hurt. Innocence is a recurring term, as well as fear that a national tradition will be lost (2016: 148). Hilhorst and Hermes (2016: 218) point to the suffering to which the mostly White Dutch Pietitie commenters bear witness in the roughly 1,000 posts they look at. A key phrase in the Pietitie material is 'children's festivity' (kinderfeest), invoked to defend a sense of the loss that children would experience if they were denied the wonder of the Sinterklaas tradition (as if this fully depended on Pete's being in blackface). Other responses focused on the alleged racism of Zwarte Piet as a total misconception (Black Pete is fun!) and the ingratitude of the accusers (with the implication that they all come from migrant backgrounds).

Wekker's analysis is built around her central concept of 'white innocence,' which refers to the way Dutch society refuses to take responsibility for its colonial history and for racist practices and references. Literally, innocence is an important theme for those who support Pietititie and link it to 'the innocence of children' (2016: 223/4) with whom they identify. Humour too is in evidence in both sets of material as a means to vent strong feelings while always also being able to claim you were 'only joking.' Online humour in pro-Pete protests as in the right-wing blogs is the property of what is known as 'geek culture' and the alt-right (as also evidenced in trolling and meme culture). The most outrageous statements, attacks and visuals are defended as 'just for the lulz' (for a laugh; Milner 2013; Phillips 2012). To take offence means not getting the joke and not having a sense of humour – exactly what

Wekker is accused of by academic colleagues when she suggests that Black Pete is an expression of racism (2016: 147). Not only does humour make possible a 'having your cake and eating it logic' in the Pietitie material and in the hate mail sent to the curators, but it is also used in a Domino or avalanche logic. First Pete has to go, then the next thing, and before you know it, it is Sharia – and clearly no longer a joke.

Both 2016 studies offer analyses of textual materials from a broad contextual and historical awareness. Both follow the emotional intensity of their material. Both reference the increased right-wing populist presence that is making nationalism acceptable again, as manifested in the forceful exclusion of the feelings of non-white Dutch. The passionate defence of national heritage appears to be built on a sense of (white) suffering, which excludes the possibility of non-white suffering. Discourse analysis here becomes part of an ethnographic effort. Wekker is an anthropologist; Hilhorst and Hermes write from a media-ethnographic perspective. It allows for recognizing and understanding affect – and the incredible speed at which unease turns into a complaint, (the appropriation of) victimhood and self-righteous and short-sighted arguments. The located phenomenon of right-wing nationalism Ahmed studied in 2004 has become a pervasive presence today. Ahmed's argument that emotion should be studied as a cultural practice that values some bodies and devalues others holds more than ever.

Anger and outrage define the politics of both Pietitie and the Kick Out Black Pete group. The wounded feelings of Black Pete supporters mirror the feelings of Moroccan youth ten years earlier, who did not feel recognized either. Pete supporters' use of humour suggests they speak from an underdog position. Mostly white Dutch, they belong to a majority group who feel vulnerable and talked down to and appear unaware of their own social power or privilege. Black Pete provides an issue that makes for a political bond rather than a previous identity or shared agenda.

Social media afford this easy bonding over (single) issues as a fleeting kind of commitment. This is very alike the sense of connection and cultural citizenship long afforded by popular culture, were it not for the intensity, the shifting of alliances within groups and the overriding negative, angry tone. Tone, intensity and pressure to declare your allegiance, moreover, are translated back into legacy media. As a result, public debate and the public sphere are changing. In the Netherlands, football chat shows on commercial television have hosts that profess their disgust with political correctness and who take great pleasure in what have been termed homophobic, racist and sexist remarks (Dongen 2017; Shownieuws 2018). Here too humour is the tool of choice for disgruntled speakers who feel disowned and sold short by both globalization and all the emancipatory movements of the 20th century. Never entirely serious, joking gives free rein to anger while it disassociates the speaker from bad intent.

Humourous non-politically aligned disgruntled letting off steam paved the way for a far more serious group of right-wing populists who have entered politics successfully. Today's hybrid mix of social and legacy media presents a new type of public sphere. It appears a more egalitarian space that is open to the voices of ordinary people. Its new elites however support exclusive rather than inclusive identity politics and new types of language and codes of conduct that threaten democratic openness and solidarity and their basic requirements of a minimum level of empathy and decency. Meanwhile, a majority of Dutch are comfortable with an updated version of Pete. Stores are ordering de-stereotyped wrapping paper. Petes in blackface are on the way out, apart from a small number of provocations by pranksters from nativist nationalist radical groups.

Storytelling beyond the fictional

In the non-fiction realm of today's media world, cultural citizenship is also easily found. As in the discussion of fiction, non-fiction content consists of cultural forms, heroes and narratives that give access to the concerns, hopes and dreams that bind groups of people. In today's world, these come with a chilling amount of anger, hatred and suspicion that infects media practices, platforms and texts that used to be reserved for the information, discussion, background and news that sustain democracy. Tracing cultural citizenship online allows us to understand that audiences were always publics: situated meaning makers who establish common culture by taking up issues while making use of popular media, whether commercial, state-financed or self-made. Digital media forms offer new ways and means to understand this (Marres et al. 2018). Now that popular media practices are losing much of the playfulness and openness they had three decades ago, there is an ongoing need to examine what appears 'simple' and is taken for granted. Ethnographic sensitivity and connecting everyday meaning making across distributed sites, online and 'IRL,' are more important than ever.

As much as early cultural studies audience research 'rescued' popular culture and its users from blanket disdain, today's right- and left-wing populism needs a counterweight. The search for hidden common ground in digital and non-digital encounters might well be the goal of cultural scholarship today. Key tools are to be found in scheduled and unscheduled 'remote ethnography' (Postill 2017). They can be participant observation, interviewing, investigative journalism or, indeed, audience ethnography. In addition, we need ongoing commitment to what Ang calls 'cultural intelligence' (2011: 789) as a counterforce against the messiness and complexities of the problems societies face today and against our tendency to oversimplify when we want to gain oversight. We need sensitivity and reflexivity, key qualities in ethnographic work (Hine 2017: 26), to bring affect and emotion into the textual domain that research is.

Ultimately, as media ethnographers, media and cultural scholars engage in 'the art of the possible' (Ang 2016: 36) by forging sincere connections with the everyday life worlds of others, regardless of their political affiliations. Given the severity of societal polarization, advocacy and commitment to singular voices may, for now, not be the best choice. All media audience research can and should help everyday conversation and debate to move beyond their current entrenched positions. Ideally placed to map and chart feelings, positions and identities, ethnographically inspired work will unlock options that open up spaces for moving forward – even if it is never clear whether forward is the right direction or one that may be even more frightening than the direction in which we are moving now.

Note

1 n-word used in original.

CONCLUSION

Democracy II: *(Searching for)* cultural citizenship as *(attending to)* worldbuilding in action

Popular culture has something to tell us. Writing about the neo-conservative and neoliberal reality of the global media industries, Larry Grossberg has poignantly asked what we can do 'to get out of this place' (Grossberg 2014). Across the chapters of this book, I have sought to use cultural citizenship as a tool to get a glimpse of such a route. The everyday use, discussion and research of popular culture – the good and the bad, the happy and the confrontational – point us to the relevance of cultural criticism and our responsibility as producers, consumers and researchers of media. 'Tooling' cultural citizenship is to weigh it towards practical use. That is, to use it for emancipatory and de-polarizing goals, for forms of empowerment that, one way or another, use (popular) culture to engage in discussion about what concerns us. Whether that is at all possible is up to the reader. Personally, I feel heartened by Henry Jenkins, Gabriel Peters-Lazaro and Sangita Shresthova's (2020) *Popular culture and the civic imagination*. It does not shy away from pain and hurt *and* offers its counterpart: the equally unbreakable spirit of fans, activists and television writers to create space for alternative imagining of the world and of the future. The case studies presented across this book, however, follow a different route – the flow of mainstream media.

Popular culture tells us something – if only we listen. Reactions to popular television drama ranging from middle to highbrow (in so far as popular culture allows for that category); concerns about children's television and its educative potential; or discussion of competition reality television on social media platforms: it is my hope that using cultural citizenship as a concept creates that little bit of distance that allows for better listening. First and foremost, this requires a measure of emotional intelligence that can only be built on respect for how we are all ruled by affect and by reasoning and engage them in making sense of the world. In his beautiful and moving elegy for Stuart Hall, David Scott (2017) speaks of receptive generosity. He comes to this concept in trying to grasp Hall's unique 'voice' in left-progressive politics and in cultural studies.

'Listening,' he argues, is the hermeneutic attitude, par excellence, of intellectual friendship. And what listening enables is the 'work of clarification' (2017: 17). Only by listening can we make the world understandable. Scott's argument is a philosophical one. It seeks to understand and cherish Hall's enduring presence in intellectual work. I feel allowed to extend his argument to the kind of audience studies that are a key part of cultural studies work, as it was nourished by Hall himself and those he worked with. Listening is what organic intellectuals who have been touched by Hall's essays and co-authored work know they can bring to the world: to understand and translate and smoothen the painful impact of colliding traditions (cf. Scott 2017: 132/3). The only way to do that well is to recognize and move beyond the conceit of omniscient Western knowledge production that thinks of itself as context-free, tradition-free and having unfettered access to the contexts of others.

For Scott, this entails the translation of whole discursive contexts rather than mere words of concepts. It seems to me that the work that cultural citizenship as a concept can do is exactly this: to understand how we form communities through inclusion and exclusion, in our own storytelling, and in our identifications, by representing all of this through the ongoing storytelling that is not owned by individuals. It means that engaging with comments about a tv character and actor, such as Skyler White/Anna Gunn, is an exercise in seeing traditions as they instruct, inspire, unfold and change in meeting with other traditions. By presenting this form as disjunctive yet collective storytelling, listening is encouraged and hopefully learned. Rather than stay with individual opinions, overrated as they are, we can find the pain and the pleasure where worlds come together.

Listening well is hard. In addition to openness to traditions, good listening requires openness to feelings and emotions and to colliding worlds and world views. I have tried to make a case for how even online comments (whether on Reddit or YouTube or Facebook) allow for such uneasy 'meetings.' Although a method that requires extensive contextualization, virtual ethnography surely provides a route to the kind of knowledge that can become a meeting space. Over time that may lead to new infrastructure which action research sees as a goal in its own right. Likewise, thinking about cultural citizenship by listening well benefits from understanding how analysis of specific texts may provide entry points for discussion. Using texts well can be an exercise in identifying what is of relevance to others. How characters, actors and presenters become lenses to do so. How they are the beginning and the relays through which popular culture provides us with stories that spawn further storytelling.

Everyday storytelling is inspired by the fictional (and non-fictional) characters that popular culture consists of. Stories are what goes around in what Du Gay and Hall (1997) called 'the circuit of culture,' moving from media platforms to everyday life and back again. Professionally made media texts are used and rewritten in everyday storytelling which in turn will feed new 'amateur,' professional and institutional media making. On platforms like YouTube and TikTok, the difference between amateur and professional media making is less and less easy to make. YouTube is watched like 'television,' whether it is gameplay (Golob 2021) or vlogs by influencers. Shared everyday storytelling cuts across different formats, genres and platforms. All of them, whether fiction or non-fiction, are popular (media) culture. Cultural citizenship can be used as a tool to find out what these stories are about. Whether in interviews, online comments or participant observation, we tend to get snippets, individual pieces of larger puzzles that can be reconstructed. As stories mix and mingle, we never know whether these reconstructed puzzles are our work of bricolage or a faithful rendering of what goes on in the world out there. It does not matter. Stories mingle and recombine and change continuously in the 'circuit of culture.' Collecting stories, plural, therefore can tell us as researchers what people feel they need to commit to in order to belong, what they fear and what they hope for.

Listening ... and then what? The stories collected in this book could have come from different parts of popular culture, from sports, quiz shows or gaming. I do not think I would find a very different kind of story when it comes to how our sexed, gendered and raced bodies become meaningful. In slightly different ways, these other texts and genres are also about identity, power, affect, culpability, innocence, confusion, storytelling, responsibility and democracy. Sports programming is a good example. One by one, women presenters are entering the fray of presenting them and their presence is allowing for new interpersonal on-screen dynamics. This is great but does not change the fact that the male bonding in sports chat can still turn into gay-bashing or lampooning of me-too activism at the flick of a wrist. This is the other side surely to the friendly face of patriarchy that is sold in *The Mentalist*. It also seems directly related to all the anger directed at women for stopping men in their mission (Skyler White in *Breaking Bad*) or stealing their legacy roles (the thirteenth Doctor Who).

Another objection to 'listening better' could be that it discounts that we are now subjected to what Jodi Dean calls 'communicative capitalism.' She argues that capitalism and democracy have converged. The values heralded as central to democracy take material form in networked communication technologies. 'Ideals of access, voice, inclusion, discussion and participation' are made to fit the logic of global telecommunications (Dean 2020: 33). Voice, engagement and participation, as a result, are captured and commodified in affective networks of mass personalized media (idem: 34). Dean agrees that affect is of crucial importance and that the lifeworld can no longer be understood as a unified domain. We differ in that I believe that paying attention to ongoing everyday storytelling will give us access *beyond* our current collective fascination with ourselves.

I take from Dean's work that there are no easy routes to a better democracy. True, popular culture is not a domain to have much faith in from the perspective of Marxist-feminist critique. I continue to believe, though, that citizenship is a process of ongoing discussion and negotiation. With Saha (2021: 13) or Jenkins et al. (2020: 8–11), I continue to lean on Stuart Hall's argument that popular media are an arena in which hegemony is never fixed but is struggled over. If we manage to take the *discussion* that popular culture gives rise to seriously, we do not need to deny its drawbacks. To wit, popular texts reinforce blatant stereotypes and offer forms of 'empowerment' that Vergès (2019) rightly denounces for being based on the exploitation and discrimination of others along lines of race and gender. Using discussion of popular culture does not mean one is not taking one's citizen responsibility seriously (as an individual or a feminist researcher): to stand up against e-bile, hating strangers, the spreading of fear and paranoid denouncement of national public broadcasting institutions or coercive gender definitions. I would always want to be critical of humour that is based on othering and intends to hurt. Citizenship implies the ethical requirement to take care of each other and the world. Further polarization does not serve these goals.

Scott suggests receptive generosity, that is: to listen with care and attention. Amia Srinivasan suggests that as feminists, we try to be realists rather than saints (2021: 171). Nina Simon (2016), an American museum director, unabashedly tells us we need to and can make connections. Relevance is not in the value of your own project, work, idea or space but in connecting with the lifeworlds of others. Only by connecting can meaning be 'unlocked' and will professional practice in the creative industries (or anywhere really) gain access to the worlds of others. Relevance, inspiration and exchange can then follow. What, then, does cultural citizenship mean for us as researchers, teachers, creative professionals, producers and consumers of media, feminists, fans or non-fans of regency romance ... ? The challenge, in the end, is to understand cultural citizenship as not just a tool but as a practice. When we find ways to practice patient listening, receptivity, generosity and kindness in bearing with the views of others, personal experience and everyday talk can be the kind of input that helps 'worldbuilding' through cultural citizenship.

World-Building in Action: Cultural Citizenship as Tool and Practice. Although often angry, upset and fearful, commenting on popular culture and using popular culture to comment on the world can also be hopeful and invested in change. In fan communities, that can become more than utopian daydreaming. Henry Jenkins and colleagues have the right of it when they see popular culture as feeding the civic imagination and as fed by creative social change (Jenkins et al. 2020). *RuPaul's Drag Race* fans (in chapter 8) did manage to shift the show's policy to become (slightly) more welcoming to trans women. Recognizing that there is always a force and voices that work towards change connects to the practice-based research I do. It is work with professionals, aimed at ameliorating and innovating communicative and social practices together with stakeholders (Kommer & Hermes 2022). I want to turn to the possible practical use of attending to cultural citizenship in practice-based (and practice-oriented) research by using the popular to make contact, exchange views and feelings and (re)build expectations.

The founding intuition is a simple one: as the educated, privileged people they are, professionals need to find planes of equality that assure others of a voice and respect for who they want to be (or identify or present as). Once we find those, we need to listen respectfully and reciprocally. That is to say, we need to engage in conversation on the terms of others rather than our own. However easy that sounds, it is difficult because it is not what we are used to doing. Or, indeed, what others will trust us, as researchers and professionals, to do, as Angela McRobbie pointed out a long time ago (McRobbie 1982). Hence the turn to popular culture: whether sports, popular music, television or romance novels, these are fields that others than the implied readers of this book feel as confident in as we do (or don't as the case may be but then *we* have a problem rather than those we want to come into contact with).

Giving up privilege, even in so minuscule a way as not being in control of what is talked about, is not easy. There are major rewards though. Engaging in conversation about popular texts is good fun and much easier than talking, e.g., about politics, as Nina Eliasoph has documented so beautifully in *Avoiding politics* (1998). The low status of popular culture makes bonding a relatively simple search for where interests overlap. Afterwards, puzzling through the stories people have to tell, even when they were angry and lashed out, is always a lovely challenge. What terms and expressions were used? What views of the world were implicitly and explicitly shared? It can, even in the case of some of the bleaker examples in this book, be a hopeful exercise. For those who are open to looking for it, there is more that is hopeful than one tends to think in dark times.

Rebecca Solnit writes about hope as an 'embrace of the unknown and unknowable' (2016: xiv). Carl DiSalvo, like me, has read about all the hope-inspiring experiments, actions and initiatives that she offers as proof. DiSalvo offers his own when pointing to how, as a design researcher, he can tilt his privilege towards an open, co-owned practice that puts what he calls 'experimental civics' in action (DiSalvo 2022). His wish is for practice-based research to be grounded in collaboration with communities. Not only is such work collective and collaborative, but it is also a form of reflective practice that counters 'those stories that mythologize the individual maker and valorize the presumed expertise of the professional designer' (2022: 7).

Inviting others into the projects and spaces that you think are relevant (as they are to you yourself) is entirely doable, Nina Simon feels – as long as you get 'to know their dreams, points of pride and fears' (2017: 99). That also happens to be the core of cultural citizenship. Nina Simon wants us to find representatives of the communities we wish to be relevant to and speak with them to learn about the community's experiences. She wants us to spend time with these communities and get to know them (idem). I want to suggest: why not also use the easy means of talking about cultural citizenship while not letting yourself be discouraged by the negativity that, at first, may come your way? Like Nina Simon, I am convinced that 'relevance is the key to a locked room where meaning lives. We just have to find the right keys, the right doors and the humility and courage to open them' (Simon 2017: 23). She adds that the rooms behind the door of relevance of course also need to be open to connection and dialogue. They may (have to) change given the experience of new others who have found their way in. Inviting 'new' others in and changing practices of representation can become just a little easier and smoother when we are aware of the value of cultural citizenship and its implicit and implied cultural and identity-related rights and responsibilities.

Context is (the) key. Beyond recognizing pre-conceived notions and practicing self-reflexivity and generous listening, it is important to contextualize well what others had to say. I like what following up on contradictions and paradoxes can do for you when you are trying to understand what it is that others are telling you. I am happy to read in David Scott's letters to Stuart Hall that he does too. Following through on paradoxes for Scott, as a matter of course, culminates in 'unlearning the conceit of omniscient privilege' (Scott 2017: 139). I am now quoting it for the second time because it so beautifully captures what 'listening well' means and therefore what is entailed in trying to reconstruct cultural citizenship. By its nature, the enormous project of 'listening well' is never a thing any one of us can own. Through the wide-angle lens of popular culture, identifying cultural citizenship is always more than any one researcher or research project can do, whether in time or in place. It is an ever-changing, ongoing set of interlocking practices that span the globe. It is the key part of the ongoing project of working on finding connections.

When one goes looking for cultural citizenship, we will, of necessity, do so in specific places. But please do not do it with overly specific goals. Cherish the surprise that is inevitably there in empirical research. 'Focus' and narrowly defined research questions are not your friend in this type of qualitative research. Any type of project that involves communities or worldbuilding will benefit from an open approach and listening as its primary methodological tool. When using popular culture and trying to find cultural citizenship, these are my humble suggestions. *Stories will start suggesting themselves.* Whether a project is aimed at understanding, appreciation, critique or as a counterpart to a design intervention, research-for-worldbuilding becomes valuable in the well-documented storytelling it allows for. As you will be aware, stories have unexpected twists and turns. All the good ones do.

I hope to have tempted readers not to mistake filter bubbles for real enclosures. Instead of defining target audiences and identifying others, I hope to have shown that it makes more sense to identify the kind of *stories* that we have at our disposal and that are shared more broadly than we think. I know that today these stories may tend towards bitterness and suspicion more than hope or solidarity. Neoliberal ideology has left a deep mark when measured against how isolation and a fend-for-yourself mentality have become common sense. Cultural citizenship though can help open up the 'new communicative spaces' that Reason and Bradbury (2006: xxii) and others quoted above believe in. Refuse, as Solnit writes, to bow to cynicism! Despair can become a habit, a reflex. Hope, she concludes, is not 'a prize or a gift but something you earn through study, through resisting the ease of despair and through digging tunnels, cutting windows, opening doors or finding the people who do these things' (2016: 142). It means accepting that, in order to do so, you also need to take the fear, the anger, the pleasures and the dignity of others into account. Listening – well and generously – and committing to understanding imperfect, unforced and ongoing conversations about popular culture is an investment in democracy. Without it, democracy remains a hollow shell.

REFERENCES

Ahmed, S. (1999). Phantasies of becoming the other. *European Journal of Cultural Studies, 2*(1), 47–63. 10.1177/136754949900200103.
Ahmed, S. (2003). In the name of love. *Borderlands E-Journal: New Spaces in the Humanities, 2*(3), 1–41.
Ahmed, S. (2004). Affective economies. *Social Text, 22*(2), 117–139.
Ahmed, S. (2004). *The cultural politics of emotion*. Edinburgh: Edinburgh University Press.
Ahmed, S. (2006). *Queer phenomenology*. London: Routledge.
Ahmed, S. (2010). Killing Joy: Feminism and the history of happiness. *Signs, 35*(3), 571–594.
Ahmed, S. (2014). The politics of good feeling. *Critical Race & Whiteness Studies, 10*(2), 1–19.
Aitkenhead, D. (2018). RuPaul: "Drag is a big f-you to male-dominated culture"' *The Guardian*. https://www.theguardian.com/tv-and-radio/2018/mar/03/rupaul-drag-race-big-f-you-to-male-dominated-culture.
Allen, K. & Mendick, H. (2013). Young people's uses of celebrity: Class, gender and 'improper' celebrity. *Discourse: Studies in the Cultural Politics of Education, 34*(1), 77–93, Doi: 10.1080/01596306.2012.698865.
Althusser, L. (1971). *Lenin and philosophy and other essays*. New York, NY: Monthly Review Press.
Andeweg, A. (2017). Novels as social media: How literature helped shape notions of sexual liberation. *Sexuality & Culture, 21*, 343–361. 10.1007/s12119-017-9419-9.
Andrejevic, M. (2004). *Reality TV: The work of being watched*. Lanham, MD: Rowman and Littlefield.
Ang, I. (1985). *Watching Dallas. Soap opera and the melodramatic imagination*. London: Methuen.
Ang, I. (2011). Navigating complexity: From cultural critique to cultural intelligence. *Continuum, 25*(6), 779–794.
Ang, I. (2016). Stuart Hall and the tension between academic and intellectual work. *International Journal of Cultural Studies, 19*(1), 29–41.

Aronoff, J. (2017). Deconstructing Clara Who. A female doctor made possible by an impossible girl. *International Journal of TV Serial Narratives*, *3*(2), 17–30.

Aspestrand Bjerke, T., & Rones, N. (2017). The fine line between funny and offensive humour in a total institution. An ethnographic study of joking relationships among army soldiers. *Res Militaris*, *7*(2), 1–23. http://resmilitaris.net.

Aufderheide, P. (Ed.). (1993). *Media literacy: A report of the national leadership conference on media literacy*. Aspen, CO: Aspen Institute.

Bacon-Smith, C. (1992). *Enterprising women: Television fandom and the creation of popular myth*. Philadelphia, PA: University of Pennsylvania Press.

Bahara, B., Kranenberg, A., & Tokmetzis, D. (2019). Hoe YouTube rechtse radicalisering in de hand werkt. Volkskrant 19 februari, https://www.volkskrant.nl/kijkverder/v/2019/hoe-youtube-rechtse-radicalisering-in-de-hand-werkt/.

Bastos, M.T., & Mercea, D. (2019). The Brexit botnet and user-generated hyperpartisan news. *Social Science Computer Review*, *37*(1), 38–54. 10.1177/0894439317734157.

Baym, N. (2000). *Tune in, log on*. London: Sage

Benhabib, S. (1992). *Situating the self*. New York, NY: Routledge.

Bennett, J., & Strange, N. (Eds.). (2011). *Television as digital media*. Durham, IL: Duke University Press.

Bennett, T. (1982). James Bond as popular hero, Unit 21. In T. Bennett et al. (Eds.), *Popular culture. Politics, ideology and popular culture 2. Block 5 units 21, 22 & 23* (pp. 5–33). Milton Keynes: Open University Press.

Bennett, T. (1986). The politics of 'the popular' and popular culture. In T. Bennett, C. Mercer & J. Woolacott (Eds.), *Popular culture and social relations* (pp. 6–21). London: Open University Press.

Bennett, T. (1995). *The birth of the museum: History, theory, politics*. New York, NY: Routledge.

Bennett, T. (1998). *Culture: A reformer's science*. London: Sage.

Bennett, T. (2003). Culture and governmentality. In J.Z. Bratich, J. Packer & C. McCarthy (Eds.), *Foucault, cultural studies, and governmentality* (pp. 47–63). Albany, NY: Suny Press.

Berg, A. van den (2010). De moraal van het verhaal: Televisie kijken is slecht, voorlezen is goed. Een discoursanalyse over het nog altijd bestaande negatieve vertoog van ouders met jonge kinderen over televisie versus het boek (The story's moral: Watching television is bad, reading to children is good). Master's thesis, Mediastudies, Universiteit van Amsterdam, available at: http://scriptiesonline.uba.uva.nl/ (Last accessed August 2012).

Berns, F.G.P. (2014). For your next drag challenge, you must do something: Playfulness without rules. In J. Deams (Ed.), *The makeup of Rupaul's drag race* (pp. 88–105). McFarland & Company, Inc., Publishers.

Blasko, D. G., Kazmerski, V. A., & Dawood, S. S. (2021). Saying what you don't mean: A cross-cultural study of perceptions of sarcasm. *Canadian Journal of Experimental Psychology/Revue canadienne de psychologie expérimentale*, *75*(2), 114.

Blevins, J., & Wood, D. (Eds.). (2014). *The methods of Breaking Bad: Essays on narrative, character and ethics*. Jefferson, NC: McFarland.

Blodgett, B., & Salter, A. (2018). Ghostbusters is for boys: Understanding geek masculinity's role in the alt-right. *Communication Culture & Critique*, *11*(1), 133–146.

Bochner, A.P., & Ellis, C. (1996). Taking ethnography into the twenty-first century: Introduction. *Journal of Contemporary Ethnography*, 25(1), 3–5.
Boer-Dirks, E. (1993). Nieuw licht op Zwarte Piet. Een kunsthistorisch antwoord op de vraag naar de herkomst van Zwarte Piet. *Volkskundig Bulletin*, 19, 1–35.
Boeschoten, T., & Ven, C.v.d. (2019). Je gaat me toch niet als genuanceerd wegzetten hè?, *Groene Amsterdammer* 35. https://www.groene.nl/artikel/je-gaat-me-toch-niet-als-genuanceerd-wegzetten-he.
Bonner, F. (2003). *Ordinary television*. London: Sage.
Booth, P. (2014). Periodising *Dr Who*. *Science Fiction Film and Television*, 7(2), 195–215.
Borghuis, P., Graaf, C.D., & Hermes, J. (2010). Digital storytelling in sex education. Avoiding the pitfalls of building a 'haram' website. *Seminar.net. Media, Technology & Lifelong Learning*, 6(2), 234–247.
Bouchallikht, K. (2018). Vrouwen zijn slachtoffer van sexy heldinnen. (Women are the victims of sexy heroines). *De Correspondent*, 2 oktober 2018, online. https://decorrespondent.nl/8466/vrouwen-zijn-slachtoffer-van-sexy-heldinnen/3302403294168-9fb468fa.
Bouchallikht, K. , & Papaikonomou, Z. (2022). *De inclusiemarathon*. Amsterdam: Amsterdam University Press.
Bourdieu, P. (1980). The production of belief: Contribution to an economy of symbolic goods. *Media, Culture & Society*, 2(3), 261–293. 10.1177/016344378000200305.
Boyd, D. (2015). *It's Complicated: The Social Lives of Networked Teens*. New Haven, CT: Yale University Press.
Boyd, D. (2018). https://points.datasociety.net/you-think-you-want-media-literacy-do-you-7cad6af18ec2 (March 9, 2018, danah boyd addresses educators at SXSW EDU conference).
Bradbury, H., & Reason, P. (2003). Action research. *Qualitative Social Work*, 2(2), 155–175.
Breek, P., Eshuis, J., & Hermes, J. (2021). Sharing feelings about neighborhood transformation on Facebook: Online affective placemaking in Amsterdam-Noord. *Journal of Urbanism: International Research on Placemaking and Urban Sustainability*, 14(2), 145–164. DOI: 10.1080/17549175.2020.1814390.
Britton, P.D. (2011). *TARDISbound: Navigating the universes of Doctor Who*. London: I.B. Tauris.
Bruijn, T.D. (2022). Urgentie van mediaopvoeding nauwelijks voelbaar bij ouders van kinderen van 0 t/m 6 jaar. Netwerk Mediawijsheid, https://netwerkmediawijsheid.nl/iene-miene-media-2022/ (last seen 29-3-2022) (Parents of 0-6 year olds feel little urgency for media education).
Brunsdon, C. (1987). Structures of anxiety. *Screen*, 39(3), 223–243.
Bucher, T., & Helmond, A. (2018). The affordances of social media platforms. In J. Burgess, A. Marwick & T. Poell (Eds.), *The SAGE handbook of social media* (pp. 233–253). London: Sage.
Buckingham, D. (1993). *Children talking television: The making of television literacy*. London: The Falmer Press.
Buckingham, D. (2000). *The making of citizens: Young people, news and politics*. London: Routledge.
Buckingham, D. (2005). The media literacy of children and young people: A review of the literature on behalf of Ofcom. London: Centre for the Study of Children,

Youth and Media Institute of Education, available at: http://eprints.ioe.ac.uk/145/1/Buckinghammedialiteracy.pdf (accessed September 2012).

Buonanno, M. (Ed.). (2017). *Television antiheroines. Women behaving badly in crime and prison drama.* Bristol: Intellect.

Burgess, J. (2006). Hearing ordinary voices: Cultural studies, vernacular creativity and digital storytelling. *Continuum, 20*(2), 201–214.

Burgess, J., & Green, J. (2009). *YouTube: Online video and participatory culture.* Cambridge: Polity Press.

Burke, P. (2009). *Popular culture in early modern Europe.* London: Ashgate.

Butler, D., Ed. (2007). *Time and relative dissertations in space: Critical perspectives on 'Doctor Who'.* Manchester: Manchester University Press.

Butler, J. (2002). Violence, mourning, politics. Lecture, feminist theory address, University College London, London, March 8, 2002.

Butler, J. (2011). *Bodies that matter: On the discursive limits of sex.* London: Routledge.

Byrne, M. (2001). Understanding life experiences through a phenomenological approach to research. *Aorn Journal, 73*(4), 830–832.

Canclini, N.G. (2001). *Consumers and citizens: Globalization and multicultural conflicts.* Minneapolis, MN: University of Minnesota Press.

Cardwell, S. (2006). Television aesthetics. *Critical Studies in Television, 1*(1), 72–80.

Cardwell, S. (2014). Television amongst friends: Medium, art, media. *Critical Studies in Television, 9*(3), 6–21.

CCCS Women's Studies Group (Eds.). (1978). *Women take issue.* London: Hutchinson.

Chang, H., Ngunjiri, F., & Hernandez, K. (2013). *Collaborative autoethnography.* Walnut Creek, CA: Left Coast Press.

Chapman, J. (2013). *Inside the Tardis: The worlds of Doctor Who.* London: I.B. Tauris.

Chen, S. (2020). The equity-diversity-inclusion complex gets a makeover. *Wired,* July 14. https://www.wired.com/story/the-equity-diversity-inclusion-industrial-complex-gets-a-makeover/.

Cherry, B. (2013). Extermi … Knit! Female fans and feminine handicrafting. In P. Booth (Ed.), *Fan phenomena: Doctor Who* (pp. 106–115). Bristol: Intellect.

Christ, W.G., & Potter, W.J. (1998). Media literacy, media education, and the academy. *Journal of Communication, 48*(1), 5–15.

Christensen, C. G., & Myford, C. M. (2014). Measuring social and emotional content in children's television: An instrument development study. *Journal of Broadcasting & Electronic Media, 58*(1), 21–41.

Citron, D. K., & Norton, H. (2011). Intermediaries and hate speech: Fostering digital citizenship for our information age. *BUL Rev., 91,* 1435.

Clifford, J., & Marcus, G.E. (Eds.). (1986). *Writing culture: The poetics and politics of ethnography.* Berkeley, CA: University of California Press.

Coe, K., Kenski, K., & Rains, S. (2014). Online and uncivil? Patterns and determinants of incivility in newspaper website comments. *Journal of Communication, 64*(2014), 658–679.

Coffey, M.K. (2003). From nation to community. Museums and the reconfiguration of Mexican society under neoliberalism. In J.Z. Bratich, J. Packer & C. McCarthy (Eds.), *Foucault, cultural studies, and governmentality* (pp. 207–242). Albany, NY: Suny.

Cohen, S., & Taylor, L. (1992). *Escape attempts*. London: Routledge.
Collins, C. (2017). Drag race to the bottom? Updated notes on the aesthetic and political economy of RuPaul's drag race. *Transgender Studies Quarterly*, *4*(1), 128–134.
Corbin, J.M., & Strauss, A. (1990). Grounded theory research: Procedures, canons, and evaluative criteria. *Qualitative Sociology*, *13*(1), 3–21.
Cordone, J., & Cordone, M. (2010). Who is the doctor? The meta-narrative of Doctor Who. In C.J. Hansen (Ed.), *Ruminations, peregrinations, and regenerations: A critical approach to Doctor Who* (pp. 8–21). Newcastle: Cambridge Scholars Publishing.
Cronin, A.M. (2005). *Advertising and consumer citizenship: Gender, images and rights*. London: Routledge.
Curran, J. (1990). The new revisionism in mass communication research: A reappraisal. *European Journal of Communication*, *5*(2), 135–164. doi:10.1177/0267323190005002002.
Dagnes, A. (2019). *Super mad at everything, all of the time*. Cham: Palgrave MacMillan, Springer.
Davies, H., Buckingham, D., & Kelley, P. (2000). In the worst possible taste: Children, television and cultural value. *European Journal of Cultural Studies*, *3*(1), 5–26.
Dean, J. (2019). Communicative capitalism. This is what democracy looks like. *RCL. Journal of Communication and Languages*, *51*, 32–49.
Dean, M. (1999). *Governmentality: Power and rule in modern society*. London: Sage.
DiAngelo, R. (2011). White fragility. *The International Journal of Critical Pedagogy*, *3*(3), 54–70.
Dibbits, H. (2007). Moroccan Dutch boys and the authentication of clothing styles. In P.J. Margry & H. Roodenburg (Eds.), *Reframing Dutch culture: Between otherness and authenticity* (pp. 11–35). London: Routledge.
Dijkman, A., & Papikonomou, Z. (2018). *Heb je een boze moslim voor mij?*. Amsterdam: Amsterdam University Press.
DiSalvo, C. (2022). *Design as democratic inquiry. Putting experimental civics into practice*. Cambridge, MA, and London: The MIT Press.
Doctor Who. "Thirteenth doctor reveal - Doctor Who." Posted July 16, (2017). YouTube video, https://www.youtube.com/watch?v=_-_bSdWEYK8. Quoted comments: Jimmy Bob Stewart, Krychick SPP, LonerStoner, Mank Deme, Mark Evans, Marta Peterson Womack, RedCowCat, RedMatter, Ryan Gunn, Scott Schinke, Sewell 27.
Dongen, M.v. (2018). Actie tegen 'homofoob' RTL-programma Voetbal Inside: 'Bedrijven, waarom adverteren jullie nog?' in Volkskrant 20-12-2017, https://www.volkskrant.nl/cultuur-media/actie-tegen-homofoob-rtl-programma-voetbal-inside-bedrijven-waarom-adverteren-jullie-nog~b70d5867/.
Donzelot, J. (1979). *The policing of families*. New York, NY: Random House.
Donzelot, J. (2008). Michel Foucault and liberal intelligence. *Economy and Society*, *37*(1), 115–134. DOI: 10.1080/03085140701760908.
Doona, J. (2020). Political comedy engagement: Identity and community construction. *European Journal of Cultural Studies*, *23*(4), 531–547.
Doona, J. (2021). News satire engagement as a transgressive space for genre work. *International Journal of Cultural Studies*, *24*(1), 15–33. 10.1177/1367877919892279.
Drazkiewicz, E., & Harambam, J. (2021). What should academics do about conspiracy theories? Moving beyond debunking to better deal with conspiratorial movements, misinformation and post-truth. *Journal for Cultural Research*, *25*(1), 1–11.

Drucker, A., Fein, O., Bergerbest, D., & Giora, G. (2014). On sarcasm, social awareness, and gender. *Humor*, *27*(4), 551–573.

Duarte, A. (2018). 'RuPaul's drag race' season 10, episode 8: The generation slap. *The New York Times*, May 10, 2018. https://www.nytimes.com/2018/05/10/arts/television/rupauls-drag-race-season-10-episode-8-recap.html.

Duits, L. (2008). Multi-girl-culture. PhD thesis, University of Amsterdam.

Dunbar, R. I. M. (1996). *Grooming, gossip, and the evolution of language*. Harvard University Press.

Dunbar, R. I. M. (2004). Gossip in evolutionary perspective. *Review of General Psychology*, *8*(2), 100–110.

Dunleavy, T. (2017). *Complex serial drama and multiplatform television*. London: Routledge.

Edwards, T. (2013). Medusa's stare: Celebrity, subjectivity and gender. *Celebrity Studies*, *4*(2), 155–168.

Eeken, S., & Hermes, J. (2021). Doctor Who, ma'am: YouTube reactions to the 2017 reveal of the new doctor. *Television & New Media*, 22(5), 447–464. 10.1177/1527476419893040

Eliasoph, N. (1998). *Avoiding politics: How Americans produce apathy in everyday life*. New York, NY: Cambridge University Press.

Enli, G. (2009). Mass communication tapping into participatory culture. *European Journal of Communication*, *24*(4), 481–493.

Enli, G. (2017). Twitter as arena for the authentic outsider: Exploring the social media campaigns of Trump and Clinton in the 2016 US presidential election. *European Journal of Communication*, *32*(1), 50–61. doi:10.1177/0267323116682802.

Felski, R. (2015). *The limits of critique*. Chicago, IL: The University of Chicago Press.

Felski, R. (2020). *Hooked. Art and attachment*. Chicago, IL: The University of Chicago Press.

Fernández Castro, J. (2017). Stuart Hall: An organic intellectual. *Middle East - Topics & Arguments, Bd.*, *7*, 23–29. doi: 10.17192/meta.2017.7.5134.

Fiske, J. (1987). *Television culture*. London: Routledge.

Fiske, J., & Hartley, J. (1978). *Reading television*. London: Methuen.

Foucault, M. (1970). *The order of things. An archeology of the human sciences*. London: Tavistock.

Foucault, M. (1972). *The archaeology of knowledge*. London: Tavistock.

Foucault, M. (1976). *The history of sexuality: An introduction*. volume I, Translated by R. Hurley. New York, NY: Random House.

Foucault, M. (1977). *Discipline and punish*. Translated by A. Sheridan. New York, NY: Pantheon.

Foucault, M. (1991). Governmentality. In G. Burchell, C. Gordon & P. Miller (Eds.), *The Foucault effect: Studies in governmentality* (pp. 87–104). London: Harvester Wheatsheaf.

Fox, J., & Ralston, R. (2016). Queer identity online: Informal learning and teaching experiences of LGBTQ individuals on social media. *Computers in Human Behavior*, *65*, 635–642. 10.1016/j.chb.2016.06.009.

Fraser, N. (2022). *Cannibal capitalism. How our system is devouring democracy, care, and the planet - and what we can do about it*. London: Verso.

Fraser, N., & Xiaoping, W. (2013). Nancy Fraser on Marx and Habermas. *International Critical Thought*, *3*(3), 259–267. DOI: 10.1080/21598282.2013.817962

Fredericks, E. [tiny_bookbot]. (2020), December 31). *People griping about nonwhite actors in Bridgerton but not fussing about the Duke wearing riding boots to a ball?* [Tweet]. Twitter. https://twitter.com/tiny_bookbot/status/1344465298552811521?s=20

Fuchs, C. (2010). Labor in informational capitalism and on the Internet. *The Information Society*, *26*(3), 179–196. 10.1080/01972241003712215.

Geertz, C. (1973). *The interpretation of cultures*. New York, NY: Basic Books.

Geraghty, C. (2003).Aesthetics and quality in popular television drama. *International Journal of Cultural Studies*, *6*(1), 25.

Gibson, M., & Hartley, J. (1998). Forty years of cultural studies: An interview with Richard Hoggart, October 1997. *International Journal of Cultural Studies*, *1*(1), 11–23. doi:10.1177/13678779980010010.

Gill, R., & Scharff, C. (Eds.). (2011). *New femininities: Postfeminism, neoliberalism and subjectivity*. Basingstoke: Palgrave Macmillan.

Gillespie, M. (1995). *Television, ethnicity and social change*. London: Routledge

Glaser, B., & Strauss, A. (1967). *The discovery of grounded theory*. Chicago, IL: Aldine.

Gn, J. (2011). Queer simulation: The practice, performance and pleasure of cosplay. *Continuum*, *25*(4), 583–593. DOI: 10.1080/10304312.2011.582937.

Golob, U., Kraševec, M., & Črnič, T. O. (2021). Video gaming spectatorship: What drives gameplay watching on YouTube?. *Media Studies*, *12*(23), 40–56.

Goodwin, J. (1989). *More man than you'll ever be: Gay folklore and acculturation in Middle America*. Bloomington, IN: Indiana University Press.

Gopnik, A. (2018). What cafés did for liberalism. *The New Yorker*, December 17. https://www.newyorker.com/magazine/2018/12/24/what-cafes-did-for-liberalism

Gramsci, A. (1971). *Selections from the prison notebooks*. Translated & Edited by Q. Hoare & G. Nowell Smith. New York, NY: International Publishers.

Gray, J. (1992). *Men are from Mars, women are from Venus*. New York, NY: HarperCollins.

Gray, A. (1992). *Video playtime. The gendering of a leisure technology*. London: Routledge.

Griswold, W., Lenaghan, E., & Naffziger, M. (2011). Readers as audiences. In V. Nightingale (Ed.), *The handbook of media audiences* (pp. 19–40). Malden, MA: Wiley Blackwell.

Grossberg, L. (1992). Is there a fan in the house? The affective sensibility of fandom. In L.A. Lewis (Ed.), *The adoring audience. Fandom and popular media* (pp. 50–68). London: Routledge.

Grossberg, L. (2010a). *Cultural studies in the future tense*. Durham, NC: Duke University Press.

Grossberg, L. (2010b). On the political responsibilities of cultural studies. *Inter-Asia Cultural Studies*, *11*(2), 241–247. DOI: 10.1080/14649371003616375

Grossberg, L. (2014). *We gotta get out of this place: Popular conservatism and post-modern culture*. London: Routledge.

Gunsteren, H.V. (1998). *A theory of citizenship. Organizing plurality in contemporary societies*. London: Sage.

Haas, H.D. (2007). Morocco's migration experience: A transitional perspective. *International Migration*, *45*(4), 39–68.

Habermas, J. (1985a). *The theory of communicative action: Reason and the rational-ization of society*. Volume 1. Boston, MA: Beacon Press.

Habermas, J. (1985b). *The theory of communicative action: Lifeword and system: A critique of functionalist reason.* Volume 2. Boston, MA: Beacon Press.

Habermas, J. (1996). *Between facts and norms.* Cambridge, MA: MIT Press.

Hadas, L. (2013). Resisting the romance: 'Shipping' and the discourse of genre uniqueness in Doctor Who fandom. *European Journal of Cultural Studies, 16*(3), 329–343.

Haidt, J. (2022). Why the past ten years of American life have been uniquely stupid. *The Atlantic,* https://www.theatlantic.com/magazine/archive/2022/05/social-media-democracy-trust-babel/629369/.

Hall, S. (1980). Encoding/decoding. In S. Hall et al. (Eds.), *Culture, media, language* (pp. 128–138). New York, NY: Hutchinson.

Hall, S. (1996). Gramsci's relevance for the study of race and ethnicity. In D. Morley & C. Kuan-Shin (Eds.), *Stuart Hall: Critical dialogues in cultural studies* (pp. 411–446). London and New York, NY: Routledge.

Hall, S. (1997). The work of representation. In S. Hall (Ed.), *Representation: Cultural representations and signifying practices* (pp. 13–74). London: Sage.

Hall, S., & Jefferson, T. (1975). *Resistance through rituals.* London: Hutchinson.

Hall, S., Lumley, R., & McLennan, G. (2007). Politics and ideology: Gramsci. In A. Gray, J. Campbell, M. Erickson, S. Hanson & H. Wood (Eds.), *CCCS selected working papers.* Volume 1, (pp. 278–305). London and New York, NY: Routledge (originally published in 1977).

Hallsworth, D. (2022). Private desires, public narratives: The intersection of sexuality and cultural citizenship in Danish state-supported cinema. *Feminist Media Studies,* DOI: 10.1080/14680777.2022.2099929.

Hammersley, M., & Atkinson, P. (1998). *Ethnography. Principles in practice. Third edition.* London: Routledge.

Hartley, J. (1999). *Uses of television.* London: Routledge.

Hall, S., & Whannell, G. (Eds.). (1964). *The popular arts.* New York, NY: Pantheon.

Hay, J. (2003). The (neo) liberalization of the domestic sphere and the new architecture of community. In J.Z. Bratich, J. Packer & C. McCarthy (Eds.), *Foucault, cultural studies, and governmentality* (pp. 165–206). Albany, NY: Suny.

Hebdige, D. (1979). *Subculture. The meaning of style.* London: Methuen.

Helsloot, J. (2012). Zwarte piet and cultural aphasia in the Netherlands. *Quotidian,* 1–20.

Henriques, J., Hollway, W., Urwin, C., Venn, C., & Walkerdine, V. (Eds.). (1984). *Changing the subject. Psychology, social regulation and subjectivity.* London: Methuen.

Henwood, K. (2007). Beyond hypercriticality: Taking forward methodological inquiry and debate in discursive and qualitative social psychology. *Discourse Studies, 9*(2), 270–275.

Herbert, D., & Gillespie, M. (Eds.). (2011). Special issue on religion, media and social change. *European Journal of Cultural Studies, 14*(4), 601–609.

Hermes, J. (1995). *Reading women's magazines.* Cambridge: Polity Press.

Hermes, J. (2005). *Rereading popular culture.* Oxford: Blackwell.

Hermes, J. (2006). The tragic success of feminism. In J. Hollows & R. Moseley (Eds.), *Feminism in popular culture* (pp. 79–95). London: Berg.

Hermes, J. (2009). Audience studies 2.0. On the theory, politics and method of qualitative audience research. *Interactions, 1*(1), 111–127.

Hermes, J. (2013). Caught. Critical versus everyday perspectives on television. In J. Teurlings & M. de Valck (Eds.), *The ends of television* (pp. 35–49). Amsterdam: Amsterdam University Press.

Hermes, J. (2018). RuPaul's drag race. Culture, politics, and fashion as affective practice. In A. Mascia, R. Menarini, S. Segre Reinach & I. Tolic (Eds.), *The size effect* (pp. 257–271). Milan: Mimesis.

Hermes, J., & Graaf, C.D. (2015). Urban stories. Producing news for urban youth. Conference Youth, Media and Diversity, IHECS Brussels.

Hermes, J., & Hill, A. (2021). Transgression in contemporary media culture. *International Journal of Cultural Studies*, 24(1), 3–14.

Hermes, J., & Kardolus, M. (2019). Occupying the intersection: RuPaul's celebration of meritocracy. *Critical Studies in Television*, 14(4), 462–467. 10.1177/1749602019875864.

Hermes, J., & Kardolus, M. (2022), The RuPaul paradox: Freedom and stricture in a competition reality TV show, *Javnost - The Public*, 29(1), 82–97. DOI: 10.1080/13183222.2021.1924541

Hermes, J., & Stoete, L. (2019). Hating Skyler White: Audience engagement, gender politics and celebrity culture. *Celebrity Studies*, 10(3), 411–426.

Hewison, R. (2014). *Cultural capital: The rise and fall of creative Britain*. London: Verso.

Hilhorst, S., & Hermes, J. (2016). 'We have given up so much': Passion and denial in the Dutch Zwarte Piet (Black Pete) controversy. *European Journal of Cultural Studies*, 19(3), 218–233.

Hill, A. (2015). *Reality television*. London: Routledge.

Hill, A. (2019). *Media experiences*. London: Routledge.

Hills, M. (2002). *Fan cultures*. London: Routledge.

Hills, M. (2010a). Mainstream cult. In S. Abbott (Ed.), *The cult TV book: From Star Trek to Dexter, new approaches to TV outside the box* (pp. 67–73). London: I.B. Tauris.

Hills, M. (2010b). *Triumph of a time lord: Regenerating Doctor Who in the twenty-first century*. London: I.B. Tauris.

Hills, M. (2012). "Proper distance" in the ethical positioning of scholar-fandoms: Between academics' and fans' moral economies? In K. Larsen & L. Zubernis (Eds.), *Fan culture: Theory/practice* (pp. 28–32). Newcastle upon Tyne: Cambridge Scholars.

Hills, M. (2015). Rebranding *Doctor Who* and reimagining *Sherlock*: 'Quality' television as 'Makeover TV Drama'. *International Journal of Cultural Studies*, 18(3), 317–331.

Hine, C. (2000). *Virtual ethnography*. London: Sage.

Hine, C. (2017). From virtual ethnography to the embedded, embodied, everyday internet. In L. Hjort et al. (Eds.), *The Routledge companion to digital ethnography* (pp. 21–28). London: Routledge.

Hochschild, A. (1979). Emotion work, feeling rules, and social structure. *The American Journal of Sociology*, 85(3), 551–575. http://www.jstor.org/stable/2778583.

Hochschild, A. (1989). *The second shift (With Anne Machung)*. London: Viking Penguin.

Hochschild, A. (2017). *Strangers in their own land*. New York: The New Press.

Hodge, R., & Tripp, D. (1986). *Children and television: A semiotic approach*. Stanford, CA: Stanford University Press.

Holladay, H.W., & Click, M. (2019). Hating Skyler White. Gender and anti-fandom in AMC's breaking bad. In M. Click (Ed.), *Anti-fandom. Dislike and hate in the digital age* (pp. 147–165). New York, NY: NYU Press.

Holmes, S. & Negra, D. (2008). Introduction. *Gender OnLine Journal*, isssue 48, 1–13. https://www.atria.nl/ezines/IAV_606661/IAV_606661_2010_51/g48_negraholmes.html

Horst, H. (2016). Being in fieldwork: Collaboration, digital media, and ethnographic practice. In *EFieldnotes: The makings of anthropology in the digital world* (pp. 153–168). Philadelphia, PA: University of Pennsylvania Press.

Hunt, L. (2013). *British low culture: From safari suits to sexploitation*. London: Routledge.

Hutcheon, L. (2002). *The politics of postmodernism*. 2nd edition. London: Routledge.

Huyssen, A. (1986). *After the great divide*. Bloomington, IN: Indiana University Press.

Jackson, S., Goddard, S., & Cossens, S. (2016). The importance of [not] being Miley: Girls making sense of Miley Cyrus. *European Journal of Cultural Studies*, *19*(6), 547–564.

Jackson, S., & Vares, T. (2015). Too many bad role models for us girls': Girls, female pop celebrities and 'sexualization'. *Sexualities*, *18*(4), 480–498.

Jenkins, H., Purushotma, R., Weigel, M., Clinton, K., & Robison, A. (2009). *Confronting the challenges of participatory culture: Media education for the 21st century (digital edition)*. Cambridge, MA: MIT Press. Available at: https://mitpress.mit.edu/books/full_pdfs/Confronting_the_Challenges.pdf (accessed August 2012).

Jacobs, J. (2001). Issues of judgement and value in television studies. *International Journal of Cultural Studies*, *4*(4), 427–447.

Jane, E. (2014). Your a ugly, whorish, slut. *Feminist Media Studies*, *14*(4), 531–546. DOI: 10.1080/14680777.2012.741073.

Jeffries, F. (2014). Reappropriating the city of fear. *Space and Culture*, *17*(3), 251–265.

Jenkins, H. (1992). *Textual poachers: Television fans and participatory culture*. New York, NY: Routledge.

Jenkins, H. (2006). *Convergence culture: Where old and new media collide*. New York, NY: New York University Press.

Jenkins, H. (2007). *The wow factor: Tracing the emotional impact of popular culture*. New York, NY: New York University Press.

Jenkins, H. (2011). Why Fiske still matters. Introduction to Fiske J., In *Reading the popular* (pp. xii–xxxviii). 2nd ed. Abingdon: Routledge.

Jenkins, H., Peters-Lazaro, G., & Shresthova, S. (Eds.). (2020). *Popular culture and the civic imagination*. New York, NY: New York University Press.

Jenner, M. (2016). Is this TVIV? On Netflix, TVIII and binge-watching. *New Media & Society*, *18*(2), 257–273.

Jenner, M. (2017). Binge-watching: Video-on-demand, quality TV and mainstreaming fandom. *International Journal of Cultural Studies*, *20*(3), 304–320.

Jensen, J. (1990). *Redeeming modernity*. London: Sage.

Jones, M. (2014). Chantal Mouffe's agonistic project: Passions and participation. *Parallax*, *20*(2), 14–30. DOI: 10.1080/13534645.2014.896546

Jowett, L. "'Is the future going to be all girl?' Doctor Who and the frustrations of a feminist." *CSTonline*, March 23, 2018, http://cstonline.net/is-the-future-going-to-be-all-girl-doctor-who-and-the-frustrations-of-a-feminist-by-lorna-jowett/.

Jowett, L. (2014). The girls who waited? Female companions and gender in Doctor Who. *Critical Studies in Television*, *9*(1), 77–94.

Jowett, L. (2017). *Dancing with the doctor: Dimensions of gender in the Doctor Who universe*. London: I.B. Tauris.

Kale, S. (2002). Women, the public sphere, and the persistence of salons. *French Historical Studies*, *25*(1), 115–148.

Karlsen, F., Schanke Sundet, V., Syvertsen, T., & Ytreberg, E. (2009). Nonprofessional activity on television in a time of digitalization: More fun for the elite or new opportunities for ordinary people? *Nordicom Review*, *30*(1), 19–36.

Kavka, M. (2012). *Reality TV*. Edinburgh: Edinburgh University Press.

Kavka, M. (2016). Celevision: Mobilizations of the television screen. In P.D. Marshall & S. Redmond (Eds.), *A companion to celebrity*. Chichester: Wiley-Blackwell.

Kellner, D., & Share, J. (2007). Critical media literacy, democracy, and the reconstruction of education. In D. Macedo & S.R. Steinberg (Eds.), *Media literacy: A reader* (pp. 3–23). New York, NY: Peter Lang Publishing.

King, S.J. (2003). Doing good by running well. Breast cancer, the race for the cure, and new technologies of ethical citizenship. In J.Z. Bratich, J. Packer & C. McCarthy (Eds.), *Foucault, cultural studies, governmentality* (pp. 285–301). Albany, NY: Suny Press.

Kommer, R.V., & Hermes, J. (2022). Aspiring to Dutchness: Media literacy, integration, and communication with eritrean status holders. *Media and Communication*, *10*(4), 317–327. 10.17645/mac.v10i4.5605.

Kozloff, S. (1992). Narrative theory and television. In R. Allen (Ed.), *Channels of discourse, reassembled. Television and contemporary criticism* (pp. 67–100). 2nd ed. London: Routledge.

Kraidy, M.M. (2016). *The naked blogger of Cairo*. Cambridge, MA: Harvard University Press.

Kulynych, J. (1997). Performing politics: Foucault, Habermas, and postmodern participation. *Polity*, *30*(2), 315–346.

Landes, J. (1988). *Women and the public sphere in the age of the French Revolution*. Ithaca, NY: Cornell University Press.

Lavik, E. (2011). The poetics and rhetoric of the wire's intertextuality. *Critical Studies in Television*, *6/1*, 52–71.

Lindlof, T.R. (1988). Media audiences as interpretive communities. *Annals of the International Communication Association*, *11*(1), 81–107.

Littler, J. (2018). *Against meritocracy. Culture, power and myths of mobility*. London: Routledge.

Livingstone, S. (2004). Media literacy and the challenge of new information and communication technologies. *Communication Review*, *1*(7), 3–14.

Livingstone, S., Van Couvering, E., & Thumim, N. (2005). *Adult media literacy: A review of the research literature*. London: Ofcom.

Lotz, A. (2007). *The television will be revolutionized*. New York, NY: New York University Press.

Lotz, A. (2018). *We now interrupt this broadcast*. Cambridge, MA: MIT Press.

Lovink, G. (2002). *Dark fibre. Tracking critical internet culture*. Cambridge, MA: The MIT Press.

Lovink, G. (2012). *Networks without a cause. A critique of social media*. Amsterdam: Institute of Network Cultures.

Luke, A. (2000). Critical literacy in Australia: A matter of context and standpoint. *Journal of Adolescent & Adult Literacy*, *43*(5), 448–461.

Lury, K. (2001). *British youth television: Cynicism and enchantment*. Oxford: Oxford University Press.
Mankekar, P. (1999). *Screening culture, viewing politics: An ethnography of television, womanhood, and nation in postcolonial India*. Durham, NC: Duke University Press.
Mankekar, P. (2015). *Unsettling India: Affect, temporality, transnationality*. Durham, NC: Duke University Press.
Marres, N., Guggenheim, M., & Wilkie, A. (2018). *Inventing the social*. Mattering Press.
Marshall, T. (1950). *Citizenship and social class and other essays*. Cambridge: Cambridge University Press.
Marshall, P. D. (1997). *Celebrity and power: Fame in contemporary culture*. Minneapolis, MN: University of Minnesota Press.
Massanari, A. (2017). #Gamergate and the fappening: How Reddit's algorithm, governance, and culture support toxic technocultures. *New Media & Society*, *19*(3), 329–346.
Matrix, S. (2014). The netflix effect. Teens, binge watching and on-demand digital media trends. *Jeunesse*, *6*(1), 119–138.
Mattel, T., & Zamolodchikova, K. (2020). *Trixie and Katya's guide to modern womanhood*. New York, NY: Penguin Random House.
Mattel, T., & Zamolodchikova, K. (2022). *Working girls. Trixie and Katya's guide to professional womanhood*. New York, NY: Penguin Random House.
Maxwell, R., & Miller, T. (2012). *Greening the media*. Oxford: Oxford University Press.
Maza, S. (1992). Women, the bourgeoisie, and the public sphere: Response to Daniel Gordon and David. *French Historical Studies*, *17*(4), 935–950.
McCabe, J., & Akass, K. (Eds.). (2007). *Quality television: Contemporary American television and beyond*. London: I.B Tauris.
McDonnell, A. (2014). *Reading celebrity gossip magazines*. John Wiley & Sons.
McGuigan, J. (2002). *Cultural populism*. London: Routledge.
McIntyre, J. (2017). Transgender idol. Queer subjectivities and Australian reality TV. *European Journal of Cultural Studies*, *20*(1), 87–103.
McKeown, B., Thomas, D. B., Rhoads, J. C., & Sundblad, D. (2015). Falling hard for Breaking Bad: An investigation of audience response to a popular television series. *Participations: Journal of Audience and Reception Studies*, *12*(2), 147–166.
McLaughlin, N. (2010). Gender redux: Bionic woman, Doctor Who, and Battlestar Galactica. In C.J. Hansen (Ed.), *Ruminations, peregrinations, and regenerations: A critical approach to Doctor Who* (pp. 117–129). Newcastle: Cambridge Scholars Publishing.
McRobbie, A. (1982). The politics of feminist research: Between talk, text and action. *Feminist Review*, *12*, 46–57.
Melzer, P. (2010). *Alien constructions: Science fiction and feminist thought*. Austin, TX: University of Texas Press.
Miklaucic, S. (2003). God games and governmentality: Civilization II and hypermediated knowledge. In J.Z. Bratich, J. Packer & C. McCarthy (Eds.), *Foucault, cultural studies, governmentality* (pp. 317–335). Albany, NY: Suny.
Miles, M.B., & Huberman, A.M. (1984). *Qualitative data analysis*. London: Sage.
Miller, D., & Horst, H. (2012). *Digital anthropology*. Oxford: Berg Publishers.
Miller, T. (1993). *The well-tempered self*. Baltimore, MD: Johns Hopkins University Press.
Milner, R.M. (2013). FCJ-156 hacking the social: Internet memes, identity antagonism, and the logic of lulz. *Fibreculture Journal*, 61–91.

Mittell, J. (2015). *Complex television*. London: Routledge.
Mol, M. (2011). Leuk, grappig, echt, spannend, leerzaam: Een onderzoek naar mediageletterdheid onder groep 8-ers (Nice, funny, real, exciting, instructive: Research into media literacy among form 8 pupils). Master's thesis, Mediastudies, Universiteit van Amsterdam, available at: http://scriptiesonline.uba.uva.nl/ (accessed August 2012).
Moran, M., & McGuigan, J. (2020). 'Tory stories': Arguing for a critical cultural populism, again. *European Journal of Cultural Studies*, *23*(6), 1005–1013.
Morley, D. (1980). *The Nationwide audience. Structure and decoding*. London: British Film Institute.
Morley, D. (1986). *Family television*. London: Comedia.
Morley, D. (1989). Changing paradigms in audience studies. In E. Seiter, H. Borchers, G. Kreutzner & E. Warth (Eds.), *Remote control. Television, audiences and cultural power* (pp. 16–43). London: Routledge.
Morris, M. (1988). Banality in cultural studies. *Discourse*, *10*(2), 3–29.
Mortensen, T. E. (2018). Anger, fear, and games: The long event of# GamerGate. *Games and Culture*, *13*(8), 787–806.
Mouffe, C. (2000). *Deliberative democracy or agonistic pluralism* (Reihe Politikwissenschaft/ Institut für Höhere Studien, Abt. Politikwissenschaft, 72). Wien: Institut für Höhere Studien (IHS). http://nbn-resolving.de/urn:nbn:de:0168-ssoar-246548.
Müller, F., & Hermes, J. (2010). The performance of cultural citizenship: Audiences and the politics of multicultural television drama. *Critical Studies in Media Communication*, *27*(2), 193–208.
Nava, M. (2002). Cosmopolitan modernity everyday imaginaries and the register of difference. *Theory, Culture & Society*, *19*(1–2), 81–99.
Negt, O., & Kluge, A. (1990). Selections from 'public opinion and practical knowledge: Toward an organisational analysis of proletariat and middle-class public opinion'. *Social Text*, *25/26*, 24–32.
Netwerk Mediawijsheid, & Nikken, P. (2022). Iene Miene Media. Een onderzoek naar omgang met en gebruik van media(apparaten) van kinderen van 0 t/m 6 jaar en de rol die ouders hierin spelen. Hilversum and Zwolle: Netwerk Mediawijsheid en Hpgeschool WIndesheim. https://netwerkmediawijsheid.nl/iene-miene-media-2022/.
Newcomb, H. (1974). *TV: The most popular art*. New York, NY: Doubleday.
Newcomb, H., & Hirsch, P.M. (1983). Television as a cultural forum. *Quarterly Review of Film & Video*, *8*(3), 45–55.
Newton, E. (1972). *Mother camp: Female impersonators in America*. Chicago, IL: University of Chicago Press.
Nicol, D. (2018). *Doctor Who: A British alien*. London: Palgrave Macmillan.
Nieuwenhuis, I., & Zijp, D. (2022). The politics and aesthetics of humour in an age of comic controversy. *European Journal of Cultural Studies*, *25*(2), 341–354.
NOS (2022). Toch Inspectie-onderzoek naar politieoptreden bij zwartepietbetoging Staphorst. https://nos.nl/artikel/2453741-toch-inspectie-onderzoek-naar-politieoptreden-bij-zwartepietbetoging-staphorst.
NRC (2019). Good idea to discuss Pete in peace time. ('Zoek in vredestijd uit waar de pijn zit'). https://www.nrc.nl/nieuws/2019/09/05/zoek-in-vredestijd-uit-waar-de-pijn-zit-a3972429.
Orthia, L. (2010). 'Sociopathetic abscess' or 'yawning chasm'?" *The Absent Postcolonial Transition in the Journal of Commonwealth Literature*, *45*(2), 207–225.

Ouellette, L. (2004). Take responsibility for yourself. Judge Judy and the neoliberal citizen. In S. Murray & L. Ouellette (Eds.), *Reality TV: Remaking television culture* (pp. 231–250). New York, NY: NYU Press.
Ouellette, L., & Hay, J. (2008). Makeover television, governmentality and the good citizen. *Continuum, 22*(4), 471–484. DOI: 10.1080/10304310801982930
Packard, V. (1957). *The hidden persuaders.* New York, NY: Pocket Books.
Papacharissi, Z. (2016). Affective publics and structures of storytelling: Sentiment, events and mediality. *Information, Communication & Society, 19*(3), 307–324.
Papacharissi, Z., & Trevey, M.T. (2018). Affective publics and windows of opportunity: Social media and the potential for social change. In G. Meikle (Ed.), *The Routledge companion to media and activism* (pp. 87–96). London: Routledge.
Pariser, E. (2011). *The filter bubble: What the Internet is hiding from you.* London: Penguin UK.
Pateman, C. (1992). *Between equality and difference.* London: Routledge.
Peacock, S. (Ed.). (2007). *Reading 24: TV against the clock.* London: I.B. Tauris.
Penman, R., & Turnbull, S. (2007). *Media literacy: Concepts, research and regulatory issues.* Canberra: Australian Communications and Media Authority.
Perloff, R. (1999). The third-person effect: A critical review and synthesis. *Media Psychology, 1*(4), 353–378.
Phillips, W.M. (2012). This is why we can't have nice things: The origins, evolution, and cultural embeddedness of online trolling. Ph.D. Dissertation, University of Oregon.
Pierson, D. P. (2014). Breaking neoliberal? Contemporary neoliberal discourses and policies in AMC's Breaking Bad. *Breaking Bad: Critical essays on the contexts, politics, style, and reception of the television series.* New York: Lexington Books, 15–31.
Postill, J. (2014). Democracy in an age of viral reality: A media epidemiography of Spain's indignados movement. *Ethnography, 15*(1), 51–69.
Postill, J. (2017). Doing remote ethnography. In L. Hjort et al. (Eds.), *The Routledge companion to digital ethnography* (pp. 61–69), London: Routledge.
Postill, J., & Pink, S. (2012). Social media ethnography: The digital researcher in a messy web. *Media International Australia, 145*(1), 123–134.
Postman, N. (1982). *The disappearance of childhood. How TV is changing children's lives.* New York, NY: Dell.
Potter, J., & Wetherell, M. (1987). *Discourse and social psychology.* London: Sage
Prins, B., & Saharso, S. (2008). In the spotlight. A blessing and a curse for immigrant women in the Netherlands. *Ethnicities, 8*(3), 365–384.
Raad voor Cultuur (2005). *Mediawijsheid. De ontwikkeling van nieuw burgerschap (Media wisdom: The development of new citizenship).* Den Haag: Raad voor Cultuur.
Radway, J. (1987 [1984]). *Reading the romance.* London: Verso.
Redmond, S. (2019). *Celebrity.* London: Routledge.
Reynolds, D. (2020). RuPaul's 2016 thoughts on Black Lives Matter and police brutality. *Advocate,* https://www.advocate.com/race/2020/6/09/rupauls-2016-thoughts-black-lives-matter-and-police-brutality
Robinson, M. (2018). *Television on demand.* New York, NY: Bloomsbury.
Rosaldo, R. (1994). Cultural citizenship and educational democracy. *Cultural Anthropology, 9*(3), 402–411.

Rottenberg, C. (2014). The rise of neoliberal feminism. *Cultural Studies*, *28*(3), 418–437.
Saha, A. (2021). *Race, culture and media*. London: Sage.
Sawicki, J. (1991). *Disciplining Foucault.: Feminism, power, and the body*. London: Routledge.
Scheffer, P. (2000). Het Multiculturele drama. *NRC Handelsblad*, 29 januari.
Schultes, P., Dorner, V., & Lehner, F. (2013). Leave a comment! An in-depth analysis of user comments on YouTube. *Wirtschaftsinformatik*, *42*, 659–673.
Scott, J. (1994). Deconstructing equality-versus-difference: Or, the uses of post-structuralist theory for feminism. In A. Herrmann & A. Stewart (Eds.), Theorizing feminisms (p. 366). Boulder, CO: Westview Press.
Scott, D. (2017). *Stuart Hall's voice. Intimations of an ethics of receptive generosity*. Durham and London: Duke University Press.
Segal, L. (1990). *Slow motion. Changing men, changing masculinities*. London: Virago.
Seigworth, G., & Gregg, M. (2010). An inventory of shimmers. In M. Gregg & G. Seigworth (Eds.), *The affect theory reader* (pp. 1–25). Durham: Duke University Press.
Seiter, E. (1999). *Television and new media audiences*. Oxford: Oxford University Press.
Seta, G.D. (2018). Trolling, and other problematic social media practices. In J. Burgess, A. Marwick & T. Poell (Eds.), *The sage handbook of social media* (pp. 390–411). London: Sage.
Seymour, R. (2016). Schadenfreude with bite [online]. *London Review of Books*, *38*(24), n.p. Available from: https://www.lrb.co.uk/v38/n24/richard-seymour/schadenfreude-with-bite [Accessed 1 February 2017].
Sheombar, A., & Hermes, J. (2022). Jongeren en de digitale leefwereld. In J. Hermes, R. van Goor & M. de. Jong (Eds.), *Leefwerelden van Jongeren. Derde herziene druk* (pp. 161–185). Bussum: Coutinho.
Shore, L.M., Cleveland, J.N., & Sanchez, D. (2018). Inclusive workplaces: A review and model. *Human Resource Management Review*, *28*(2), 176–189.
Shownieuws (2018). 'D66: excuses van VI over "transgendergrap"' https://www.shownieuws.nl/top-nieuws/2018/d66-excuses-van-vi-transgendergrap/
Sidore, D. (2015). Spectacularly ignorant. In Carlson, A. L. (Ed.), *Genius on television: Essays on small screen depictions of big minds*. Jefferson, NC: McFarland, 12–31.
Sikkema, P. (Ed.). (2009). *Jongeren09. We laten ons niet gek maken (Young people 09: No one is going to drive us mad)*. Amsterdam: Qrius.
Silverstone, R. (1994). *Television and everyday life*. London: Routledge.
Sim, B. (2019). RuPaul's drag race: Every season & spin-off currently in development. *ScreenRant*, November 10, 2019. https://screenrant.com/rupauls-drag-race-every-season-spin-off-currently-development/.
Simon, N. (2016). *The art of relevance. Museum 2.0*. www.artofrelevance.org.
Skeggs, B. (1997). *Formations of class and gender*. London: Sage.
Skeggs, B., & Helen Wood, H. (2012). *Reacting to reality television: Performance, audience and value*. London: Routledge.
Skeggs, B., Thumim, N., & Wood, H. (2008). Oh goodness, I am watching reality TV": How methods make class in audience research. *European Journal of Cultural Studies*, *11*(1), 5–24. 10.1177/1367549407084961.
Snickars, P., & Vonderau, P. (2009). *The YouTube reader*. Stockholm: Kungliga biblioteket.

Sontag, S. (1983 [1964]). "Notes on camp" in idem. In *The Susan Sontag reader* (pp. 295–314). Harmondsworth: Penguin.
Spigel, L., & Olsson, J. (Eds.). (2004). *Television after TV: Essays on a medium in transition*. Durham: Duke University Press.
Spot (2010). Alles over tijd. Tijdbestedingsonderzoek 2010 (All about time: Time allocation research). Available at: http://spot.nl/docs/tijdsbestedingsonderzoek-2012/boekje-alles-over-tijd-2010.pdf?sfvrsn=0 (accessed September 2012).
Srinivasan, A. (2021). *The right to sex*. London: Bloomsbury.
Stallybrass, A., & White, P. (1986). *The politics and poetics of transgression*. Ithaca, NY: Cornell University Press.
Steger, M.B., & James, P. (2019). *Globalization matters: Engaging the global in unsettled times*. Cambridge: Cambridge University Press.
Stevenson, N. (2000). *Culture and citizenship*. London: Sage
Stevenson, N. (2003). *Cultural citizenship: Cosmopolitan questions*. Maidenhead: Open University Press.
Storey, J. (2018). *Cultural theory and popular culture*. 8th revised ed. London: Routledge.
Street, M. (2021). "RuPaul announces name of Australian 'drag race,' confirmed to host," January 8, 2021. https://www.out.com/television/2021/1/08/apparently-rupaul-might-host-drag-race-australia-after-all.
Tally, J. (1999). The agonic freedom of citizens. *Economy and Society*, 28(2), 161–182. DOI: 10.1080/03085149900000001
Tasker, Y. (2012). *Spectacular bodies: Gender, genre and the action cinema*. London: Routledge.
Taylor, V., & Rupp, L.J. (2004). Chicks with dicks, men in dresses: What it means to be a drag queen. *Journal of Homosexuality*, 46(3-4), 113–133.
Terranova, T. (2000). Free labor: Producing culture for the digital economy. *Social Text*, 63(18), 33–58.
Teurlings, J. (2010). On savvy viewers and critical apathy. *European Journal of Cultural Studies*, 13(3), 359–373.
Teurlings, J. (2018). Social media and the new commons of TV criticism. *Television & New Media*, 19(3), 208–224.
The Critical Drinker (2020). "Fugitive of the Judoon" - Doctor Who's most stunning and brave episode ever. https://www.youtube.com/watch?v=l_-hqqcS_xg (last seen May 2022).
Thelwall, M. (2018). Social media analytics for YouTube comments: Potential and limitations. *International Journal of Social Research Methodology*, 21(3), 303–316.
Thomsen, C., & Essig, L. (2022). Lesbian, feminist, TERF: A queer attack on feminist studies. *Journal of Lesbian Studies*, 26(1), 27–44. DOI: 10.1080/10894160.2021.1950270.
Thomsen, C., & Finley, J. (2019). On intersectionality: A review essay. *Hypatia*, 34(1), 155–160. 10.1111/hypa.12450.
Thorburn, D. (1987). Television as an aesthetic medium. *Critical Studies in Mass Communication*, 4, 161–173.
Thornton, S. (1995). *Club cultures. Music, media, and subcultural capital*. Cambridge: Polity Press.
Tufekci, Z. (2014). Engineering the public: Big data, surveillance and computational politics. *First Monday*, 19(7). 10.5210/fm.v19i7.4901.

Turner, B. (1993). *Citizenship and social theory*. London: Sage.
Turner, G. (2010). *Ordinary people and the media: The demotic turn*. London: Sage.
Valck, M. de, & Teurlings, J. (Eds.). (2013). *After the break. Television theory today*. Amsterdam: AUP.
Ven, C.V.D. (2019). Worstelend ten onder aan het eigen gelijk. *Groene Amsterdammer* 5, 30 januari. (https://www.groene.nl/artikel/worstelend-ten-onder-aan-het-eigen-gelijk)
Vergès, F. (2021). *A decolonial feminism*. Translated by A.J. Bohrer with the author. London: Pluto Press.
Vivona, B. (2014). "To laugh or not to laugh": Understandings of the appropriateness of humour and joking in the workplace. *European Journal of Humour Research*, 2(1), 1–18. 10.7592/EJHR2014.2.1.vivona.
Walkerdine, V. (1986). Video replay: Families, films and fantasy. In V. Burgin, J. Donald & C. Kaplan (Eds.), *Formations of fantasy* (pp. 167–199). London: Methuen.
Wallace, R. (2010). But doctor? – A feminist perspective of Doctor Who. In C.J. Hansen (Ed.), *Ruminations, peregrinations, and regenerations: A critical approach to Doctor Who* (pp. 102–116). Newcastle: Cambridge Scholars Publishing.
Warner, M. (2022). Publics and counter publics. *Public Culture*, 14(1), 49–90.
Warren, C. (1974). *Identity and community in the gay world*. New York, NY: John Wiley & Sons.
Wekker, G. (2016). *White innocence. Paradoxes of colonialism and race*. Amsterdam: AUP.
Wetherell, M. (2012). *Affect and emotion*. London: Sage.
Wetherell, M. (2013). Affect and discourse – What's the problem? From affect as excess to affective/discursive practice. *Subjectivity*, 6(4), 349–368.
Wetherell, M. (2015). Trends in the turn to affect: A social psychological critique. *Body & Society*, 21(2), 139–166.
Wetherell, M., & Potter, M. (1988). Discourse analysis and the identification of interpretative repertoires. In C. Antaki (Ed.), *Analysing everyday explanation* (pp. 168–183. London: Sage.
Wilder, A. (2013). The Forgotten Rape of Skyler White. HuffPost College (blog.), September 13, 2013. Accessed November 15, 2015. http://www.huffingtonpost.com/alice-wilder/the-forgotten-rape-of-sky_b_4013319.html
Williams, R. (1974). *Television: Technology as cultural form*. London: Fontana.
Williams, R. (2011). Desiring the doctor: Identity, gender and genre in online science-fiction fandom. In T. Hochscherf & J. Leggott (Eds.), *British science fiction in film and television* (pp. 167–177). Jefferson, NC, and London: McFarland.
Wilson, J. (2010). Star testing. The emerging politics of celebrity gossip. *The Velvet Light Trap*, 65(Spring), 25–38.
Winlow, S., & Hall, S. (2007). Book review: Resistance through rituals (2nd edn). *Crime, Media, Culture*, 3(3), 394–397. doi:10.1177/174165900700030030902.
Wood, H. (2017). The politics of hyperbole on Geordie Shore: Class, gender, youth and excess. *European Journal of Cultural Studies*, 20(1), 39–55. 10.1177/1367549416640552.
Wood, M. (2019). On 'telling better stories'. *Cultural Studies*, 33(1), 19–28. 10.1080/09502386.2018.1542014.
Young, I. (1990). *Foucault and feminism*. London: Routledge.

Ytreberg, E. (2004). Formatting participation within broadcast media production. *Media, Culture & Society*, *26*, 677–692.
Yudice, G. (2004). *The expediency of culture*. Durham, NC: Duke University Press.
Yuval-Davis, N. (2006). Belonging and the politics of belonging. *Patterns of Prejudice*, *40*(3), 197–214. DOI: 10.1080/00313220600769331.
Zervignon, A. (2002). Drag shows: Drag queens and female impersonators. *GLBTQ Encyclopedia*. Available at: http://www.glbtq.com (accessed 8 August 2019).
Zoonen, L.v. (1994). *Feminist media studies*. London: Sage.

INDEX

abuse 98
aca-fans & fandom 8, 37, 134
access 162
accountability 55, 74, 91, 146
action 82
action research (definition) 47
activism, anti-Black Pete 155
activist/activism 125, 146
'activists of affect' 144
actor(s) 62, 70
addicts 76
advocacy 159
affect 8, 9; (definition) 28, 34, 39, 40, 43, 62, 73, 76, 78, 84; (as axis) 85, 117–8, 124, 135, 146–7, 150, 163
affective bonds 6
affective interpellation 72
affective practice 98
affective speech 144
affective-discursive practice 46
affordance 85
affordance as axis 84
affordance of social media 71
agency 4, 8
aggression 156
aggressive woman 139
agonistic appeal 142
agonistic conversation 142, 144
agonistic dialogue 129
agonistic politics 21
Ahmed, S. 40, 44, 48, 55, 99, 107
Aitkenhead, D. 132

Alfageeh, S. 17
algorithms 155
allegiance 71–2, 135
allegiance, counter- 71, 73
allegiances 156
Allen, K. 63, 74
alt-right 155
Althusser, L. 33
Amhali, Najib 153
analysis, comment-by-comment 98
Andeweg, A. 41
Andrejevic, M. 65
Ang, I. 34, 36, 39, 65, 145
anger 96, 142, 146, 147, 151, 154–5, 157
ANT (Actor Network Theory) 125
anti-intellectualism 124
antihero, amoral 72
appreciation 117
appreciative inquiry 8, 56, 83, 113–5, 122, 124, 127, 142
appreciative media literacy 93
appropriation 134, 136
archetype, popular-cultural 120
archetypes 65
Aronoff, J. 97
arrogance 114
art 84
Atkinson, P. 36, 48, 50, 55
attachment(s) 9, 113, 115, 116, 125, 130
audience ethnography 6, 158
audience research 6, 27, 33
audience studies 42, 161

audience work 56
audience-led textual analysis 130, 131
aura of distance 74
aura of intimacy 74
authenticity 24, 46
authoritarianism 119
authority 127, 136
autism spectrum disorder 123
auto-ethnographic collaboration 135
auto-ethnography 127, 132

babysitter, tv as 79
Bacon-Smith, C. 145
'bad faith' 116
bad ratings 106
Bahara, H. 155
Baker, Simon 114
Bastos, M. 29
Bauwel, S. van 86
Beckys 17
becoming 40
Beek, Gijs van 78, 84
behaviour, extreme abnormal 92
belonging 7, 16, 146
Bennett, T. 38
Berg, Annika van den 78, 79, 80
Berns, F. 134
betrayal 105
'big bad world' 88
binge watching 61
black behavior 139
Black Lives Matter 116, 138
Black Pete is racism 156
Black Pete, *see* Pete
Blackface 41
blackness 139
Blasko, D. 107
Blevins, J. 64
blocking (telephone contacts) 85
blogging 154
blogs 145
Bob the Drag Queen 134
body 48
Boer-Dirks, E. 147
Boeschoten, T. 155
Bolkestein 148
Bonner 145
book reading 79, 80, 81
Borghuis, P. 47
boring (the news) 82, 83
botnets 29
Bouchalikht 17, 18
Bourdieu, P. 38, 141

boyd, d. 58, 71, 84
boys 77
bracketing 55
Bradbury, H. 47, 166
Breaking Bad 8, 61, 66, 72, 73, 75
Breek, P. 5
Breitbart 150
Bridgerton 1, 2, 27–8, 42
bridging cultural capital 128
Britton, P. 97
Brunsdon, C. 120
Brusse, Bert 154, 155
Buckingham 80
Buffy studies 37
building shared worlds 49
bullied 88, 90
bullying 31, 93
Buonanno, M. 120
bureaucracies 120
Burgess, J. 7, 146
business models 134
Butler, D. 97
Byrne, M. 44

calculated ignorance 36
camp 131; (definition)
capitalism 144
capitalism, communicative 162
Cardwell, S. 118
carnival 41
casting 99, 101
CCCS 33, 35
CDA (critical discourse analysis) 55
celebrities 69, 74
celebrity 62, 63, 70, 118
celebrity affect 118
celebrity culture 134
celebrity hating 65
celebrity, composite 62, 65, 73
Chads 17
Chang, H. 135, 143 ff
Chaplin, Charlie 122
Chapman, J. 97
character consistency 135
character(s) 65, 66, 67, 70, 86, 132, 135
characters, most-hated female 61
characters, non-straight 116
Cherry, B. 97
child rearing 24, 51
children 50, 76
children's television 86
Christensen, C. 86
circuit of culture 162

Index   **187**

cis-gender 89, 135
cis-gender behaviour 77, 88
citizen 46, 120
citizen disengagement 3
citizen role repertoire 46
citizens, producing well-behaved 85
citizenship 21; (definition) 38, 62
citizenship and media 2
citizenship and media literacy 76
citizenship, civic 22
citizenship, cultural 1, 2; (definition) 6, 7, 13–4; (definition) 17, 18, 21; (definition Rosaldo) 19, 25, 27, 43, 74, 93, 104, 125, 127, 129, 145–7; (definition) 152, 158, 160–166
citizenship, cultural, as alignment, appreciation and attachment 115
citizenship, cultural, as collaborative effort 142
citizenship, cultural, as conversation 96, 130
citizenship, cultural, as everyday democracy 4
citizenship, cultural, as fierce discussion
citizenship, cultural, as performance 24
citizenship, cultural, as unforced reflection 75
citizenship, cultural, from a feminist perspective 13
citizenship, definition 2, 5
citizenship, DIY 14
citizenship, performance of cultural 65
citizenship, political 22, 54
citizenship, social 22
Citron, D.K. 13
civic discussion 9
civic imagination 9, 29, 160
civil societ33
civility 133
claims, irrational 129
class 84
Click, M. 64
client 24, 46
Clifford, J. 36
close reading 114, 125
co-create 145
co-ownership 7, 134
code(s), moral 65, 70
codes 65, 142
coding (open, axial, selective) 51, 64, 98
Coe, J. 146
coffee houses 22, 47
Coffey, M. 37

Cohen, S. 133
cohesion, social 62
collaboration with communities 164
collage art 84
collectives, rights of 70
Collins, C. 134
colonialism 22
colonies 22
color 101
color, queen of 134
commercial television 157
commercialism 56, 153
commercialization 31
commercials 81
common folk 141
common sense 33, 35, 54
communicative action 19
communitarian outlook 136
communities of use 45
community 19, 49, 64, 129, 132, 138, 142
community building 44, 150
community website 151
community, destabilized 101
community, queer 130
community, sense of 73
competence 15
competition 142
competitive reality tv show 130, 132–3
complaint 157
complexity 65
composite celebrity 73; ch 4
conceit of omniscient Western knowledge production 161
concern 77
condensation (of codes) 87
condescension 114
confusion 8, 74, 152
consciousness, false 33
consensus 129
consent 1
conservatism 55
conservatism, gender 52
conservatism, populist 9
conservative forces 144
conservative populist politics 13
conspiracy 98, 103
conspiracy thinking 2, 44, 147, 155
consumer 14, 24, 46
consumption 33
contestation 133
context is key 165
contextualization 39, 44, 148
contextualizing well 56

contradiction 33, 52, 56
contradictory challenges 94
contradictory emotions 153
control 74, 85
control, democratic 73
controversy online 136
Corbin, J. 51, 64, 98
Cordone, J. 97
Corner, J. 13
corruption 120
Cossens, S. 63
couch potatoes 76
Couldry, N. 14
counter stories 144
counterpublics 20
craft 142
creative industries policy 40
critical mindset 113, 122
criticism, feminist social 45
critique 114
Cronin, A. 14
cross-media presence 131
culpability 8
cult texts 103
cultural capital 128, 131
cultural capital 131
cultural citizenship, *see* citizenship, cultural
cultural critique 6
cultural knowledge 52
cultural knowledge, shared underlying 65
cultural logic 52
cultural policy 133
cultural studies 27
cultural studies, histories of 30
culture 6
culture as expedient 40
culture, capitalist 56
culture, celebrity 65
culture, celebrity 70
culture, celebrity 75
culture, consumer 34, 35
culture, gossip 62
culture, high 37, 38
culture, women's 35
cultured, being 141
curation 4
cynicism 166

Dahlgen, P. 3, 56
Dallas 34
dandyism 122
data collection 43

Davies, H. 76, 82
De Jaap 145, 154–5
De Joop 145, 154
Dean, J. 162
Dean, M. 8
debate, public 62
deep truth 124
Deleuze, G. 40
deliberation 24
democracy 5, 133, 147, 158, 166
democracy, inclusive 129
democracy, requirements for 25
democracy, semiotic 14
democratic duty 76
democratic sensibility 2
demotic turn 156
dependence 104
depoliticization 139
Detox 129, 132
Dhaenens, F. 86
dialogue 129
dialogue across divides 58
Dibbits, H. 151
difference 44, 45, 84, 149
digital ethnography 149, 150
dignity 13, 16
Dijkman, A. 18
DiSalvo, C. 164
disappointment 54, 142
disarticulation 16
discourse 37, 73, 78, 118
discourse analysis 44, 65, 150, 157
discourse-analytical approach 108
discourse, incitement to 104
discrepancy between tv talk and use 80
discrimination 21, 147, 153
disengagement 118
disgust 96–7
disinterest 58
distinction 141
distrust 124, 128, 153
diversity 1, 84, 148
diversity, ethnic and cultural 130
diversity, gender 78, 86
diversity, racial 42
diversity, sexual 51
DIY citizenship 14
Doctor Who 8, 20, 95
Donzelot, J. 23
Doona, J. 7
drag 130-1, 132; (definition) 138
drag as a political statement 142
drag culture 131

drag kings 132
drag queen 132, 133
drama 71, 72, 83
drama series 69; (rich) 74; (high quality) 118
dramatization 25
Draper, Betty 63
Drazkiewicz, E. 19
dream world 142
Driessens, O. 62
Drucker, A. 107
DuGay , P. 162
Duits, L. 81, 83, 84, 154, 155
Dunbar, R. 73
Dusen, Cris van 42

e-bile 96
ecstacy 118
Edwards, T. 73–4
Eeken, S. van 96
effects, perverse 147
effeminacy, male 126
Eliasoph, N. 164
Ellis, J. 74
emancipation 62, 100, 131, 147
emerging narratives 56
emotion(s) 2, 9, 43, 46, 48, 62, 95, 98, 145–8, 150–1
emotional intelligence 144, 161
emotional realism 65
emotions, inappropriate 129
empathetic understanding 50
empathy 125, 144
empowerment 49, 58, 160, 163
encoding-decoding 146
energy 39
engagement 35; (personal) 56, 127–8
entanglements 114
entertainment 7
entrepreneurial self 133
equality 130
Essig, L. 20
ethnicity 138
ethnographic participatory design methods 145
ethnographic research among girls 81
ethnographic sense making 158
ethnography 6, 30, 36, 48, 55, 158; (remote)
everyday experience 150
everyday media experience 118
evil 125, 127
excess 84; (as axis) 85

exclusion 7, 50, 73, 85, 93, 141
exclusions 137, 138
exclusivity 142
exhilaration 41
experimental civics 164
extremist threat 99

Facebook 9, 62–3, 97–8, 155
fact-checking 4
failure 55
fake 81–3
fame, female 74
family 58, 69, 71; (patriarchal) 127
fan base 105
fan co-authorship 73
fan community 8, 129, 163
fan discussion 130
fandom 8, 118
fan(s) 20, 104, 139, 142
fantasies of new selves 41
fear 50, 85–6, 93, 95, 119–20, 151
fear of guns 123, 125
fear of Islam 147
feeling(s) 6, 46, 48, 62, 78, 153; (paradoxical) 156
Felski, R. 48, 56, 83, 113, 115,117–8, 125, 127, 130
female Doctor Who 95
feminine qualities 123
femininity 63, 120, 132; (codes of) 138
femininity, policing of 73
femininization 120
feminism 17-8, 35; (proto) 63, 99
feminism as radically anti-male 103
feminism, post-structuralist 44
feminist 120, 123
feminist agenda 127
feminist and queer politics 136
feminist ideology 98
feminist joke 114
feminist legacy 115
feminist man 122
feminist perspective 49
feminist project, progressive 20
fieldwork memos 152
fieldwork notes 153
'fight or flight' 152
filking 107
filter bubbles 148
Finley, J. 21
Fiske, J. 13, 31–2, 36, 133, 146
Flockhard, Callista 49
food 122–3

football chat shows 157
force of law 120
Fortuyn, Pim 151
Foucault, M. 23, 25, 30, 37, 104, 133
Fox, J. 41
fragility 103
frames 55, 122, 125; (comedy, feminism, genius)
frameworks of knowledge 146
Fraser, N. 19, 24, 45, 74, 91
freedom 8, 34, 90, 93, 133; (culture as domain of)
friendship 107
frustration 152
Fuchs, C. 29
fun 84, 107, 127

Gamergate 154
gamers 31
games, educational 85
gaslighting 56, 58
gay 90, 91, 135
gay community 131–2
gay rights 140
geek fragility 103
GeenStijl 150
Geertz, C. 36
gender 23, 44, 46, 51, 58, 74, 77, 84, 86, 126; (definition)
gender anxiety 98, 101
gender as a category 132
gender as Achilles heel 93
gender change 99
gender codes, heteronormative 88
gender coding 132
gender coding, hetereonormative 130
gender confusion 74, 77, 95, 96
gender conservatism 49, 52, 104
gender distinction, overgeneralized 107
gender diversity 78, 86
gender roles 77, 86; (conformist)
gender values, traditional 75
gender-conservative disenchantment 107
gender 17, 55; (policing) 64; (attitudes towards) (ideology) 68; (conservative notions) 74; (conservative agenda) 77; (conventions) 78; (fluid) 90; (vulnerable) (hieerarchy) 93; (performance) 101; (innate) (instability) 108; (binary definition) (identity) 131; (freedom) 142; (normativity)

gendered identity 52
generosity 4
generosity, receptive 161
genius 122–4
gentleman 121
Geraghty, C. 118
'ghetto' black woman 139
Gibson, M. 35
Gill, R. 46, 74, 93
Gillespie, M. 36, 145, 149
Gilligan, Vince 61
girls 77, 88
Glaser, B. 51
Gn, J. 41
Goddard, S. 63
Goffman, E. 14
Gogh, Theo van 151
Golob, U. 162
Goodwin, J. 132
Gopnik, A. 22
gossip 73, 62, 69; (magazines) 135
gossip, celebrity 65, 73
governmentality 8, 28, 37, 38, 63, 131; (neoliberal)
Graaf, Christa de 78, 84, 152
gradual focusing 50
Gramsci, A. 33, 41
Gray, A. 36, 49, 145
Gray, J. 20, 28, 86
Green, J. 7
Gregg, M. 62, 150
grief 103, 105
Grossberg, L. 9, 20, 34, 39, 160
Grounded Theory 50, 64
Gunn, Anna 62
Gunsteren, H. van 5, 14

Habermas, J. 19, 22, 23, 25, 44, 45, 47, 129
Haidt, J. 4, 6, 28
Halberstam, J. 86
Hall, Stephen 35, 36
Hall, Stuart 4, 15, 30, 33, 35, 37, 133, 146, 161–3
Hallsworth , D. 25
Hammersley , M. 36, 48, 50, 55
happiness 95
happiness, promise of 99, 107
Harambam, J. 19
Hartley, J. 7, 14, 30, 34–5
hate speech 44, 147, 154
hatred 66, 74, 95, 96, 146, 147, 158
Hay, J. 37, 133
Hebdige, D. 33, 34

hegemonic rule 28
hegemony 27, 42, 133
helplessness 50, 54
Helsloot, J. 147
Henwood, K. 52, 54
hermeneutics, suspicious 56
Hernandez, K. 135, 143 ff
hero
heroine, tragic 73
heteronormative 88, 108; (contract)
heteronormativity 132
Hilhorst, S. 49, 156
Hill, A. 3, 56, 57, 108, 117–8, 133
Hills, M. 37, 97, 134
Hine, C. 149, 158
Hirsch, P. 29
Hochschild, A. 8. 9 13, 147
Hodge, R. 80
Hoeksma, S. 50, 78, 86
Hoggart, R. 35
holding to account 73
Holmes, S. 63
home, at 5
homophobia 136
hope 100, 120; (politics of) 127
Horst, H. 149, 150
hostility 98, 152
Huberman, A. 54
humour 25, 33, 82; (value of) 106, 107; (anti-female bias) 108, 116, 146, 156; (online) 157
hurt 156
Hutcheon, L. 131
Huyssen, A. 3, 120
hypocrisy 116, 125

ideal speech situation 25
identification 14, 43
identifying-as 4, 16
identities 43; (imagined) 77; (non-binary) 129, 146
identities, hard 18, 150, 151
identities, soft 18, 151
identity 4, 7–8, 14; (definition)-17 19, 39, 40, 45, 49, 52, 101, 142, 146, 150, 152; (construction)
identity formation 41, 44, 62
identity politics 152
identity, fluid 150
ideology 14, 15, 33, 34; (dominant) 44; (neoliberal) 63; (gender)
imaginaries, new 56
implicit references 108

incels 17
inclusion 16, 21, 51, 73, 85, 106, 142, 162
inclusions 137, 138
inclusivity, feigned 129
individualism 93, 73; (neoliberal) 123
inequality 13, 136
infidelity 68, 69
influencer 31
injustice 104
innocence 8, 121
innocence, white 156
inquiry, appreciative 8
insecurities 119
institutional governance 97
integrity 24, 49, 120
intellectuals, organic 33
intensity 48
interpellation 40
interpellation, affective 72
intersectional logic 101
interviews 6, 152
intuition 76
investigative journalism 158
investment 128
investment portfolio 20
irony 107
Islam 147–8, 153
Islamophobia 147, 153
Islamic threat 152

Jackson, S. 63, 73
Jacob, J. 117
James, P. 148
Jane, E. 96
Jane, Patrick 114–127
Janus-faced monster 7
Jefferson, T. 35
Jeffries, F. 119
Jenkins, H. 29, 145, 160, 163
Jensen, J. 7, 34
Jihad 152
Johansson, S. 65
Johnson, R. 78
joke 151; (self-deprecative) 156
joke, self-deprecative 151
joking 157
Jones, M. 129
Jowett, L. 97
judgements 113
judging others 73

Kale, S. 22
Kardolus, M. 129, 132

Katya 134, 135
Kavka, M. 74, 134
Kellner, D. 80
Kemmis, S. 45–7
Kick Out Black Pete 147, 157
killjoys 99
King, S. 37
Kluge, A. 19
knowledge, reflexive 48
knowledge, technical cultural 68
Koch, Karel 78, 84
Kohl, H. 40
Kommer, R. 164
Kooijman, J. 62
Kozloff, S. 125
Kraidy, M. 146
Kulynych, J. 24, 25

labelling 19
Labour party 40
labour, free 46
Landes, J. 23
language 108
language learning 77
latino 136
Lavik 120
learning from television 82
learning, incidental 83
legacy figure(3) 95, 108
legacy figures in media entertainment 97
legacy male roles 108
lesbian 105
lesbian love object 108
LGBTQI+ politics 116
liberation 131
liberty 130
life worlds 84
life, the good 84
lifeworld 22, 44, 46
Lindlof, T. 45
listening 3,4, 14, 43, 113, 115, 125, 161
listening better 160
listening generously 56
literacy 28, 35, 56; (critique) 83; (negative form of)
Littler, J. 3, 41, 46, 133
logic, associative and appreciative 118
logic, cultural 51
love 98, 105, 127
lulz 70, 156

macho 115
magic 130

maker knowledge 114
male body 138
male bonding 162
male disenfranchisement 108
male roles 95
male supremacy 116
man skirt 121
man, traditional ways of being a 115
Mankekar, P. 149
Marcus, G. 36
markets 74
Maroc.nl 151
Marokko.nl web community 7, 144, 150, 152–4
Marres, N. 158
Marshall, T. 22, 23
Marshall, P.D. 62, 70, 74
Marxism 30
Marxist-feminist critique 163
masculine poses and mannerisms 115
masculinity 3, 63, 71; (threatened) 95; (fragile) 115; (post-feminist) 120; (as strength) 123; (modern) 127
mash-up videos 146
Massanari, A. 154
materiality 150
Mattel, Trixie 134, 135
Maza, S. 23
McDonnell, A. 65
McGuigan, J. 32
McKeown, B. 64
McMillan Cottom 15, 18
McRobbie, A. 34, 164
meaning making 15, 28, 29, 49, 117; (embodied) 146, 150, 158; (situated)
meaning making, everyday 33, 43, 47
meaning making, local patterns 44
meanings 145
media as a civic space 77
media as assemblage of affect and effects 85
media culture, digital 148
media education 78, 128; (as training ground)
media effects 67
media ethnography 148–9, 157
media industries, male-dominated 101
media influence 6
media interpretation 127
media literacy 7, 9, 47, 76, 77, 80, 84; (intercultural) 85, 93, 144
media literacy as appreciative inquiry 115
media platforms 146

media representation 97, 146
media sphere, hybrid 146
media use, everyday 8
media wisdom 85, 113, 144
Media Wizards (game) 84, 93
media 7; (powerful) 8; (dangerous) 53; (power of the)
media, demonizing social 7
media, spreadable 7
melodrama 36, 65, 73, 74
Melzer, P. 97
memes 146
memo 50
Mendick, H. 63, 74
mentalist (definition) 113, 121
Mentalist, the 8, 113–128
Mercea, D. 29
meritocracy 3, 41
methodological challenge 108, 117
methodology 43, 44
Meyer Spacks, P. 73
Miles, M. 54
Miller T. 7, 14, 131, 133, 144, 149–50
Milner, R. 156
misinformation 58
misogynist frame 71
misogyny 62, 106
Mittell, J. 61–2, 71–2, 135
moderators 148
modernist apprehension of media effects 76
modernist legacy 2, 3, 6
modernity 120, 125
Moffat, S. 99
Mol, M. 78, 81, 82
money 24
moral imperatives 93
moral realism 65, 68, 73
morality 55; (conservative) 65, 120
Morley, D. 34, 52, 145
Morris, M. 32,34, 52, 145
Mortensen, T. 154
Mouffe, C. 20, 129
mulitcultural drama 148
Müller, F. 108
multiculturalism 148
'musculinity' 97
music fandom 39
myth 14

narrative 49
narrative development 66
narratives 56, 113
nation 76

national broadcast media 153
nationalism 151
nature 92
nature/nurture 51, 55
Nava, M. 14
negotiation 35
Negra, D. 63
Negt, O. 19
neo-conservatism 8
neoliberal ideology 123
neoliberal reasoning 133
neoliberal, Ru as 140
neoliberalism 8, 15, 40–1
nerd 122, 126
Netflix 1, 61, 81
Netwerk Mediawijsheid 77, 79, 86
Newcomb, H. 29
news media (and democracy) 13
news program 82
news, boring 82
news, fake 58
news, the 76, 83, 158
Newton, E. 132
Ngundjiri, F. 135, 143 ff
Nicol, D. 97
Nikken, P. 77, 79, 86
non-binary 77; (identities) 135, 137
non-fiction 144
normality 14, 24, 150
normalization 28
nostalgia 51, 98–100, 108
nurture 92

O'Hara, Eureka 134
obedience 133
obligations 58
observation 6
online life worlds 84
online world 144
ontological security 101
oppression 28, 136
ordinary people 156
ordinary television 145
orientation 48
oriented, being 78
Ouellette, L. 133
outcomes, tragic 147
outliers 54
outrage 71, 155, 157
ownership 70, 108, 135; (collaborative)

Packard, V. 38
pain 146

Papacharissi, Z. 146
Papaikonomou Z. 18
paradox (es) 56, 133, 142
paradoxes, following through on 165
paradoxical identity 123
parenting 91
parenting style 91
parents 8, 50, 51, 54, 55, 58, 76, 86, 94
parents, gay 86
Pariser, E. 148
participant design 6
participant observation 158
participants 136
participation 162
participative forms of research 6
particularity 149
patience 98–100
patriarchal family 69, 71
patriarchal imprint 115
patriarchal structures 96
patriarchy 22
patronizing 35, 125
patterns 56
people of colour 101
people, the 32
performance 24, 45, 141, 142
performance of cultural citizenship
performativity 24, 25
permissive populism 132
personal 153
personal engagement 35
personal life 44–6, 65
personal space 152
perspective, feminist 49
pessimism 56, 81; (cultural)
Pete 9, 41, 144, 147, 155, 156, 158
Pete controversy 147, 148
Peters-Lazaro, G. 29, 160
phenomenology 48, 55
Philips, W. 156
Pierson, D. 64
Piet 148; (and, see Pete)
Pietietie 9, 144, 145, 148–9, 155–7
pillarization 148
pink is for girls 88
place as context 90
placemaking 5
planes of equality 164
platform capitalism 144
platforms, social media 65, 147, 155
pleasure 1, 28, 113, 127, 132; (nostalgic) 142; (escapist or passionate)
pleasures 145

plot 66
polarization 2,44, 147, 150, 159
police procedural 118, 120
police series 119
policing 73, 131; (of gender, race and national culture) 139
policy 133
political agenda 35, 98
political citizenship 145
political correctness 157
political energy 132
political engagement 20
political platform 108
politics 21; (agonistic) 29; (gender) 44; (identitarian) 65; (of accountability) 75, 101; (emancipatory) 116 120; (of fear) 134, 136; (feminist and queer) 140, 142; (of difference) 153, 161; (left-progressive)
politics, populist 65, 124
politics, Ru's 132, 141
polylogue 148
popular culture 1, 3, 6, 17, 18, 20, 27–42, 116, 160
popular culture as arena for informal reflection 3
popular culture project 13
popular media culture 95
popular music 34
popular television magic 114
populism 9, 32; (cultural) 132, 151, 153–4; (right-wing)
populist 29; (leaders) 65; (politics) 144; (right)
positions, speaking 65
Post Online 145, 154
post-scripting in reality tv 135
post-structuralism 48
post-television 131
Postill, J. 146, 158
Postman, N. 81
Potter, J. 51, 52, 65, 152
poverty 136
power 5, 8, 13–4, 24–5, 39, 43–4, 101; (social) 107
power of television 39
power structures 29, 146
power/knowledge 37, 48
powerful media 6
powerlessness 104
practice-based research 164
praise 98

pranking 71
pre-conceived notions 55, 56
Prins, B. 148
privacy 46, 66
privilege 16, 44, 115; (male) 155
production team 100
professional 52; (practice) 63, 66; (persona) 74; (as intermediary) 126; (female strength) 146; (codes of conduct)
professionalism 65, 74
professionals 5, 84, 94, 114, 145, 154
programming 135
progress 98
progressive feminist project 20
protection 53, 90
proto-feminism 35
pseudonyms 66
psycho-analysis 39, 122
public debate 62, 157
public discussion 147
public figures 65, 74
public knowledge project 13
public logic 156
public service television 98
public shaming 65–6, 70, 73
public space 157–8
public sphere 19, 129
public television for children 78

Qader, Soraya 17
QAnon 41
qualitative audience researcg 149
queens, latin-american 141
queer 77, 130
quiz shows 83

rabbit hole 155
race 44
racism 136, 140, 147, 156
Radway, J. 34–6, 123, 145
Ralston, R. 41
Ramadan 152
rationality 3
reading 56 127; (as a fan) 127; (as a feminist)
Reagan, Ronald 40
real 82
realism, emotional 65
reality genres 40
reality tv formats 133
Reason, P. 47, 166
recognition 33, 45, 130, 153
Red John 114, 117, 119, 120, 122, 124–6

Reddit 62, 64, 74, 124–7, 154
Redmond, S. 118
reflection 6, 62–3, 146
reflexivity 48, 158
refugee groups 147
relations of production 146
relativism 48
relevance 161, 163, 165
religious observance 151
repertoire analysis 153
repertoire(s), interpretative 51, 65, 87
representation 7, 37, 39, 54; (gender) 97, 129, 136, 142, 153; (negative)
reproduction 45
Republiek Allochtonië 154
reruns 81
research memo 50
research, participative forms of 6
resentment 155
resistance 28, 34, 128, 133
respect 13, 128, 152
response videos 95
responsibilities 2, 5, 19, 62, 74
responsibility 54, 73–4, 93; (abdication of) 134; (method) 160
Reveal, the 95, 105, 107, 108
revenge 123, 124
reward 68
Rhimes, Shonda 1, 42
rights 2, 5, 19, 58, 62, 70; (of collectives) 74, 140
rigour 50
risk 53
role models 97, 108; (gendered)
roles, male 95, 108
romance novels 1, 27, 36
romance readers 123
romance reading 34, 35
romantic fantasy 107
romantic hero 123
romantic interest, lesbian 108
Rosaldo, R. 21, 44
rules, generic 73
RuPaul 129–143
RuPaul's Drag Race 8, 31, 129–143

safe space 154
safety 152
Saha, A. 163
Saharso, S. 148
salons, Parisian 22
sarcasm 106–9, 116, 122
saturation 98

savvy viewing 6–6, 68
sceens as babysitter 77
Scharff, C. 46, 74, 93
Scheffer, P. 147
school as research environment 81, 83
Schultes, P. 97
Scott, D. 4, 161
screen time 77
script writing 124
scripts, social 21
Segal, L. 3, 90, 120
Seigworth, G. 62, 150
Seiter, E. 80
self-actualization 9
self-identification 19; (right to) 21
self-management 133
self-reflection 43
self-reflexivity 54; (radical)
semiotic democracy 14, 133
semiotics 30
sensational 153
sensibility 39; (affective) 131
sensitivity 158
sensitizing concepts 56
sentiment 78
Sesame Street 78
Seta, G. 146
sex worker 139
sexism 63; (everyday) 74, 96; (underlying)
sexist stereotype 126
Seymour, R. 31
Shangela 134
Sharia 157
Sheombar, A. 85
Shklar, J. 116, 125
Shondaland 1, 42
Shore, L. 16, 80
Shrestova, G. 29, 160
Sidore, D. 124
Sikkema, P. 81
Simon, N. 163, 165
sincerity 116, 125
Sinterklaas 9, 41, 147–8
Skeggs, B. 41, 74
Skyler 8, 61, 70, 72, 74–5
slavery 22
slut-shaming 73
smoking 68
soaps (fake and real) 82
social change 19
social justice warrior(s) 96, 99, 105
social media affordances 157
social media logic 66

social power inequality 107
sociality 146
solidarity 49, 119, 127, 142
solidity in tradition 100
Solnit, R. 164, 166
Sontag, S. 131–2
Soprano, Carmela 63
space, public 88
Spinoza 39
sports programming 162
spreadable media 7
Srinivasan, A. 17, 18, 21, 163
Staceys 17
Stallybrass 41, 133
standards, moral 73
State, the 38
status 1, 67, 98
Steger, M. 148
stereotype(s) 126, 139, 163
Stevenson, N. 5, 14
Storey, J. 41, 42
stories 4; (shared) 6, 8; (deep) 56; 1444 (sensational)
story worlds 135
storytelling 44, 49, 120, 144; (online)
storytelling, collective 145, 161
storytelling, everyday 162–3
straight 135
Strauss, A. 51, 64, 98
strength 127
structure of feeling 29, 39; (tragic)
structure, social 44
subculture 34; (youth) 103–4; (geek)
subjectivity as fixed 118
success 55
suffering, white 157
suitability 84
surprise 54
suspense 82
suspicion 114, 124, 128
suspicion, hermeneutics of 115
suspicious reading 56, 83
system 22, 44, 46

tactility 118
Tally, J. 133
target groups 19
Tasker, Y. 97
taste 1; (hierarchies of) 28, 76, 131
Taylor, E 126, 133
technical infrastructures 146
telenovela 153
telenovela project 145, 152

television 14; (as transcultural teacher) 39, 51; (use) 51–2; (viewing) 53; (fear of) 68; (storytelling) 72; (series) 73; (quality) 81, 82; (learning from) 86, 106; (history) 118; (texture) 127; (attractive) 132; (logic)
television drama 98, 135
television, children's 51, 86
television, public (service) 61, 98
television's manipulation 54
tension 67
TERF 20
Terranova, T. 29, 45
Teurlings, J. 27, 46, 65–6
textual analysis 127, 130, 138
textual criticism 114, 125
texturality 118
texture of television 118, 122
Thatcher, Margaret 40
theorization 44, 56
Thirteenth Doctor 95
Thomsen, C. 20, 21
Thornton, S. 36
threat (s) 98, 120
Thumin, N. 41
TikTok 76, 162
togetherness 152
tomboyishness 77
tone-policing 4
tradition 100
trans (ness) 20, 77, 105, 136
trans man 138
trans woman 138
transgender characters 76
transitioning 138
transphobia 97, 108
trauma 98, 103
treason 98, 104
Tripp, D. 80
trolling 153–4
trust 4, 84, 153
truth 48; (objective) 124
truths 56
Tufecki, Z. 29
Turner, B. 14
Turner, G. 156
tv diaries 81
tv production 82
tv viewing 86
tv, old-fashioned 84
Twitter 154–5
Twitter controversies (and public debate) 29

typical boy, girl 87

understanding 50
unease 157

validation 56
validity 24, 54, 95
valorization 9
value 50, 74; (subject of)
Vanlee, F. 86
Vares, T. 73
VCR 36
Ven, C. van de 154, 155
venting 18
Verba, S. 3
Vergès, F. 163
verifiability 146
vernacular creativity 146
victimhood 157
viewer 120
vigilante avenger 124
Vixen, the 139, 140
vlogs 145
voice 4, 32, 161–2
Vries, M. de 73
vulnerability 7, 127
vulnerable 71; (as a woman) 157

Wallace, R. 97
Warner, M. 20
Warren, C. 132
weaponization of social media commentary 4
Wekker, G. 41, 156
Wetherell 8
Wetherell, M. 8, 9, 39, 46, 48, 51–2, 65, 71, 152
Whannell, G. 30
white 133, 135
white fragility 103
white male 120
White, A. 41
White, Skyler 8, 61
White, Walter 61, 72
Whittaker, Jodie 96–99, 103, 105, 108–9
Wij Blijven Hier 154
Wilder, A. 73
Wilders, Geert 151
Williams, R. 97; (on dr Who)
Williams, Alex 63
Williams, R. 29; (on structure of feeling)
Wilson, J. 63
Winslow, S. 35, 36

women's emancipation 98
Wood, D. 64
Wood, H. 41, 74
Woodward, K. 14
worker 24, 46
world building 6, 49, 160, 163
worry 100

Yasmina.nl 148, 151
youth culture, Moroccan 151

YouTube 95–98, 105, 109, 134, 136, 146, 152
YouTube comments 97
Yudice, G. 7, 40, 133
Yuval-Davis, N. 17

Zamolodchikova, K. 134
Zervignon, A. 132
Zoonen, L. van 101

Printed in the United States
by Baker & Taylor Publisher Services